A
PRACTICAL DICTIONARY
OF THE
PERSIAN LANGUAGE

BY

JOHN ANDREW BOYLE, Ph.D.

LUZAC & COMPANY, LTD.
46 GREAT RUSSELL STREET,
LONDON, W.C.1.
1949

PRINTED BY
STEPHEN AUSTIN AND SONS, LIMITED,
ORIENTAL AND GENERAL PRINTERS,
1, FORE STREET, HERTFORD, ENGLAND.

PREFACE

The chief purpose of this dictionary is to provide the student of Persian, in a compendious form and at a moderate price, with the means of reading books and newspapers in the modern language. In addition, therefore, to the general vocabulary, an attempt has been made to incorporate as many as possible of the political, economic, and scientific terms most widely current at the present day. These terms include, on the one hand, words of European (mainly French) origin introduced into the language to represent ideas for which there was no corresponding Persian expression; and, on the other hand, neologisms adopted by the Persian Academy (*Farhangestān-e-Irān*) to provide purely Persian equivalents for Arabic and, to a lesser extent, Turkish and European words.

Of the authorities consulted during the compilation of this work, by far the most important was the Persian–English dictionary of Haïm.[1] For the neologisms I had recourse to the publication of the Persian Academy: *Vāzheh hā-ye-nou keh tā pāyān-e-sāl-e-1319 dar Farhangestān-e-Irān paẕirofteh shodeh ast* ("New words adopted by the Persian Academy up to the end of 1319 [2]"). I also utilized a glossary of scientific terms compiled by the Russian Orientalist Arends and published in Leningrad in 1928, and a Persian–Russian–Azerbaijani dictionary which appeared in Baku in 1945, under the auspices of the Azerbaijani Academy of Sciences.

The system of transliteration is based on the practice of the Persians themselves when using the Roman character. The letters, therefore, are given their modern Persian as distinct from their classical Arabic values. I have, however, thought it useful to distinguish between the different *s*'s, *z*'s, etc., by means of the usual diacritical points. Final *hamzeh* in such words as فضلاء has been omitted not only in the transliteration but also in the original Arabic character: it serves no purpose in this position except when followed by the *eẕāfat*, and even then is often replaced by ی.

The abbreviations for the most part require no explanation. The following indicate borrowings from foreign languages: A. = Arabic,

[1] Tehran, 1934–6, 2 vols.
[2] *i.e.* March, 1941.

a. = partly Arabic,[1] AR. = Armenian, E. = English, F. = French, G. = German, H. = Hịndustani, M. = Mongolian, R. = Russian, and T. = Turkish (Turki). It should be borne in mind that these letters refer only to the language from which the word in question was introduced into Persian and not necessarily the language from which the word was originally taken. Thus, *qānun* "law" and *eter* "ether" are both Greek words by origin, but the former being borrowed from the Arabic and the latter from the French they are marked A. and F. respectively. A more extreme example is the word *lider* "political leader", which is as obviously borrowed from the French as its origin is unmistakably English. With respect to foreign words introduced into the language in the pre-Islamic period, it has not been thought necessary to indicate their provenance: such borrowings as *sim* "silver", from the Greek ἄσημος, are treated as though they were native Persian words.

It remains to thank those who have helped me in the production of this work, in particular my teacher, Professor V. Minorsky, who read through the first proofs and made a great number of suggestions, almost all of which have been adopted in the text. My thanks are also due to Colonel J. I. Eadie and Mr. A. J. Seltman, who read through the subsequent proofs and suggested a number of valuable emendations. In conclusion, I should like to express my appreciation of the able manner in which the printers, Messrs. Stephen Austin and Sons, have acquitted themselves of a difficult and tedious task.

[1] It has not been thought necessary to indicate in similar fashion the words partly derived from other languages.

J. A. B.

LONDON.
November, 1948.

PRONUNCIATION

a (اَ, ـَ), like the *a* in *cat.*

ā (آ, ـَا), like the *a* in *wash.*

b (ب), as in English.

ch (چ), like the *ch* in *church.*

d (د), softer than in English.

e (ـِ), like the *e* in *bell.*

ei (اَی, ـَی), like the *ei* in *reign.*

f (ف), as in English.

g (گ), as in English before *ā, o, ou,* and *u,* but palatalized before *a, e, ei,* and *i,* and also finally.

gh (غ), the French *r grasseyé.*

h (ه) and *ḥ* (ح), as in English. *ḥ* is pronounced in every position, but *h* is silent finally after *e*, except in a few cases, all of which are indicated in the text.

i (اِی, ـِی), like the *i* in *machine,* but with a shorter pronunciation before a vowel (e.g. *siāh*) or final *n* (e.g. *zamin*).

j (ج), like the *j* in *jam.*

k (ک), as in English before *ā, o, ou,* and *u,* but palatalized under the same conditions as *g.*

kh (خ), like the Scotch *ch* in *loch.*

l (ل), like the *l* in *lean,* never like the *l* in *feel.*

m (م), as in English.

n (ن), as in English, but pronounced *m* before *b* (e.g. *donbāl* is pronounced *dombāl*).

o (اُ, اُو, ـُ, ـُو), between the English *u* in *pull* and the French *o* in *pomme*.

ou (آو, ـَو), like the *ou* in *mould*.

p (پ), as in English.

q (ق), like *gh*.

r (ر), always trilled.

s (س), *ṣ* (ص) and *ṡ* (ث), like the *s* in *sun*, never like *s* in *rose*.

sh (ش), as in English.

t (ت) and *ṭ* (ط), softer than the English *t*.

u (اُو, ـُو), like the *u* in *rule*.

v (و), as in English, but silent in the combination *khvā*.

y (ى), as in English.

z (ز), *ẕ* (ذ), *ẓ* (ض) and *ẓ̈* (ظ), all like the English *z*.

zh (ژ), like the *s* in *pleasure* or the French *j* in *jour*.

ʻ (ع) and ʼ (ء) represent the glottal stop.

ا

آب (*āb*) water; lustre. آب و هوا climate.

آباد (*ābād*), آبادان (*ābādān*) inhabited, cultivated, flourishing.

آبادانی (*ābādāni*), آبادی (*ābādi*) populousness, flourishing condition; inhabited place; reconstruction.

آبان (*ābān*) *name of the eighth month of the Persian year.*

آب انبار (*āb anbār*) cistern.

آب پاش (*āb pāsh*) watering-can.

آبجو (*ābjou*) beer.

آبدار (*ābdār*) juicy; lustrous.

آبدست (*ābdast*) ablution.

آبرو (*ābru*) reputation.

آبستن (*ābestan*) pregnant.

آبشار (*ābshār*) waterfall.

آبگیر (*ābgir*) pool.

آبگینه (*ābgineh*) glass, mirror.

آبله (*ābeleh*) small pox. آبله کوبیدن to vaccinate.

آبله کوب (*ābeleh kub*) vaccinator.

آبله کوبی (*ābeleh kubi*) vaccination.

آبنوس (*ābnus*) ebony.

آبی (*ābi*) watery, aquatic; blue.

آبیاری (*ābyāri*) irrigation. آبیاری کردن to irrigate.

آتاشه (*ātāsheh*) F. attaché.

آتش (*ātesh*) fire. آتش زدن to set fire to.

آتشبار (*āteshbār*) battery (*of artillery*).

آتشخانه (*āteshkhāneh*) fire-box.

آتش فشان (*ātesh feshān*) volcanic; volcano.

آتشکده (*āteshkadeh*) fire-temple.

آتش نشان (*ātesh neshān*) fireman.

آتش نشانی (*ātesh neshāni*) fire-brigade.

آتشین (*āteshin*) fiery.

آتن (*āten*) F. Athens.

آتیه (*ātieh*) A. future.

آثار (*āṣār*) A. traces, relics; (literary) works. (*Pl. of* اثر.)

آجر (*ājor*) A. brick.

آجودان (*ājudān*) F. adjutant, aide-de-camp.

آجیل (*ājil*) nuts, dried fruit.

آچار (1) (*āchār*) pickles; fruit preserved in salt, vinegar or sugar.

آچار (2) (*āchār*) T. screwdriver.

آحاد (*āḥād*) A. units. (*Pl. of* احد.)

آخ (*ākh*) ah!

آختن (*ākhtan*) to draw, unsheathe.

آخر (*ākher*) A. last; last part, end, result; finally.

آخر الامر (*ākhero'l-amr*) A. at last.

آخرت (*ākherat*) A. the future, the next world.

آخرین (*ākherin*) *a.* last.

آخور (*ākhor*) manger.

آخوند (*ākhond*) tutor; theologian.

آداب (*ādāb*) A. etiquette. (*Pl. of* ادب.)

آدرس (*ādres*) F. address.

آدم (*ādam*) A. Adam; man(kind).

آدمخور (*ādamkhor*) *a.* cannibal.

آدمی (*ādami*) A. man(kind).

آدمیت (*ādamiyyat*) A. humanity; civility.

آدمیزاد (*ādamizād*) *a.* human being.

آدینه (*ādineh*) Friday.

آذر (*āẕar*) fire; *name of the ninth month of the Persian year.*

آذربایجان (*āẕarbāyjān*) Azerbaijan.

آذوقه (*āẕuqeh*) provisions.

آرا (*ārā*) A. votes. (*Pl. of* رأی.)

آراستن (*ārāstan*) to decorate; to arrange.

آرام (*ārām*) rest, repose, tranquillity; quiet(ly) آرام گرفتن to rest; to quieten down.

آرامش (*ārāmesh*) tranquillity, peace.

آرایش (*ārāyesh*) adornment, decoration.

آرتش (*ārtesh*) *i. q.* ارتش.

آرد (*ārd*) flour.

آرزو (*ārzu*) wish.

آرژانتین (*ārzhāntin*) F. Argentine.

آرمان (*ārmān*) longing, yearning; ideology.

آرنج (*āranj*) elbow.

آری (*āre*) yes.

آز (*āz*) greed.

آزاد (*āzād*) free. در هوایِ آزاد in the open air.

آزادی (*āzādi*) freedom, liberty.

آزادیخواه (*āzadikhvāh*) democratic, liberal.

آزار (*āzār*) injury, molestation. آزار کردن to torment, tease.

آزردن (*āzordan*) to injure, annoy.

آزرم (*āzarm*) shame, modesty; reverence.

آزمایش (*āzmāyesh*) trial, experiment.

آزمایشگاه (*āzmāyeshgāh*) laboratory.

آزمودن (*āzmudan*) to try, test.

آزموده (*āzmudeh*) tried, tested.

آژان (*āzhān*) F. policeman.

آژانس (*āzhāns*) F. newsagency.

آژیر (*āzhir*) alarm, (air-raid) warning.

آس (*ās*) mill; (act of) grinding. آس کردن to grind.

آسان (*āsān*) easy.

آسانی (*āsāni*) ease.

آسایش (*āsāyesh*) rest, tranquillity.

آسایش گاه (*āsāyesh gāh*) sanatorium.

آستانه (*āstāneh*) threshold.

آستر (*āstar*) lining.

آستین (*āstin*) sleeve.

آسمان (*āsmān*) heaven, sky.

آسودن (*āsudan*) to rest.

آسوده (*āsudeh*) quiet, peaceful.

آسه (*āseh*) axis.

آسیا (1) (*āsiā*) mill.

آسیا (2) (*āsiā*) Asia.

آسیا بان (*āsiā bān*) miller.

آسیب (*āsib*) damage.

آسید (*āsid*) F. acid.

آش (*āsh*) potage.

آشامیدن (*āshāmidan*) to drink.

آشپز (*āshpaz*) cook.

آشتی (*āshti*) reconciliation.

آشفتن (*āshoftan*) to disturb, to be disturbed.

آشکار (*āshkār*) evident, manifest, open.

آشکارا (*āshkārā*) openly.

آشکوب (*āshkub*) storey ; layer.
آشنا (*āshnā*) acquainted, familiar.
آشنائی (*āshnā'i*) acquaintance, friendship.
آشوب (*āshub*) tumult, confusion, riot.
آشور (*āshur*) Assyria.
آشوری (*āshuri*) Assyrian.
آشیانه (*āshiāneh*) nest ; hangar.
آغاز (*āghāz*) beginning. آغاز کردن to begin.
آغشتن (*āgheshtan*) to moisten ; to smear ; to pollute.
آغل (*āghel*) T. sheep-cote.
آفاق (*āfāq*) A. horizons ; the (whole) world. (*Pl. of* افق.)
آفت (*āfat*) A. plague, calamity.
آفتاب (*āftāb*) sun.
آفتاب رو (*āftāb ru*) sunny.
آفتاب گیر (*āftāb gir*) parasol ; sunny.
آفتابه (*āftābeh*) ewer.
آفریدگار (*āferidegār*) Creator.
آفریدن (*āferidan*) to create.
آفرین (*āferin*) bravo ! praise.
آفرینش (*āferinesh*) creation.
آقا (*āqā*) T. sir, gentleman. —آقایِ Mr. —.
آگاه (*āgāh*) informed aware.
آگاهی (*āgāhi*) information, knowledge ; secret police.
آگندن (*āgandan*) to fill, cram, stuff.
آگهی (*āgahi*) announcement.
آلاف (*ālāf*) A. thousands. (*Pl. of* الف.)
آلام (*ālām*) A. griefs. (*Pl. of* الم.)
آلت (*ālat*) A. tool, instrument.
آلمان (*ālmān*) F. Germany ; German.
آلو (*ālu*) plum.
آلوبالو (*ālubālu*) cherry.
آلودن (*āludan*) to pollute, contaminate.
آلوده (*āludeh*) polluted ; embarrassed.
آماج (*āmāj*) target.
آمادگاه (*āmādgāh*) training centre.
آماده (*āmādeh*) ready, prepared.
آمار (*āmār*) statistics.
آماس (*āmās*) swelling, inflammation.
آمال (*āmāl*) A. hopes, wishes. (*Pl. of* امل.)
آمپر (*āmper*) F. ampère.
آمپر سنج (*āmper sanj*) ammeter.
آمدن (*āmadan*) to come.
آمرزش (*āmorzesh*) forgiveness.
آمرزیدن (*āmorzidan*) to forgive.
آمریکا (*āmrikā*) America.
آموختن (*āmukhtan*) to teach ; to learn.
آموزشگاه (*āmuzeshgāh*) school.
آموزگار (*āmuzgār*) teacher.
آمیختن (*āmikhtan*) to mix, mingle.
آمیزش (*āmizesh*) intercourse.
آمیزشی (*āmizeshi*) venereal.
آن (1) (*ān*) that.
آن (2) (*ān*) A. moment.
آناً (*ānan*) A. instantaneously.
آنتن (*ānten*) F. antenna, aerial.
آنچه (*āncheh*) that which, what.
آنی (*āni*) A. momentary.
آواره (*āvāreh*) vagrant.
آواز (*āvāz*), آوازه (*āvāzeh*) voice, sound ; song.
آوازه خوان (*āvāzeh khvān*) singer.
آورد (*āvard*) battle.

آوردگاه (*āvardgāh*) battlefield.
آوردن (*āvardan*) to bring.
آوريل (*āvril*) F. April.
آويختن (*āvikhtan*) to hang.
آويخته (*āvikhteh*) hanging.
آه (*āh*) sigh. آه كشيدن to sigh.
آهار (*āhār*) starch.
آهسته (*āhesteh*) slowly.
آهک (*āhak*) lime. سنگِ آهک limestone.
آهن (*āhan*) iron.
آهنربا (*āhanrobā*) magnet.
آهنگ (*āhang*) melody, harmony; intention.
آهنگر (*āhangar*) blacksmith.
آهنى (*āhani*) pertaining to iron.
آهو (*āhu*) gazelle, antilope; deer.
آهيختن (*āhikhtan*) to draw, unsheathe.
آيا (*āyā*) *interrogative particle.*
آيش (*āyesh*) fallow.
آينده (*āyandeh*) coming, future.
آئين (*ā'in*) rite, ceremony, custom.
آئين نامه (*ā'in nāmeh*) regulations.
آئينه (*ā'ineh*) mirror.
اب (*ab*) A. father.
ابا (*ebā*) A. refusal. ابا كردن to refuse.
ابتدا (*ebtedā*) A. beginning.
ابتلا (*ebtelā*) A. (state of) being attacked (*by diseases, etc.*).
ابتهاج (*ebtehāj*) A. joy, gladness.
ابتياع (*ebtiā'*) A. (act of) purchasing.
ابد (*abad*) A. eternity without end.
ابداً (*abadan*) A. never (*with neg.*).
ابدال (*ebdāl*) A. exchange.
ابدى (*abadi*) A. eternal.
ابر (*abr*) cloud; cloudy.
ابراز (*ebrāz*) A. (act of) divulging, expressing.
ابرام (*ebrām*) A. importunity.
ابراهيم (*ebrāhim*) A. Abraham.
ابرص (*abraṣ*) A. leper, leprous.
ابرو (*abru*) eyebrow.
ابرى (*abri*) cloudy.
ابريشم (*abrishom*) silk.
ابريق (*ebriq*) A. ewer.
ابزار (*abzār*) tool.
ابعاد (*ab'ād*) A. dimensions. (*Pl. of* بُعْد.)
ابعد (*ab'ad*) A. more, most distant.
ابلاغ (*eblāgh*) A. communication. ابلاغ كردن to communicate.
ابله (*ablah*) A. stupid, foolish; idiot.
ابليس (*eblis*) A. Devil, Satan.
ابن (*ebn*) A. son.
ابنا (*abnā*) A. sons. (*Pl. of* ابن.)
ابواب (*abvāb*) A. doors; chapters. (*Pl. of* باب.)
ابهام (*ebhām*) A. ambiguity; thumb; great toe.
ابهت (*obbahat*) A. magnificence, grandeur.
ابيات (*abyāt*) A. verses. (*Pl. of* بيت.)
ابيض (*abyaẓ*) A. white.
اپيدمى (*epidemi*) F. epidemic.
اتابک (*atābak*) T. guardian, tutor; prime minister.
اتازونى (*etāzuni*) F. United States.
اتاق (*otāq*) T. room.
اتباع (*atbā'*) A. followers; subjects. (*Pl. of* تابع.)

اتحاد (*ettehād*) A. union ; alliance.

اتحادیه (*ettehādiyyeh*) A. league.

اتحاف (*ettehāf*) A. making a present of, dedication.

اتخاذ (*ettekhāz*) A. (act of) adopting, choosing for oneself. اتخاذ کردن to adopt.

اتر (*eter*) F. ether.

اتراک (*atrāk*) A. Turks. (*Pl. of* ترک.)

اتریش (*otrish*) F. Austria.

اتساع (*ettesā'*) A. dilatation.

اتصاف (*ettesāf*) A. characterization, qualification.

اتصال (*ettesāl*) A. connection, continuity.

اتصالاً (*ettesālan*) A. constantly, continuously.

اتفاق (*ettefāq*) A. agreement ; event, incident. باتفاقِ together with. باتفاقِ آرا unanimously.

اتفاقاً (*ettefāqan*) A. accidentally, by chance ; together ; unanimously.

اتفاقی (*ettefāqi*) A. accidental.

اتکا (*ettekā*) A. reliance.

اتکال (*ettekāl*) A. reliance ; resignation.

اتلاف (*etlāf*) A. (act of) wasting, ruining. اتلاف کردن to waste, ruin.

اتم (*atom*) F. atom.

اتمام (*etmām*) A. completion.

اتمی (*atomi*), اتمیک (*atomik*) F. atomic.

اتوبوس (*otobus*) F. omnibus.

اتومبیل (*otomobil*) F. motor car.

اتهام (*ettehām*) A. accusation.

اثاث (*asās*) A. furniture, movable goods.

اثاثیه (*asāsiyyeh*) A. furniture.

اثبات (*esbāt*) A. (act of) proving, proof اثبات کردن to prove.

اثر (*asar*) A. trace ; impression, effect ; literary work. در اثرِ as the result of.

اثنا (*asnā*) A. middle ; interval. در این اثنا meanwhile.

اجابت (*ejābat*) A. (act of) answering favourably, acceptation.

اجاره (*ejāreh*) A. rent ; lease.

اجازه (*ejāzeh*) A. permission.

اجبار (*ejbār*) A. compulsion.

اجباری (*ejbāri*) A. compulsory.

اجتماع (*ejtemā'*) A. meeting, gathering, congregation.

اجتماعی (*ejtemā'i*) A. social.

اجتناب (*ejtenāb*) A. avoidance. اجتناب کردن to avoid.

اجتهاد (*ejtehād*) A. effort, endeavour ; office of a مجتهد.

اجحاف (*ejhāf*) A. extortion.

اجداد (*ajdād*) A. ancestors. (*Pl. of* جد.)

اجر (*ajr*) A. reward.

اجرا (*ejrā*) A. execution, enforcement. اجرا کردن to carry out ; to obey, observe.

اجرام (*ajrām*) A. bodies. (*Pl. of* جِرم.)

اجرائی (*ejrā'i*) A. executive.

اجرت (*ojrat*) A. wages.

اجزا (*ajzā*) A. parts, ingredients ; employees. (*Pl. of* جزء.)

اجسام (*ajsām*) A. bodies. (*Pl. of* جسم.)

اجل (*ajal*) A. doom, death.

اجل (*ajall*) A. more, most glorious

اجلاس (*ejlās*) A. sitting, session.

اجلال (*ejlāl*) A. glory.

اجماع (*ejmā'*) A. assembly, gathering.

اجمال (*ejmāl*) A. abridgement.

اجمالاً (*ejmālan*) A. briefly.

اجمالی (*ejmāli*) A. brief, compendious.

اجناس (*ajnās*) A. goods. (*Pl. of* جنس.)

اجنبی (*ajnabi*) A. foreign(er).

اجنحه (*ajneḥeh*) A. wings. (*Pl. of* جناح.)

اجوف (*ajvaf*) A. hollow.

اجیر (*ajir*) A. hired labourer.

احادیث (*aḥādiṣ*) A. traditions. (*Pl. of* حدیث.)

احاطه (*eḥāṭeh*) A. (act of) surrounding; comprehension. احاطه کردن to surround.

احباب (*aḥbāb*) A. friends. (*Pl. of* حبیب.)

احتذار (*eḥteẕār*) A. avoidance.

احتراز (*eḥterāẕ*) A. avoidance. احتراز کردن to avoid.

احتراق (*eḥterāq*) A. combustion, oxidation.

احترام (*eḥterām*) A. respect.

احتساب (*eḥtesāb*) A. calculation; office of a محتسب.

احتشام (*eḥteshām*) A. pomp, magnificence.

احتکار (*eḥtekār*) A. (act of) buying up and hoarding.

احتمال (*eḥtemāl*) A. probability. احتمال دادن to consider probable.

احتیاج (*eḥtiāj*) A. need, requirement.

احتیاط (*eḥtiāṭ*) A. caution; care; precaution.

احتیاطی (*eḥtiāṭi*) A. precautionary.

احجار (*aḥjār*) A. stones, rocks. (*Pl. of* حجر.)

احد (*aḥad*) A. one; (*with neg.*) no one.

احداث (*eḥdāṣ*) A. creation.

احدیت (*aḥadiyyat*) A. unity.

احراز (*eḥrāz*) A. (act of) obtaining. احراز کردن to obtain.

احزاب (*aḥzāb*) A. parties. (*Pl. of* حزب.)

احسان (*eḥsān*) A. beneficence.

احسن (*aḥsan*) A. better, best.

احسنت (*aḥsant*) A. bravo!

احصائیه (*eḥṣā'iyyeh*) A. statistics.

احضار (*eḥẓār*) A. summons, recall. احضار کردن to summon, recall.

احضاریه (*eḥẓāriyyeh*) A. subpœna.

احقاق (*eḥqāq*) A. adjudication. احقاق حق administration of justice.

احکام (*aḥkām*) A. orders, commands. (*Pl. of* حکم.)

احمد (*aḥmad*) A. *masc. proper name.*

احمر (*aḥmar*) A. red.

احمق (*aḥmaq*) A. fool(ish).

احوال (*aḥvāl*) A. conditions, states; state of health. (*Pl. of* حال.)

احوال پرسی (*aḥvāl porsi*) *a.* inquiry after one's health.

احیا (*eḥyā*) A. revival.

احیاناً (*aḥyānan*) A. occasionally; in the event (that).

اخبار (*akhbār*) A. news, reports. (*Pl. of* خبر.)

اختتام (*ekhtetām*) A. completion, conclusion.

اختر (*akhtar*) star.

اختراع (*ekhterā'*) A. discovery. اختراع کردن to discover.

اختصار (*ekhteṣār*) A. abbreviation; brevity.

اختصاص (*ekhteṣāṣ*) A. appropriation. اختصاص داشتن به — to be exclusively devoted to —.

اختفا (*ekhtefā*) A. concealment.

اختلاس (*ekhtelās*) A. embezzlement.

اختلاط (*ekhtelāṭ*) A. mixture.

اختلاف (*ekhtelāf*) A. difference; dispute.

اختلال (*ekhtelāl*) A. disorder, confusion.

اختناق (*ekhtenāq*) A. strangulation.

اخته (*akhteh*) castrated.

اختیار (*ekhtiār*) A. choice, option; authority.

اخذ (*akhẕ*) A. (act of) taking.

اخراج (*ekhrāj*) A. expulsion, dismissal.

اخص (*akhaṣṣ*) A. more, most special.

اخطار (*akhṭār*) A. dangers. (*Pl. of* حطر.)

اخطار (*ekhṭār*) A. notification; warning. اخطار کردن to notify; to warn.

اخفا (*ekhfā*) A. (act of) concealing.

اخگر (*akhgar*) embers.

اخلاص (*ekhlāṣ*) A. sincerity.

اخلاصمند (*ekhlāṣmand*) *a.* sincere.

اخلاف (*akhlāf*) A. successors, descendants. (*Pl. of* خلف.)

اخلاق (*akhlāq*) A. morals; ethics.

اخلاقی (*akhlāqi*) A. moral; ethical.

اخم (*akhm*) frown.

اخمو (*akhmu*) morose, surly.

اخوان (*akhavān*) A. brethren.

اخوت (*okhovvat*) A. brotherhood.

اخوی (*akhavi*) *a.* my brother.

اخیر (*akhir*) A. last, recent.

اخیراً (*akhiran*) A. recently.

ادا (*adā*) A. payment; performance; pronunciation.

اداره (*edāreh*) A. administration, management.

اداری (*edāri*) A. administrative.

ادامه (*edāmeh*) A. continuation. ادامه داشتن to continue.

ادب (*adab*) A. politeness, courtesy; culture.

ادبا (*odabā*) A. men of letters. (*Pl. of* ادیب.)

ادبار (*edbār*) A. adversity.

ادبی (*adabi*) A. literary.

ادبیات (*adabiyyāt*) A. literature.

ادخال (*edkhāl*) A. introduction, insertion.

ادرار (*edrār*) A. urine.

ادراک (*edrāk*) A. perception.

ادعا (*edde'ā*) A. claim. ادعا کردن to claim.

ادعا نامه (*edde'ā nāmeh*) *a.* bill of indictment.

ادوات (*adavāt*) A. tools.

ادوار (*advār*) A. periods, ages. (*Pl. of* دَوْر.)

ادویه (*advieh*) A. drugs, spices. (*Pl. of* دوا.)

ادیان (*adyān*) A. religions. (*Pl. of* دین.)

ادیب (*adib*) A. man of letters.

اذعان (*ez̲ʻān*) A. acknowledgement; submission. اذعان کردن to acknowledge.

اذن (*ez̲n*) A. leave, permission.

اذهان (*az̲hān*) A. opinion. (*Pl. of* ذهن.)

اذیت (*az̲iyyat*) A. harm, injury. اذیت کردن to hurt, harm.

ارابه (*arābeh*) T. cart, waggon; tank.

اراده (*erādeh*) A. will.

اراضی (*arāẕi*) A. lands, territories. (*Pl. of* ارض.)

ارامنه (*arāmeneh*) A. Armenians. (*Pl. of* ارمنی.)

ارباب (*arbāb*) A. possessors, owners; master, landlord. (*Pl. of* رب.)

ارتباط (*ertebāṭ*) A. connection, communication.

ارتباطی (*ertebāṭi*) A. pertaining to communications.

ارتجاع (*ertejāʻ*) A. reaction.

ارتجاعی (*ertejāʻi*) A. reactionary.

ارتش (*artesh*) army.

ارتشا (*erteshā*) A. (act of) taking a bribe.

ارتعاش (*erteʻāsh*) A. trembling.

ارتفاع (*ertefāʻ*) A. height, elevation.

ارتقا (*erteqā*) A. elevation, promotion. ارتقا کردن to raise, promote.

ارتکاب (*ertekāb*) A. commission, perpetration (*of a crime*).

ارث (*ers̱*) A. inheritance.

ارثی (*ers̱i*) A. hereditary.

ارج (*arj*) worth, value.

ارجاع (*erjāʻ*) A. (act of) referring, assigning.

ارجح (*arjaḥ*) A. more, most preferable.

ارجمند (*arjmand*) valuable, dear.

اردن (*ordonn*) A. Jordan.

اردو (*ordu*) T. camp; Urdu.

اردوگاه (*ordugāh*) camp.

اردیبهشت (*ordibehesht*) *name of the second month of the Persian year.*

ارز (*arz*) value, price; currency.

ارزاق (*arzāq*) A. provisions. (*Pl. of* رزق.)

ارزان (*arzān*) cheap.

ارزانی (*arzāni*) cheapness; (act of) giving, (thing) given. ارزانی داشتن to grant, bestow.

ارزش (*arzesh*) value.

ارزن (*arzan*) millet.

ارزیدن (*arzidan*) to be worth, to cost.

ارسال (*ersāl*) A. (act of) sending. ارسال کردن to send.

ارسطو (*arasṭu*) A. Aristotle.

ارشاد (*ershād*) A. orthodoxy.

ارشد (*arshad*) A. elder, senior.

ارض (*arẕ*) A. earth, land, territory.

ارضِ روم (*arẕe rum*) A. Erzerum.

ارضی (*arẕi*) A. territorial.

ارغوان (*arghavān*) Judas-tree; purple (colour).

ارغوانی (*arghavāni*) purple.

ارقام (*arqām*) A. figures. (*Pl. of* رقم.)

ارکان (*arkān*) A. pillars (of state); fundamentals. ارکانِ حرب (military) staff.

ارکستر (*orkestr*) F. orchestra.

ارگ (*arg*) citadel.

ارگان (*orgān*) F. organ (*of a political party*).

ارمغان (*armaghān*) present, souvenir.

ارمنستان (*armanestān*) Armenia.

ارمنی (*armani*) Armenian.

ارواح (*arvāḥ*) A. souls, spirits. (*Pl. of* روح.)

اروپا (*orupā*) Europe.

ارّه (*arreh*) saw.

از (*az*) from, out of; than.

ازدواج (*ezdevāj*) A. marriage. ازدواج کردن to marry.

ازدحام (*ezdeḥām*) A. crowd.

ازدیاد (*ezdiād*) A. increase. augmentation.

ازل (*azal*) A. eternity without beginning.

ازمنه (*azmeneh*) A. times. (*Pl. of* زمان.)

ازمیر (*ezmir*) Smyrna.

ازواج (*azvāj*) A. pairs. (*Pl. of* زوج).

اژدها (*azhdahā*) dragon.

اژدر (*azhdar*) dragon; torpedo.

اساتید (*asātid*) *a.* masters. (*Pl. of* استاد.)

اساس (*asās*) A. basis, foundation; principle.

اساساً (*asāsan*) A. fundamentally, essentially, in principle.

اساسنامه (*asāsnāmeh*) *a.* statute.

اساسی (*asāsi*) A. basic, fundamental.

اسامی (*asāmi*) A. names. (*Pl. of* اسم.)

اسانسور (*asānsor*) F. lift.

اسب (*asb*) horse.

اسباب (*asbāb*) A. instruments, goods, chattels. (*Pl. of* سبب.)

اسب دوانی (*asb davāni*) horse race.

اسبق (*asbaq*) A. previous.

اسپانی (*espāni*) F. Spain.

اسپرس (*esperes*) sainfoin.

اسپریس (*aspris*) racecourse.

استا (*ostā*) master.

استاد (*ostād*) master; professor.

استان (*ostān*) province.

استاندار (*ostāndār*) governor of a province.

استبداد (*estebdād*) A. despotism.

استتار (*estetār*) A. concealment.

استثمار (*esteṣmār*) A. exploitation.

استثنا (*esteṣnā*) A. exception. باستثناءِ except.

استحصال (*esteḥṣāl*) A. production.

استحقاق (*esteḥqāq*) A. merit.

استحکام (*esteḥkām*) A. firmness; fortification.

استحمام (*esteḥmām*) A. (act of) taking a bath.

استخدام (*estekhdām*) A. engagement, employment. استخدام کردن to engage, employ.

استخر (*estakhr*) lake, pond.

استخراج (*estekhrāj*) A. extraction. استخراج کردن to extract, to work (*a mine*).

استخوان (*ostokhvān*) bone ; stone (*of fruits*).

استخوان بندی (*ostokhvān bandi*) skeleton.

استدعا (*ested'ā*) A. request.

استدلال (*estedlāl*) A. demonstration.

استراحت (*esterāḥat*) A. rest. استراحت کردن to rest.

استرداد (*esterdād*) A. restoration.

استسقا (*estesqā*) A. dropsy.

استطاعت (*esteṭā'at*) A. ability, power.

استعداد (*este'dād*) A. talent.

استعفا (*este'fā*) A. resignation. استعفا دادن to resign.

استعمال (*este'māl*) A. use, employment.

استغاثه (*esteghāṣeh*) A. supplication.

استفاده (*estefādeh*) A. (act of) taking advantage, use, profit.

استفراغ (*estefrāgh*) A. (act of) vomiting.

استفسار (*estefsār*) A. inquiry, interrogation.

استفهام (*estefhām*) A. interrogation.

استقامت (*esteqāmat*) A. perseverance.

استقبال (*esteqbāl*) A. going to meet ; (official) welcome ; future.

استقرا (*esteqrā*) A. deduction.

استقرار (*esteqrār*) A. settlement, establishment.

استقراض (*esteqrāẓ*) A. (act of) borrowing.

استقراع (*esteqrā'*) A. drawing (*of lots, etc.*).

استقلال (*esteqlāl*) A. independence.

استکان (*estekān*) R. tumbler.

استمداد (*estemdād*) A. (act of) seeking help.

استنباط (*estenbāṭ*) A. deduction.

استنساخ (*estensākh*) A. transcription, copying.

استنطاق (*estenṭāq*) A. cross-examination, interrogation.

استوا (*estevā*) A. equality ; equator.

استوار (*ostovār*) firm, solid, fixed ; warrant officer.

استوارنامه (*ostovārnāmeh*) credentials.

استوانه (*ostovāneh*) cylinder.

استهزا (*estehzā*) A. mockery.

استیضاح (*estiẓāḥ*) A. interpellation.

استیلا (*estilā*) A. domination, ascendancy.

استیناف (*estināf*) A. appeal.

اسحق (*esḥāq*) A. Isaac.

اسد (*asad*) A. lion ; Leo.

اسرا (*osarā*) A. prisoners. (*Pl. of* اسیر.)

اسرار (*asrār*) A. secrets. (*Pl. of* سرّ.)

اسرار آمیز (*asrār āmiz*) *a.* mysterious.

اسراف (*esrāf*) A. extravagance.

اسرع (*asra'*) A. quicker, quickest.

اسطبل (*esṭabl*) A. stable.

اسعار (*as'ār*) A. prices ; rates of exchange. (*Pl. of* سعر.)

اسف (*asaf*) A. regret.

اسفالت (*asfālt*) F. (act of laying with) asphalt.

اسف انگیز (*asaf angiz*) *a.* regrettable, deplorable.

اسفل (*asfal*) A. lower, lowest ; inferior.

اسفناج (*esfenāj*) spinach.

اسفند (*esfand*) *name of the last month of the Persian year.*

اسقف (*osqof*) A. bishop.

اسکلت (*eskelet*) F. skeleton.

اسکناس (*eskenās*) R. bank-note.

اسکندر (*eskandar*) A. Alexander.

اسکندرون (*eskandarun*) A. Alexandretta.

اسکندریه (*eskandariyyeh*) A. Alexandria.

اسکی (*eski*) F. ski.

اسلاف (*aslāf*) A. forefathers. (*Pl. of* سلف.)

اسلام (*eslām*) A. Islam.

اسلامبول (*eslāmbol*) *a.* Constantinople.

اسلامی (*eslāmi*) A. Islamic.

اسلاو (*eslāv*) F. Slav.

اسلحه (*asleḥeh*) A. arms. (*Pl. of* سلاح.)

اسلوب (*oslub*) A. style.

اسم (*esm*) A. name.

اسما (*asmā*) A. names. (*Pl. of* اسم.)

اسمعیل (*esmā'il*) A. Ishmael; *masc. proper name.*

اسم نویسی (*esm nevisi*) *a.* enrolment.

اسناد (*asnād*) A. documents. (*Pl. of* سند.)

اسواران (*asvārān*) troop (*of cavalry, etc.*).

اسود (*asvad*) A. black.

اسهال (*es-hāl*) A. diarrhœa.

اسهام (*as-hām*) A. shares. (*Pl. of* سهم.)

اسیر (*asir*) A. prisoner.

اسیری (*asiri*) *a.* captivity.

اشباع (*eshbā'*) A. saturation.

اشتباه (*eshtebāh*) A. mistake.

اشتعال (*eshte'āl*) A. conflagration.

اشتغال (*eshteghāl*) A. occupation.

اشتقاق (*eshteqāq*) A. derivation.

اشتها (*eshtehā*) A. appetite, desire.

اشتیاق (*eshtiāq*) A. desire, longing.

اشجار (*ashjār*) A. trees. (*Pl. of* شجر.)

اشخاص (*ashkhāṣ*) A. persons. (*Pl. of* شخص.)

اشرار (*ashrār*) A. insurgents, rebels. (*Pl. of* شریر wicked.)

اشراف (*ashrāf*) A. nobles, aristocrats. (*Pl. of* شریف.)

اشرافی (*ashrāfi*) *a.* aristocratic.

اشربه (*ashrebeh*) A. drinks. (*Pl. of* شراب.)

اشرف (*ashraf*) A. more, most noble.

اشرفی (*ashrafi*) A. *name of a gold coin.*

اشعار (*ash'ār*) A. poems (*Pl. of* شعر).

اشعار (*esh'ār*) A. (act of) stating, notifying.

اشعه (*ashe''eh*) A. rays, sunbeams. (*Pl. of* شعاع)

اشغال (*ashghāl*) A. occupations, affairs. (*Pl. of* شغل.)

اشغال (*eshghāl*) A. occupation. اشغال کردن to occupy.

اشغالگر (*eshghālgar*) *a.* occupier.

اشک (*ashk*) tear.

اشکال (*ashkāl*) A. forms, shapes.

اشکال (*eshkāl*) A. difficulty.

اشکانی (*ashkāni*) Arsacide.

اشمئزاز (*eshme'zāz*) A. repugnance.

اشهر (*ashhar*) A. more, most famous.

اشیا (*ashyā*) A. things ; goods. (*Pl. of* شیء.)

اصابت (*eṣābat*) A. (act of) overtaking ; hitting.

اصحاب (*aṣḥāb*) A. owners. (*Pl. of* صاحب.)

اصرار (*eṣrār*) A. insistence. اصرار کردن to insist.

اصطبل (*eṣṭabl*) A. stable.

اصطکاک (*eṣṭekāk*) A. friction.

اصطلاح (*eṣṭelāḥ*) A. (technical) term; idiom.

اصغر (*aṣghar*) A. smaller, smallest.

اصفار (*aṣfār*) A. ciphers, zeros. (*Pl. of* صفر.)

اصفر (*aṣfar*) A. yellow.

اصل (*aṣl*) A. origin ; principal ; foundation.

اصلاً (*aṣlan*) A. (*with neg.*) at all.

اصلاح (*eṣlāḥ*) A. correction, reform, improvement. اصلاح کردن to correct, reform, improve.

اصلح (*aṣlaḥ*) A. more, most advisable.

اصلی (*aṣli*) A. original, fundamental.

اصناف (*aṣnāf*) A. guilds, classes. (*Pl. of* صنف.)

اصول (*oṣul*) A. elements, principles ; method. (*Pl. of* اصل.)

اضافه (*eẓāfeh*) A. addition ; *name of a grammatical particle.* اضافه کردن to add.

اضطراب (*eẓṭerāb*) A. disturbance, agitation, anxiety.

اضمحلال (*eẓmeḥlāl*) A. overthrow, disappearance.

اطاعت (*eṭā'at*) A. obedience. اطاعت کردن to obey.

اطاق (*oṭāq*) T. room, chamber.

اطاله (*eṭāleh*) A. (act of) lengthening.

اطبا (*aṭebbā*) A. physicians. (*Pl. of* طبیب.)

اطراف (*aṭrāf*) A. sides ; suburbs. (*Pl. of* طرف.) در اطرافِ about.

اطعمه (*aṭ'emeh*) A. victuals. (*Pl. of* طعام.)

اطفا (*eṭfā*) A. extinction, quenching. اطفا کردن to extinguish.

اطفال (*aṭfāl*) A. children. (*Pl. of* طفل.)

اطفائیه (*eṭfā'iyyeh*) A. fire-brigade.

اطلاع (*eṭṭelā'*) A. information. اطلاع دادن to report.

اطلاق (*eṭlāq*) A. liberation ; general acceptation (*of a word*).

اطلس (1) (*aṭlas*) A. satin.

اطلس (2) (*aṭlas*) A. Atlantic.

اطمینان (*eṭminān*) A. confidence, assurance.

اطو (*oṭu*) T. flatiron. اطو کشیدن to iron.

اطوار (*aṭvār*) A. ways, fashions. (*Pl. of* طور.)

اطو کش (*oṭu kash*) ironer.

اظهار (*eẓhār*) A. statement, expression. اظهار داشتن to state.

اظهر (*aẓhar*) A. more, most evident ; clearer, clearest.

اعاده (*e'ādeh*) A. restoration, restitution.

اعانه (*e'āneh*) A. assistance, relief, relief fund.

اعتبار (*e'tebār*) A. credit, repute.

اعتدال (*e'tedāl*) A. moderation; equilibrium; equinox.

اعتراض (*e'terāẓ*) A. objection, protest. اعتراض كردن to object, protest.

اعتراف (*e'terāf*) A. confession. اعتراف كردن to confess.

اعتصاب (*e'teṣāb*) A. strike. اعتصاب كردن to go on strike.

اعتقاد (*e'teqād*) A. belief.

اعتماد (*e'temād*) A. confidence, trust.

اعتنا (*e'tenā*) A. attention.

اعداد (*a'dād*) A. numbers. (*Pl. of* عدد.)

اعدام (*e'dām*) A. execution. اعدام كردن to execute.

اعراب (*a'rāb*) A. Arabs. (*Pl. of* عرب.)

اعرابى (*a'rābi*) A. Bedouin Arab.

اعزام (*e'zām*) A. dispatch. اعزام كردن to send.

اعصاب (*a'ṣāb*) A. nerves. (*Pl. of* عصب.)

اعصار (*a'ṣār*) A. ages. (*Pl. of* عصر.)

اعضا (*a'ẓā*) A. members. (*Pl. of* عضو.)

اعطا (*e'ṭā*) A. (act of) granting. اعطا كردن to grant.

اعظم (*a'ẓam*) A. greater, greatest.

اعلام (*e'lām*) A. announcement. اعلام كردن to announce.

اعلاميه (*e'lāmiyyeh*) A. communiqué.

اعلان (*e'lān*) A. advertisement; declaration.

اعلى (*a'lā*) A. higher, highest; upper; superior.

اعليحضرت (*a'lāḥaẓrat*) A. His Majesty.

اعم (*a'amm*) A. ***used only in the phrase*** اعم از — يا — whether — or —.

اعمال (*a'māl*) A. works, actions. (*Pl. of* عمل.)

اعمال (*e'māl*) A. application, exertion.

اعياد (*a'yād*) A. festivals. (*Pl. of* عيد.)

اعيان (*a'yān*) A. nobles; wealthy. (*Pl. of* عين.) مجلسِ اعيان Senate, House of Lords.

اغتشاش (*eghteshāsh*) A. riot, rebellion.

اغذيه (*aghẕieh*) A. foods. (*Pl. of* غذا.)

اغراض (*aghrāẓ*) A. designs, personal interests. (*Pl. of* غرض.)

اغراق (*eghrāq*) A. exaggeration.

اغشيه (*aghshieh*) A. membranes. (*Pl. of* غشا.)

اغفال (*eghfāl*) A. (act of) deluding.

اغلاط (*aghlāṭ*) A. mistakes, errors. (*Pl. of* غلط.)

اغلب (*aghlab*) A. more, most.

اغماض (*eghmāẓ*) A. connivance.

اغنام (*aghnām*) A. sheep. (*Pl. of* غنم.)

اغنيا (*aghniā*) A. the rich. (*Pl. of* غنى.)

اغوا (*eghvā*) A. seduction, enticement.

اغيار (*aghyār*) A. others, strangers. (*Pl. of* غير.)

افاده (*efādeh*) A. conveying (*of meaning*); showing off.

افاغنه (*afāgheneh*) A. Afghans. (*Pl. of* افغان.)

افتادگى (*oftādegi*) humility.

افتادن (*oftādan*) to fall.

افتتاح (*eftetāḥ*) A. opening, inauguration.

افتخار (*eftekhār*) A. honour, glory.

افترا (*efterā*) A. calumny.

افخم (*afkham*) A. greater, greatest.

افراختن (*afrākhtan*) to raise, exalt.

افراد (*afrād*) A. individuals. (*Pl. of* فرد.)

افراسیاب (*afrāsiāb*) *name of a mythical king.*

افراشتن (*afrāshtan*) to raise, exalt.

افراط (*efrāṭ*) A. excess.

افراطی (*efrāṭi*) A. extreme, extremist.

افروختن (*afrukhtan*) to kindle, light.

افریقا (*efriqā*) Africa.

افزار (*afzār*) tool.

افزایش (*afzāyesh*) increase, augmentation.

افزودن (*afzudan*) to increase.

افسار (*afsār*) bridle.

افسانه (*afsāneh*) fable.

افسانه آمیز (*afsāneh āmiz*) fabulous.

افسر (1) (*afsar*) crown.

افسر (2) (*afsar*) officer.

افسردن (*afsordan*) to depress.

افسرده (*afsordeh*) depressed, dejected.

افسوس (*afsus*) alas !

افسون (*afsun*) spell, incantation; deceit.

افسونگر (*afsungar*) magician.

افشا (*efshā*) A. divulgence. افشا کردن to divulge.

افشاندن (*afshāndan*) to scatter.

افشردن (*afshordan*) to press, to squeeze.

افشره (*afshoreh*) fruit juice, sherbet.

افطار (*efṭār*) A. breaking a fast.

افعال (*af'āl*) A. actions. (*Pl. of* فعل.)

افعی (*af'i*) A. viper.

افغان (*afghān*) Afghan.

افغانستان (*afghānestān*) Afghanistan.

افق (*ofoq*) A. horizon.

افقی (*ofoqi*) A. horizontal.

افکار (*afkār*) A. thoughts, ideas. (*Pl. of* فکر.) افکارِ عامه public opinion.

افکندن (*afkandan*) to throw, cast.

افلاس (*eflās*) A. bankruptcy, poverty.

افلاطون (*aflāṭun*) A. Plato.

افواج (*afvāj*) A. armies, troops, regiments. (*Pl. of* فوج.)

افواه (*afvāh*) A. mouths; hearsay. (*Pl. of* فم.)

اقارب (*aqāreb*) A. kinsmen. (*Pl. of* قریب.)

اقامت (*eqāmat*) A. residence. اقامت کردن to reside.

اقامه (*eqāmeh*) A. (act of) setting up, adducing.

اقبال (*eqbāl*) A. prosperity, good fortune.

اقتباس (*eqtebās*) A. excerption, borrowing.

اقتدار (*eqtedār*) A. power.

اقتصاد (*eqteṣād*) A. economy.

اقتصادی (*eqteṣādi*) A. economic.

اقتضا (*eqteẓā*) A. exigency.

اقدام (*eqdām*) A. step, action. اقدام كردن to take action.

اقدس (*aqdas*) A. more, most sacred.

اقرار (*eqrār*) A. confession.

اقسام (*aqsām*) A. kinds, sorts. (*Pl. of* قسم.)

اقصى (*aqṣā*) A. farthest.

اقطار (*aqṭār*) A. regions. (*Pl. of* قطر.)

اقل (*aqall*) A. least.

اقلاً (*aqallan*) A. at least.

اقليت (*aqalliyyat*) A. minority.

اقليم (*eqlim*) A. clime.

اقمار (*aqmār*) A. moons; satellites. (*Pl. of* قمر.)

اقناع (*eqnā'*) A. (act of) satisfying; persuasion. اقناع كردن to satisfy; to persuade.

اقوام (*aqvām*) A. peoples, tribes. (*Pl. of* قوم.)

اكبر (*akbar*) A. greater, greatest; *masc. proper name.*

اكتبر (*oktobr*) F. October.

اكتساب (*ektesāb*) A. acquisition.

اكتشاف (*ekteshāf*) A. discovery, exploration; reconnaissance.

اكتفا (*ektefā*) A. (state of) being contented. اكتفا كردن to be contented.

اكثر (*akṣar*) A. more, most; greater, greatest.

اكثريت (*akṣariyyat*) A. majority.

اكراد (*akrād*) A. Kurds. (*Pl. of* كُرد.)

اكراه (*ekrāh*) A. aversion, reluctance.

اكل (*akl*) A. (act of) eating.

اكليل (*eklil*) A. crown; garland.

اكنون (*aknun*) now.

اكيد (*akid*) A. strict; emphatic.

اكيداً (*akidan*) A. strictly; emphatically.

اگر (*agar*) if.

اگرچه (*agarcheh*) although.

الا (*ellā*) A. except. والا otherwise.

الاغ (*olāgh*) T. donkey.

الان (*al-ān*) A. now; presently.

البته (*al-batteh*) A. of course, certainly.

البسه (*albeseh*) A. clothes. (*Pl. of* لباس.)

التجا (*eltejā*) A. (act of) taking refuge.

التزام (*eltezām*) A. obligation, undertaking; attendance.

التفات (*eltefāt*) A. favour, kindness.

التقا (*elteqā*) A. meeting, confluence.

التماس (*eltemās*) A. entreaty, supplication.

التهاب (*eltehāb*) A. inflammation.

الجزاير (*al-jazāyer*) A. Algeria, Algiers.

الحاق (*elḥāq*) A. annexation.

الحمد لله (*al-ḥamdo lellāh*) A. thank God!

السنه (*alseneh*) A. tongues, languages. (*Pl. of* لسان.)

الغا (*elghā*) A. concellation, annulment.

الف (*alf*) A. thousand.

الف با (*alef bā*) A. ABC, alphabet.

الغرض (*al-gharaẓ*) A. in a word.

الفت (*olfat*) A. familiarity.

القاب (*alqāb*) A. titles. (*Pl. of* لقب.)

الک (*alak*) T. sieve.

الکتریسیته (*elektrisiteh*) F. electricity.

الکتریکی (*elektriki*) electrical.

الکل (*alkol*) F. alcohol.

الکلی (*alkoli*) alcoholic.

الله (*allāh*) A. God.

الم (*alam*) A. grief.

الماس (*almās*) diamond.

الوار (*alvār*) A. Lurs. (*Pl. of* لر.)

الواط (*alvāṭ*) A. rascal(s); rascally.

الوان (*alvān*) A. colours; kinds. (*Pl. of* لون.)

الوهیت (*oluhiyyat*) A. deity, divinity.

الهام (*elhām*) A. inspiration.

الهی (*elāhi*) A. O God!

الی (*elā*) A. to, until.

الی الابد (*elā 'l-abad*) A. for ever.

الیاف (*alyāf*) A. filaments. (*Pl. of* لیف.)

اما (*ammā*) A. but.

اماکن (*amāken*) A. places. (*Pl. of* مکان.)

اماله (*emāleh*) A. clyster, enema.

امام (*emām*) A. religious leader, *imam.*

امان (*amān*) A. safety; quarter.

امانت (*amānat*) A. honesty; deposit, trust.

امانتی (*amānati*) *a.* deposit(ed).

امپراتور (*emperātur*), امپراطور (*emperaṭur*) R. emperor.

امپراتوری (*emperāturi*), امپراطوری (*emperāṭuri*) empire.

امت (*ommat*) A. nation, people, sect.

امتثال (*emteṣ̤āl*), A. conformity, obedience.

امتحان (*emteḥān*) A. examination, test.

امتداد (*emtedād*) A. extension.

امتعه (*amte'eh*) A. goods. (*Pl. of* متاع.)

امتناع (*emtenā'*) A. refusal.

امتنان (*emtenān*) A. obligation.

امتیاز (*emtiāz*) A. privilege, concession.

امثال (*amṣ̤āl*) A. proverbs. (*Pl. of* مثل.)

امجد (*amjad*) A. more, most glorious.

امداد (*emdād*) A. assistance.

امر (*amr*) A. matter, affair; command.

امرا (*omarā*) A. chiefs, leaders. (*Pl. of* امیر).

امرار (*emrār*) A. (act of) passing (*time*), earning (*one's livelihood*).

امراض (*amrāẓ*) A. diseases. (*Pl. of* مرض).

امرداد (*amordad*) *i.q.* مرداد.

امروز (*emruz*) to-day.

امروزه (*emruzeh*) nowadays.

امریکا (*amrikā*) America.

امزجه (*amzejeh*) A. temperaments, constitutions. (*Pl. of* مزاج.)

امساک (*emsāk*) A. parsimony.

امسال (*emsāl*) this year.

امشب (*emshab*) to-night.

امضا (*emẓā*) A. signature. امضا کردن to sign.

امعا (*am'ā*) A. intestines. (*Pl. of* معا.)
امکان (*emkān*) A. possibility.
امکنه (*amkeneh*) A. places. (*Pl. of* مکان.)
امل (*amal*) A. hope, desire.
املا (*emlā*) A. orthography.
املاح (*amlāḥ*) A. salts. (*Pl. of* ملح.)
املاک (*amlāk*) A. properties, lands. (*Pl. of* ملک.)
امن (*amn*) A. safety, security; safe.
امنا (*omanā*) A. trustees. (*Pl. of* امین.)
امنیت (*amniyyat*) A. security.
امنیه (*amniyyeh*) A. civil guard.
امواج (*amvāj*) A. waves. (*Pl. of* موج.)
اموال (*amvāl*) A. goods, possessions. (*Pl. of* مال.)
امور (*omur*) A. affairs. (*Pl. of* امر) امورِ خارجه foreign affairs.
امی (*ommi*) A. illiterate.
امید (*omid*) hope.
امیدوار (*omidvār*) hopeful.
امیر (*amir*) A. prince, commander, emir.
امیر البحر (*amiro'l-baḥr*) A. admiral.
امین (*amin*) A. trustworthy, trustee.
اناث (*enāṣ*) A. females. (*Pl. of* انثی.)
انار (*anār*) pomegranate(-tree).
انبار (*anbār*) storehouse, shed.
انباره (*anbāreh*) accumulator.
انباشتن (*anbāshtan*) to fill (up); to store.
انبر (*anbor*) tongs, pincers.
انبساط (*enbesāṭ*) A. expansion.

انبوه (*anbuh*) crowd(ed); thick, bushy; numerous.
انبیا (*anbiā*) A. prophets. (*Pl. of* نبی.)
انتحار (*enteḥār*) A. suicide. انتحار کردن to commit suicide.
انتخاب (*entekhāb*) A. choice, selection, election. انتخاب کردن to choose, elect.
انتخابات (*entekhābāt*) A. general election.
انتساب (*entesāb*) A. relation, connection.
انتشار (*enteshār*) A. propagation, publication. انتشار دادن to propagate, publish. انتشار یافتن to be propagated, published.
انتصاب (*enteṣāb*) A. appointment.
انتظار (*enteẓār*) A. expectation, waiting. انتظار داشتن to expect.
انتظام (*enteẓām*) A. order, discipline.
انتفاعی (*entefā'i*) A. profit-making.
انتقاد (*enteqād*) A. criticism.
انتقال (*enteqāl*) A. removal, transfer. انتقال دادن to remove. انتقال یافتن to be removed.
انتقام (*enteqām*) A. revenge.
انتها (*entehā*) A. end.
انثی (*onṣā*) A. female.
انجام (*anjām*) completion, fulfilment. انجام دادن to complete, fulfil. انجام یافتن to be completed, fulfilled.
انجماد (*enjemād*) A. congelation, solidification.

انجمن (*anjoman*) society, council, assembly, conference, committee.

انجیر (*anjir*) fig.

انجیل (*enjil*) A. gospel.

انحا (*anḥā*) A. ways, manners. (*Pl. of* نحو.)

انحراف (*enḥerāf*) A. deviation.

انحصار (*enḥeṣār*) A. monopoly.

انحصاری (*enḥeṣāri*) A. pertaining to monopolies.

انحطاط (*enḥeṭāṭ*) A. decline.

انحلال (*enḥelāl*) A. dissolution.

انداختن (*andākhtan*) to throw, cast.

اندازه (*andāzeh*) size, measure(ment). اندازه گرفتن to measure.

اندام (*andām*) body ; limb.

اندرز (*andarz*) advice.

اندرون (*andarun*) interior ; harem.

اندک (*andak*) little, few.

اندوختن (*andukhtan*) to amass, hoard.

اندوخته (*andukhteh*) amassed, hoarded ; deposit ; reserve.

اندونزی (*andonezi*) F. Indonesia.

اندوه (*anduh*) grief, sorrow.

اندوهگین (*anduhgin*) sad, sorrowful.

اندیشه (*andisheh*) reflection ; anxiety.

اندیشیدن (*andishidan*) to think, reflect.

انرژی (*enerzhi*) F. energy.

انزال (*enzāl*) A. seminal effusion.

انزجار (*enzejār*) A. aversion.

انزوا (*enzevā*) A. seclusion.

انس (*ons*) A. familiarity. انس گرفتن to become familiar ; to become tame.

انساج (*ansāj*) A. tissues. (*Pl. of* نسج.)

انسان (*ensān*) A. man(kind).

انسانیت (*ensāniyyat*) A. humanity, courtesy.

انشا (*enshā*) A. style, composition.

انشأ الله (*enshā' allāh*) A. God willing.

انصاف (*enṣāf*) A. justice.

انضباط (*enẓebāṭ*) A. order ; restraint, discipline.

انضمام (*enẓemām*) A. annexation, junction, conjunction. بانضمامِ together with.

انطباق (*enṭebāq*) A. conformity.

انظار (*anẓār*) A. looks, glances, views. (*Pl. of* نظر.) انظارِ عمومی public opinion.

انعام (*en'ām*) A. gratuity, tip.

انعقاد (*en'eqād*) A. conclusion (*of an agreement*) ; holding (*of a meeting*).

انعکاس (*en'ekās*) A. reflection, repercussion.

انفجار (*enfejār*) A. explosion.

انفراد (*enferād*) A. isolation.

انفرادی (*enferādi*) A. isolated, individual.

انفصال (*enfeṣāl*) A. separation, dismissal.

انفیه (*anfieh*) A. snuff.

انفیه دان (*anfieh dān*) *a.* snuff-box.

انقباض (*enqebāẓ*) A. contraction.

انقراض (*enqerāẓ*) A. overthrow, extinction.

انقضا (*enqeẓā*) A. termination, expiration.

انقلاب (*enqelāb*) A. revolution.

انقلابی (*enqelābi*) A. revolutionary.

انقوزه (*anquzeh*) asafœtida.

انکار (*enkār*) A. denial. انکار کردن to deny.

انکسار (*enkesār*) A. fracture; despondency.

انکشاف (*enkeshāf*) A. discovery.

انگاشتن (*angāshtan*) to suppose, to consider.

انگبین (*angabin*) honey.

انگشت (*angosht*) finger.

انگشتانه (*angoshtāneh*) thimble.

انگشتر (*angoshtar*), انگشتری (*angoshtari*) ring.

انگل (*angal*) loop, button-hole; parasite.

انگلستان (*englestān*) England, Great Britain.

انگلی (*angali*) parasitic.

انگلیس (*englis*) English(man), British.

انگور (*angur*) grape(s).

انگیختن (*angikhtan*) to excite, rouse.

انوار (*anvār*) A. lights. (*Pl. of* نور.)

انواع (*anvā'*) A. kinds, sorts. (*Pl. of* نوع.)

انوشه (*anusheh*) happy, blessed.

انوشیروان (*anoushirvan*) *name of a Sassanian king; masc. proper name.*

انهار (*anhār*) A. rivers. (*Pl. of* نهر.)

انهدام (*enhedām*) A. destruction.

انیس (*anis*) A. companion, friend.

او (*u*) he, she.

اواخر (*avākher*) A. last parts, end. (*Pl. of* آخر.)

اواسط (*avāseṭ*) A. middle parts, middle. (*Pl. of* اوسط.)

اوامر (*avāmer*) A. orders.

اوان (*avān*) A. times. (*Pl.* of آن.)

اوایل (*avāyel*) A. first parts, beginning. (*Pl. of* اول.)

اوباش (*oubāsh*) A. rogues, ruffians.

اوت (*ut*) F. August.

اوج (*ouj*) A. zenith.

اوراق (*ourāq*) A. leaves; papers, documents. (*Pl. of* ورق.)

اورنگ (*ourang*) throne.

اورشلیم (*urshelim*) A. Jerusalem.

اوصاف (*ouṣāf*) A. qualities, attributes. (*Pl. of* وصف.)

اوسط (*ousaṭ*) A. middle, medium.

اوضاع (*ouẓā'*) A. conditions, state of affairs. (*Pl. of* وضع.)

اوطان (*ouṭān*) A. countries, homes. (*Pl. of* وطن.)

اوقات (*ouqāt*) A. times; state of mind. (*Pl. of* وقت.)

اوقاف (*ouqāf*) A. pious legacies, foundations. (*Pl. of* وقف.)

اول (*avval*) A. first.

اولاً (*avvalan*) A. firstly, in the first place.

اولاد (*oulād*) A. sons, children. (*Pl. of* ولد.)

اولی (*avvali*) A. first.

اولیا (*ouliā*) A. saints; guardians; administrators.

اولین (*avvalin*) *a.* first.

اولیه (*avvaliyyeh*) A. primary.

اونیورسیته (*universiteh*) F. university.

اهالی (*ahāli*) A. people, population. (*Pl. of* اهل.)

اهانت (*ehānat*) A. contempt; insolence.

اهتزاز (*ehtezāz*) A. agitation, vibration.

اهتمام (*ehtemām*) A. care, diligence.

اهدا (*ehdā*) A. presentation; dedication.

اهرام (*ahrām*) A. pyramids. (*Pl. of* هرم.)

اهرم (*ahrom*) lever.

اهل (*ahl*) A. people.

اهلی (*ahli*) A. tame.

اهم (*ahamm*) A. more, most important.

اهمال (*ehmāl*) A. negligence.

اهمیت (*ahammiyyat*) A. importance.

ای (*ei*) O!

ایالت (*eyālat*) A. province.

ایالتی (*eyālati*) *a.* provincial.

ایام (*ayyām*) A. days. (*Pl. of* یوم.)

ایتالیا (*itāliā*) Italy.

ایتام (*eitām*) A. orphans. (*Pl. of* یتیم.)

ائتیلاف (*e'tilāf*) A. alliance, coalition; agreement.

ایجاب (*ijāb*) A. exigency.

ایجاد (*ijād*) A. creation, establishment. ایجاد کردن to create, to establish.

ایدآل (*ideāl*) F. ideal.

ایراد (*irād*) A. objection; adduction; delivery (*of a speech*).

ایران (*irān*) Persia.

ایرانی (*irāni*) Persian.

ایرانیت (*irāniyyat*) *a.* "Persiandom."

ایرج (*iraj*) *name of a legendary king of Persia; masc. proper name.*

ایزد (*izad*) God.

ایستادن (*istādan*) to stand.

ایستاده (*istādeh*) standing.

ایستگاه (*istgāh*) station.

ایشان (*ishān*) they.

ایضاً (*eiẓan*) A. ditto.

ایفا (*ifā*) A. fulfilment. ایفا کردن to fulfil.

ایل (*il*) T. tribe.

ایلچی (*ilchi*) T. ambassador.

ایما (*imā*) A. signal, sign, hint.

ایمان (*imān*) A. faith, belief.

ایمن (*iman*) A. safe.

این (*in*) this.

اینجا (*injā*) here.

اینک (*inak*) now.

ایوان (*eivān*) veranda, balcony; palace.

ایوب (*ayyub*) A. Job.

ب

ب (*be*) to, with, by.

با (*bā*) with. با آنکه although.

با ادب (*bā adab*) *a.* polite, courteous.

باب (1) (*bāb*) father; suitable.

باب (2) (*bāb*) going, in working order. باب کردن to set going, to start.

باب (3) (*bāb*) A. door, gate; affair, matter; chapter. در بابِ concerning.

بابا (*bābā*) papa.

بابت (*bābat*) A. concern, account. بابتِ on account of.

باب زن (*bāb zan*) spit.

بابونه (*bābuneh*) camomile.

باج (*bāj*) tribute, tax.

باختر (*bākhtar*) west.

باختری (*bākhtari*) western.

باختن (*bākhtan*) to lose.

باد (*bād*) wind.

بادام (*bādām*) almond.

باد آورده (*bād āvardeh*) windfall.

بادبان (*bādbān*) sail.

بادپا (*bādpā*) (swift) horse.

بادکوبه (*bādkubeh*) Baku.

بادنجان (*bādenjān*) egg-plant.

با دوام (*bā davām*) *a.* durable.

باده (*bādeh*) wine.

بادی (*bādi*) pertaining to the wind. قایقِ بادی a sailing boat.

بادیه (*bādieh*) A. desert.

بار (*bār*) burden, load; fruit; fœtus; time, turn; audience.

باران (*bārān*) rain.

باردار (*bārdār*) fruitful; pregnant.

بارز (*bārez*) A. manifest.

بارش (*bāresh*) rain.

بار کش (*bār kash*) carrying loads. حیوانِ بار کش beast of burden.

بارندگی (*bārandegi*) rainfall.

بارو (*bāru*) rampart.

باروت (*bārut*) gunpowder.

باره (1) (*bāreh*) respect, regard. در بارهٔ with respect to.

باره (2) (*bāreh*) rampart.

باره (3) (*bāreh*) horse.

باری (1) (*bāri*) anyhow.

باری (2) (*bāri*) pertaining to loads. اتوموبیلِ باری lorry.

باریدن (*bāridan*) to rain.

باریک (*bārik*) narrow, thin; delicate, subtle.

باز (1) (*bāz*) open(ed); again.

باز (2) (*bāz*) hawk.

بازار (*bāzār*) market.

باز پرس (*bāz pors*) cross-examiner, examining magistrate.

باز پرسی (*bāz porsi*) cross-examination, interrogation.

باز جوئی (*bāz ju'i*) investigation, inquiry.

باز خواست (*bāz khvāst*) investigation.

باز داشت (*bāz dāsht*) prevention; detention. باز داشت کردن to prevent; to detain.

بازداشتگاه (*bāzdāshtgāh*) concentration camp.

بازدید (*bāzdid*) return visit; inspection; audit(ing), checking.

بازرس (*bāzras*) inspector.

بازرسی (*bāzrasi*) inspection, investigation.

بازرگان (*bāzergān*) merchant.

بازرگانی (1) (*bāzergāni*) trade, commerce.

بازرگانی (2) (*bāzergāni*) commercial.

باز گشت (*bāz gasht*) return. باز گشت کردن to return.

باز گشتن (*bāz gashtan*) to return.

باز مانده (*bāz māndeh*) detained; left behind; exhausted.

بازو (*bāzu*) (upper) arm.

بازو بند (*bāzu band*) amulet.

بازی (*bāzi*) game, play. بازی کردن to play.

باز یافت (*bāz yāft*) recovery.

باز یافتن (*bāz yāftan*) to recover.

بازیچه (*bāzicheh*) toy, plaything.

بازیگر (*bāzigar*) actor.

باستان (*bāstān*) ancient.

باستان شناس (*bāstān shenās*) archaeologist.

باستان شناسی (*bāstān shenāsi*) archaeology.

باستانی (*bāstāni*) ancient.

باسمه (*bāsmeh*) T. press.

باشگاه (*bāshgāh*) club.

باشه (*bāsheh*) sparrow-hawk.

باصره (*bāṣereh*) A. sight.

با صفا (*bā ṣafā*) *a.* pleasant.

باطری (*bāṭri*) F. battery.

باطل (*bāṭel*) A. null and void; vain, false.

باطلاق (*bāṭlāq*) T. marsh, swamp.

باطن (*bāṭen*) A. interior; heart, mind; secret.

باطنی (*bāṭeni*) A. interior, inward, esoteric.

باعث (*bā'eṣ*) A. cause, motive.

باغ (*bāgh*) garden.

باغبان (*bāghbān*) gardener.

باغچه (*bāghcheh*) little garden, orchard.

بافتن (*bāftan*) to weave.

باقر (*bāqer*) A. *masc. proper name.*

باقی (*bāqi*) A. remaining, remainder. باقی ماندن to remain.

باک (*bāk*) fear.

باکره (*bākereh*) A. virgin.

بال (1) (*bāl*) wing.

بال (2) (*bāl*) whale.

بالا (*bālā*) above. بالا بردن to raise. از — بالا رفتن to climb —.

بالا پوش (*bālā push*) overcoat; quilt.

بالا خانه (*bālā khāneh*) balcony.

بالاخره (*be'l-akhereh*) A. at last, finally.

بالاخص (*be'l-akhaṣṣ*) A. most especially.

بالارو (*bālārou*) lift.

بالجمله (*be'l-jomleh*) A. in short.

بالش (*bālesh*), بالشت (*bālesht*) pillow, bolster.

بالصراحه (*be'ṣ-ṣarāḥeh*) A. explicitly.

بالطبع (*be'ṭ-ṭab'*) A. naturally.

بالعکس (*be'l-'aks*) A. vice versa; on the contrary.

بالغ (*bālegh*) A. adult, full-grown; amounting.

بالکل (*be'l-koll*) A. entirely.

بالمره (*be'l-marreh*) A. gradually.

بالنتیجه (*be'n-natijeh*) A. consequently.

بالنسبه (*be'n-nesbeh*) A. comparatively.

بام (*bām*) roof.

بامداد (*bāmdād*) morning.

بامدادان (*bāmdādān*) (in the) morning.

بامیه (*bāmieh*) okra, lady's finger.

بانک (*bānk*) F. bank.

بانکدار (*bānkdār*) banker.

بانگ (*bāng*) cry, clamour.

بانو (*bānu*) lady.

بانی (*bāni*) A. founder.

باور (*bāvar*) belief. باور کردن to believe.

با وفا (*bā vafā*) *a.* faithful.

باه (*bāh*) A. sperm; virility.

باهم (*bāham*) together.

با هوش (*bā hush*) intelligent.

بایر (*bāyer*) A. arid.

بایستن (*bāyestan*) to be necessary.

بایگان (*bāyegān*) guardian; treasurer; archivist.

ببر (*babr*) tiger.

بت (*bot*) idol.

بت پرست (*bot parast*) idolater.

بچگی (*bachchegi*) childhood.

بچه (*bachcheh*) child.

بحار (*beḥār*) A. seas. (*Pl. of* بحر).

بحث (*baḥṣ*) A. dispute, argument, debate.

بحر (*baḥr*) A. sea.

بحر الروم (*baḥro'r-rum*) A. the Mediterranean.

بحران (*boḥrān*) A. crisis.

بحران آمیز (*boḥrān āmiz*) *a.* critical.

بحری (*baḥri*) A. marine.

بحل (*beḥel*) *a.* pardon.

بخار (*bokhār*) A. vapour, steam.

بخاری (*bokhāri*) A. pertaining to steam; stove.

بخت (*bakht*) luck, fortune.

بخت آزمائی (*bakht āzmā'i*) lottery.

بختیار (*bakhtyār*) fortunate, lucky.

بخش (*bakhsh*) division; sub-district.

بخشش (*bakhshesh*) present, gift.

بخشنامه (*bakhshnāmeh*) circular.

بخشنده (*bakhshandeh*) forgiving, merciful.

بخشودگی (*bakhshudegi*) exemption.

بخشیدن (*bakhshidan*) to forgive; to grant, bestow.

بخل (*bokhl*) A. avarice.

بخیل (*bakhil*) A. avaricious, miser(ly).

بخیه (*bakhyeh*) stitch(ing).

بد (*bad*) bad.

بدایت (*bedāyat*) A. beginning.

بد بخت (*bad bakht*) unfortunate.

بد بختانه (*bad bakhtāneh*) unfortunately.

بدبین (*badbin*) pessimistic.

بد خواه (*bad khvāh*) malevolent.

بد خو (*bad khu*) bad-tempered.

بدر (*badr*) A. full moon.

بدرقه (*badraqeh*) escort, convoy.

بدرود (*bedrud*) farewell.

بدعت (*bed'at*) A. innovation; heresy.

بد گو (*bad gu*) slanderous, slanderer.

بد گوئی (*bad gu'i*) slander.

بدل (*badal*) A. substitute.

بد مست (*bad mast*) blind drunk.

بد مستی (*bad masti*) drunkenness, drunken brawling.

بدن (*badan*) A. body.

بد نام (*bad nām*) infamous.

بد نامی (*bad nāmi*) ill repute.

بدو (*badv*) A. beginning.

بدواً (*badvan*) A. in the beginning, first.

بدونِ (*bedune*) A. without.

بدهکار (*bedehkār*) debtor.

بدهی (*bedehi*) debt.

بدی (*badi*) badness, wickedness.

بدیع (*badi'*) A. strange, wonderful.

بدیهی (*badihi*) A. self-evident.

بذر (*bazr*) A. seed.

بذل (*bazl*) A. munificence, giving freely. بذل کردن to give freely.

بذله (*bazleh*) A. jest.

بر (1) (*bar*) on.

بر (2) (*bar*) breast.

بر (3) (*bar*) fruit.

برّ (*barr*) A. land.

برابر (*barābar*) equal(ly). در برابرِ before, in front of. سه برابر three times as much.

برابری (*barābari*) equality.

برات (*barāt*) A. draft, bill of exchange.

برادر (*berādar*) brother.

برادر زاده (*berādar zādeh*) nephew.

برادری (*berādari*) brotherhood, fraternity.

براده (*borādeh*) A. filings.

براری (*barāri*) A. deserts. (*Pl. of* بریه.)

بر آشفتن (*bar āshoftan*) to be agitated.

بر افراشتن (*bar afrāshtan*) to raise.

براق (*barrāq*) A. bright, glittering.

بر آمدگی (*bar āmadegi*) swelling, projection.

بر انداختن (*bar andākhtan*) to overthrow; to abolish.

بر آورد (*bar āvard*) estimate.

براهین (*barāhin*) A. proofs. (*Pl. of* برهان).

برایِ (*barāye*) for, on account of. برایِ اینکه because.

بربری (*barbari*) A. barbarian.

بربط (*barbaṭ*) A. harp.

بر پیچیدن (*bar pichidan*) to roll up.

برتر (*bartar*) higher.

برتری (*bartari*) superiority.

برج (*borj*) A. tower; sign of the zodiac.

بر جستگی (*bar jastegi*) relief, projection.

بر جستن (*bar jastan*) to leap.

بر جسته (*bar jasteh*) embossed; outstanding, eminent.

برجیس (*berjis*) the planet Jupiter.

بر چیدن (*bar chidan*) to pick up.

بر خواستن (*bar khvāstan*) to rise.

برخوردار (*barkhordār*) enjoying, successful. برخوردار شدن to enjoy.

بر خوردن (*bar khordan*) to come in contact with, encounter.

برخی (*barkhi*) some.

بر داشتن (*bar dāshtan*) to take (up); to remove.

بردبار (*bordbār*) meek, patient.

بردگی (*bardegi*) slavery, servitude.

بردن (*bordan*) to take (away). نام — بردن to mention —.

برده (*bardeh*) slave, captive.

بر رسی (*bar rasi*) review, study.

برز (*barz*) agriculture; seed.

برزگر (*barzgar*) agriculturalist.

برش (*boresh*) cut; coupon.

برشته (*bereshteh*) roasted. برشته کردن to roast.

بر علیهِ (*bar 'aleihe*) *a.* against.

برف (*barf*) snow.

برق (*barq*) A. lightning; electricity.

بر قرار (*bar qarār*) *a.* established; in working order.

برکت (*barakat*) A. blessing.

برکه (*berkeh*) A. pool.

برگ (*barg*) leaf.

بر گردانیدن (*bar gardānidan*) to turn; to change; to return, restore.

بر گرفتن (*bar gereftan*) to remove, carry off.

بر گزیدن (*bar gozidan*) to choose, select.

بر گشتن (*bar gashtan*) to return; to be changed; to apostatize.

بر گشته (*bar gashteh*) changed, inverted. بر گشته اختر ill-starred.

بر لهِ (*bar lahe*) *a.* in favour of, for.

برنا (*barnā*) young (man).

برنامه (*barnāmeh*) model; programme.

برنج (1) (*berenj*) rice.

برنج (2) (*berenj*) brass.

برنده (*barandeh*) bearer; winner.

برنده (*borandeh*) cutting, sharp.

برنشیت (*bronshit*) F. bronchitis.

بروج (*boruj*) A. towers; signs of the zodiac. (*Pl. of* برج.)

برودت (*borudat*) A. cold(ness).

بروز (*boruz*) A. appearance. بروز کردن to appear.

برومند (*barumand*) fruitful; fortunate.

بره (*barreh*) lamb.

برهان (*borhān*) A. proof, demonstration.

برهم (*barham*) together, against one another.

برهم خوردگی (*barham khordegi*) indisposition.

برهنه (*berahneh*) naked, bare.

بری (*barri*) A. terrestrial.

بریان (*beryān*) roasted. بریان کردن to roast.

بریتانیا (*britāniā*) Britain.

بریدن (*boridan*) to cut (off).

برین (*barin*) highest, supreme.

بریه (*barriyyeh*) A. desert.

بز (*boz*) goat.

بزاز (*bazzāz*) A. cloth-dealer.

بزاق (*bozāq*) A. saliva.

بز دل (*boz del*) coward(ly).

بزرک (*bazrak*) *a.* linseed.

بزرگ (*bozorg*) great, large.

بزرگی (*bozorgi*) greastnes, size.

بزغاله (*bozghāleh*) kid.

بزم (*bazm*) banquet, feast.

بزمجه (*bozmajjeh*) lizard.

بزه (*bezeh*) sin, crime.

بزه کار (*bezeh kār*) sinful, criminal.

بس (*bas*) enough. از بس که ,بس که inasmuch as.

بسا (*basā*) many (a).

بساط (*besāṭ*) A. carpet; goods exposed for sale.

بسامد (*basāmad*) frequency. پر بسامد high frequency. کم بسامد low frequency.

بست (*bast*) fastening, knot; sanctuary; dyke.

بستان (*bostān*) garden.

بستر (*bestar*) bed.

بستری (*bestari*) bedridden.

بستگی (*bastegi*) relationship; dependence.

بستن (*bastan*) to bind, tie; to close; to conclude (*a treaty*).

بسته (*basteh*) bound, tied; frozen; dependent; package, parcel.

بسط (*basṭ*) A. extension, expansion. بسط دادن to extend, expand.

باسم الله (*besme'llāh*) A. in the name of God!

بسمل (*besmel*) *a.* (ritually) slaughtered.

بسی (*basi*) many, much.

بسیار (*besyār*) many, much; very.

بسیج (*basij*) preparation; mobilization. بسیج کردن to prepare; to mobilize.

بشارت (*beshārat*) A. good tidings.

بشاشت (*bashāshat*) A. cheerfulness.

بشر (*bashar*) A. mankind.

بشریت (*bashariyyat*) A. humanity.

بشقاب (*boshqāb*) T. plate, dish.

بصره (*baṣreh*) A. Basra.

بصیرت (*baṣirat*) A. intelligence, insight.

بضاعت (*bez̤ā'at*) A. merchandise; stock, capital; means.

بط (*baṭṭ*) A. duck.

بطالت (*baṭālat*) A. vanity; absurdity.

بطری (*boṭri*) E. bottle.

بطن (*baṭn*) A. belly, womb.

بطی (*baṭi*) A. slow, dull.

بعد (*ba'd*) A. afterwards. بعد از after.

بعد (*bo'd*) A. distance.

بعداً (*ba'dan*) A. subsequently.

بعدها (*ba'dhā*) A. afterwards.

بعض (*ba'z̤*) A. part, some. بعضی some.

بعید (*ba'id*) A. distant, remote; strange, improbable.

بعینه (*be'eineh*) A. exactly.

بغاز (*boghāz*) T. strait.

بغتةً (*baghtatan*) A. suddenly.

بغداد (*baghdād*) Baghdad.

بغرنج (*boghranj*) complicated, intricate.

بغض (*boghz̤*) A. hatred.

بغل (*baghal*) arm-pit.

بقا (*baqā*) A. duration, permanence, eternity.

بقال (*baqqāl*) A. grocer.

بقالی (*baqqāli*) *a.* grocery.

بقچه (*boqcheh*) bundle, knapsack.

بقم (*baqam*) A. logwood.
بقیه (*baqiyyeh*) A. remainder.
بکارت (*bakārat*) A. virginity.
بکر (*bekr*) A. virgin.
بلا (*balā*) A. misfortune, calamity.
بلا (*belā*) A. without.
بلاد (*belād*) A. cities, countries. (*Pl. of* بلد).
بلاغ (*balāgh*) A. (delivery of) message.
بلا فاصله (*belā fāṣeleh*) A. immediately.
بلبل (*bolbol*) nightingale.
بلد (1) (*balad*) A. city, country.
بلد (2) (*balad*) T. guide. بلد بودن to know, be conversant with.
بلدان (*boldān*) A. cities, countries. (*Pl. of* بلد.)
بلدرچین (*belderchin*) T. quail.
بلدیه (*baladiyyeh*) A. municipality.
بلژیک (*belzhik*) F. Belgium.
بلعیدن (*bal'idan*) *a.* to swallow.
بلغا (*bolaghā*) A. the eloquent. (*Pl. of* بلیغ).
بلغارستان (*bolghārestān*) Bulgaria.
بلکه (*balkeh*) *a.* but; even, perhaps.
بلند (*boland*) high, tall; long; loud. بلند کردن to raise. بلند شدن to rise.
بلندی (*bolandi*) height, tallness; loudness.
بلوا (*balvā*) disturbance, riot.
بلور (*bolur*) A. crystal.
بلوط (*baluṭ*) A. acorn; oak.
بلوغ (*bolugh*) A. puberty.
بلوک (*boluk*) T. rural district.
بله (*baleh*) *a.*, بلی (*bale*) A. yes.
بلیط (*beliṭ*) F. ticket.
بلیغ (*baligh*) A. eloquent.
بلیه (*baliyyeh*) A. misfortune, calamity.
بم (*bam*) bass.
بمب (*bomb*) F. bomb.
بمباران (*bombārān*) bombardment. بمباران کردن to bomb(ard).
بمب افکن (*bomb afkan*), بمب انداز (*bomb andāz*) bomber (aircraft).
بمبئی (*bamba'i*) Bombay.
بمحض (*bemaḥze*) *a.* immediately upon. بمحض اینکه as soon as.
بن (*bon*) root.
بنا (*benā*) A. building. بنا کردن to build. بنا بر according to. بنا بر این therefore. بنا بودن to be arranged.
بنا (*bannā*) A. mason, builder.
بنادر (*banāder*) A. ports. (*Pl. of* بندر.)
بنائی (*bannā'i*) *a.* masonry.
بن بست (*bon bast*) cul-de-sac.
بند (*band*) band, bond(s); paragraph; dam, dyke.
بندر (*bandar*) port, harbour.
بنزین (*benzin*) F. petrol.
بنفش (*benafsh*) violet (*colour*).
بنفشه (*benafsheh*) violet (*flower*). بنفشهٔ فرنگی pansy.
بنگاه (*bongāh*) storehouse; luggage; institution; firm.
بنه (*boneh*) baggage.
بنی (*bani*) A. sons. (*Pl. of* ابن.) بنی آدم mankind.
بنیاد (*bonyād*) foundation.

بنیان (*bonyān*) A. structure, building.

بنیه (*bonyeh*) A. frame, structure.

بو (*bu*) smell, scent.

بوته (1) (*buteh*) bush, shrub.

بوته (2) (*buteh*) crucible.

بودن (*budan*) to be.

بورس (*burs*) F. exchange, market.

بوزینه (*buzineh*) monkey.

بوس (*bus*) kiss.

بوستان (*bustān*) garden.

بوسه (*buseh*) kiss.

بوسیدن (*busidan*) to kiss.

بو قلمون (*bu qalamun*) *a.* chameleon ; turkey.

بوکس (*boks*) F. boxing.

بول (*boul*) A. urine.

بوم (1) (*bum*) A. owl.

بوم (2) (*bum*) region, country.

بومی (*bumi*) native ; endemic.

بوئیدن (*bu'idan*) to smell.

به (1) (*beh*) to, in, with.

به (2) (*beh*) better. (*The* h *is pronounced.*)

به (3) (*beh*) quince. (*The* h *is pronounced.*)

بها (*bahā*) price.

بهار (*bahār*) spring.

بهانه (*bahāneh*) pretext, excuse.

بهبود (*behbud*), بهبودی (*behbudi*) improvement.

بهتر (*behtar*) better.

بهترین (*behtarin*) best.

بهداری (*behdāri*) health (department).

بهداشت (*behdāsht*) hygiene.

بهرام (*bahrām*) *masc. proper name* ; the planet Mars.

بهره (*bahreh*) share.

بهره برداری (*bahreh bardāri*) exploitation utilization.

بهره مند (*bahreh mand*) participating.

بهشت (*behesht*) paradise.

بهم (*beham*) together.

بهمن (*bahman*) *name of the eleventh month of the Persian year.*

بهنجار (*behanjār*) normal.

بی (*bi*) without (*in compounds*).

بیابان (*biābān*) desert.

بیان (*bayān*) A. statement, expression.

بیانیه (*bayāniyyeh*) A. manifesto.

بی آزار (*bi āzār*) harmless.

بی بی (*bi bi*) mistress of the house.

بی پایان (*bi pāyān*) endless, infinite.

بیت (*beit*) A. house ; distich.

بیت المقدس (*beito'l-moqaddas*) A. Jerusalem.

بیجا (*bijā*) out of place ; inopportune.

بیجان (*bijān*) lifeless.

بیچاره (*bichāreh*) helpless, unfortunate.

بی چیز (*bi chiz*) poor.

بیخ (*bikh*) root.

بیختن (*bikhtan*) to sift.

بید (1) (*bid*) moth.

بید (2) (*bid*) willow.

بیداد (*bidād*) oppression.

بیدار (*bidār*) awake. بیدار شدن to wake up.

بی درد (*bi dard*) painless.

بی درمان (*bi darmān*) irremediable.
بیدرنگ (*biderang*) without delay.
بیدین (*bidin*) A. irreligious.
بیراه (*birāh*) astray; by-way.
بیرق (*beiraq*) T. flag.
بیرون (*birun*) out. بیرون کردن to drive out, expel.
بیزار (*bizār*) wearied, disgusted.
بیزاری (*bizāri*) weariness, disgust.
بیست (*bist*) twenty.
بیستم (*bistom*) twentieth.
بی سیم (*bi sim*) wireless.
بیش (*bish*) more.
بیشتر (*bishtar*) more.
بی شرم (*bi sharm*) shameless.
بیشک (*bishakk*) A. doubtless.
بیشمار (*bishomār*) innumerable.
بیشه (*bisheh*) thicket.
بی صبر (*bi ṣabr*) A. impatient.
بی صبری (*bi ṣabri*) A. impatience.
بیضوی (*beiẓavi*) A. oval.
بیضه (*beiẓeh*) A. egg; testicle.
بیطار (*beiṭār*) A. veterinary surgeon.
بیطرف (*biṭaraf*) A. impartial, neutral.
بیطرفی (*biṭarafi*) A. impartiality, neutrality.
بیع (*bei'*) A. sale.
بیعانه (*bei'āneh*) A. earnest-money.
بیغم (*bighamm*) A. free from grief.
بیفایده (*bifāyedeh*) A. useless, futile.
بی قرار (*bi qarār*) A. restless, inconstant.
بی قید (*bi qeid*) A. unrestrained, careless.
بیکار (*bikār*) unemployed, idle.
بیکاری (*bikāri*) unemployment, idleness.
بیکس (*bikas*) friendless.
بیگار (*bigār*) statute labour.
بیگانه (*bigāneh*) strange(r), foreign(er).
بیگمان (*bigomān*) doubtless.
بیگناه (*bigonāh*) innocent.
بیل (*bil*) spade.
بیم (*bim*) fear.
بیمار (*bimār*) ill.
بیمارستان (*bimārestān*) hospital.
بیماری (*bimāri*) illness.
بیمروت (*bimorovvat*) A. ungenerous, unjust.
بیمزه (*bimazeh*) tasteless, insipid.
بیمعنی (*bima'ni*) A. meaningless, insignificant.
بیمقدار (*bimeqdār*) A. insignificant.
بیمه (*bimeh*) insurance. بیمه کردن to insure.
بین (*bein*) A. interval. بینِ between.
بینا (*binā*) seeing; clear-sighted.
بین المللی (*beino'l-melali*) A. international.
بینائی (*binā'i*) sight; clear-sightedness.
بی نظیر (*bi naẓir*) A. matchless, incomparable.
بینوا (*binavā*) indigent, poor.
بینی (*bini*) nose.
بی نیاز (*bi niāz*) contented.
بی وجود (*bi vojud*) A. useless; mean, humble.
بیور (*beivar*) ten thousand.

بیوفا (*bivafā*) *a.* unfaithful.

بیوقت (*bivaqt*) *a.* untimely.

بیوه (*biveh*) widow(er).

بیهوده (*bihudeh*) vain ; useless.

بیهوش (*bihush*) unconscious ; unintelligent.

پ

پا (*pā*) foot, leg. پا شدن to get up. برپا کردن to erect, to establish.

پاپ (*pāp*) F. Pope.

پاداش (*pādāsh*) reward, retribution.

پادزهر (*pādzahr*) bezoar-stone.

پادشاه (*pādshāh*) king.

پادشاهی (*pādshāhi*) reign, rule.

پادگان (*pādegān*) garrison.

پارابلوم (*pārābelum*) (Parabellum) pistol.

پاراف (*pārāf*) F. initial(ling).

پارچه (*pārcheh*) cloth ; piece.

پارس (1) (*pārs*) Pars, Fars.

پارس (2) (*pārs*) leopard.

پارس (3) (*pārs*) bark(ing).

پارسا (*pārsā*) pious.

پارسال (*pārsāl*) last year.

پارسی (*pārsi*) Persian.

پارکه (*pārkeh*) F. office of the public prosecutor.

پارلمان (*pārlemān*) F. parliament.

پارو (*pāru*) oar. پارو زدن to row.

پاره (*pāreh*) piece, part, some. پاره کردن to tear.

پاس (*pās*) watch, guard.

پاسبان (*pāsbān*) guard, sentinel ; policeman.

پاسبانی (*pāsbāni*) (act of) watching, guarding.

پاسخ (*pāsokh*) answer, reply. پاسخ دادن to answer, reply.

پاسگاه (*pāsgāh*) (sentry) post.

پاشنه (*pāshneh*) heel.

پاشیدن (*pāshidan*) to sprinkle, scatter.

پا فشاری (*pā feshāri*) persistence.

پاک (*pāk*) pure.

پاکت (*pākat*) R. envelope ; letter.

پاکستان (*pākestān*) Pakistan.

پاکی (*pāki*) purity.

پاکیزه (*pākizeh*) clean.

پالایش (*pālāyesh*) filtration.

پالتو (*pāltou*) F. overcoat.

پالشگاه (*pāleshgāh*) refinery.

پالودن (*pāludan*) to filter, strain, refine.

پالیز (*pāliz*) kitchen garden.

پامال (*pāmāl*) trampled.

پاندول (*pāndul*) F. pendulum.

پانزده (*pānzdah*) fifteen.

پانزدهم (*pānzdahom*) fifteenth.

پانسمان (*pānsemān*) F. dressing (*of wound*).

پانصد (*pānṣad*) five hundred.

پاياپاى (*pāyāpāy*) compensation, set-off.

پايان (*pāyān*) end, conclusion.

پايان نامه (*pāyān nāmeh*) thesis, dissertation.

پايتخت (*pāyetakht*) capital.

پايدار (*pāyedār*) permanent; firm.

پايه (*pāyeh*) foundation; leg, pillar; degree.

پائيدن (*pā'idan*) to be firm, to last; to watch.

پائيز (*pā'iz*) autumn.

پائين (*pā'in*) down.

پتو (*patu*) blanket.

پختن (*pokhtan*) to cook, to bake.

پخش (*pakhsh*) distribution; broadcasting.

پدر (*pedar*) father.

پدرى (*pedari*) paternal.

پديد (*padid*) visible, evident. پديد آمدن to appear. پديد آوردن to cause to appear.

پديدار (*padidār*) appearing, evident.

پذيرا (*pazirā*) accepting.

پذيرائى (*pazirā'i*) reception.

پذيرش (*paziresh*) agrément.

پذيرفتن (*paziroftan*) to accept, admit.

پر (*par*) feather.

پر (*por*) full, filled. پر از — كردن to fill with —.

پر افتخار (*por eftekhār*) *a.* glorious.

پراكندن (*parākandan*) to scatter, disperse.

پرت (*part*) prostrate; outlying.

پرتاب (*partāb*) (act of) shooting.

پرتقال (*portoqāl*) Portugal.

پرتگاه (*partgāh*) precipice.

پرتو (*partou*) ray, beam.

پرچم (*parcham*) flag.

پرخاش (*parkhāsh*) battle, quarrel.

پرداخت (*pardākht*) payment, issue.

پرداختن (1) (*pardākhtan*) to pay.

پرداختن (2) (*pardākhtan*) to polish; to accomplish; to be occupied.

پرده (*pardeh*) curtain; veil.

پر زور (*por zur*) strong, powerful.

پرستار (*parastār*) attendant, nurse.

پرستار خانه (*parastār khāneh*) infirmary.

پرستارى (*parastāri*) attendance, nursing. پرستارى كردن to nurse.

پرستش (*parastesh*) worship.

پرستنده (*parastandeh*) worshipper.

پرستو (*parastu*) swallow.

پرستيدن (*parastidan*) to worship.

پرسش (*porsesh*) question.

پرسيدن (*porsidan*) to ask.

پرش (*paresh*) flight; jump(ing).

پر فايده (*por fāyedeh*) *a.* useful.

پرگار (*pargār*) pair of compasses.

پرنده (*parandeh*) bird, flying (creature).

پرنس (*prans*) F. prince.

پرنسس (*pranses*) F. princess.

پرنيان (*parniān*) shot silk.

پرو (*peru*) F. Peru.

پروا (*parvā*) care; fear.

پروار (*parvār*) fattened (animal).

پرواز (*parvāz*) flight. پرواز كردن to fly.

پروانه (1) (*parvāneh*) butterfly, moth.

پروانه (2) (*parvāneh*) licence, permit.

پروردگار (*parvardegār*) Providence, God.

پروردن (*parvardan*) to nourish, bring up, educate.

پرورش (*parvaresh*) fostering, training, education. پرورش دادن to foster, train, educate.

پروژه (*prozheh*) F. plan, project.

پروفسور (*profesor*) F. professor.

پروقار (*porvaqār*) *a.* grave, serious.

پروگرام (*progrām*) F. programme, syllabus.

پرونده (*parvandeh*) bundle, wallet; file, dossier.

پروریدن (*parvaridan*) *i. q.* پروردن

پرویز (*parviz*) *name of a Sassanian king; masc. proper name.*

پروین (*parvin*) Pleiades.

پره (*parreh*) paddle, wing; blade (*of a propeller*).

پرهیز (*parhiz*) abstinence.

پرهیزگار (*parhizgār*) abstinent, chaste.

پرهیزگاری (*parhizgāri*) abstinence, chastity.

پری (*pari*) peri.

پری (*pori*) fullness.

پریدن (*paridan*) to fly.

پریروز (*pariruz*) the day before yesterday.

پریشان (*parishān*) scattered, dishevelled; disturbed, distressed.

پریشانی (*parishāni*) dispersion, disturbance, distress.

پریشب (*parishab*) the night before last.

پزشک (*pezeshk*) doctor, physician.

پزشکی (1) (*pezeshki*) medicine.

پزشکی (2) (*pezeshki*) medical.

پزشکیار (*pezeshkyār*) medical assistant.

پژمرده (*pezhmordeh*) withered, faded.

پژوهش (*pezhuhesh*) inquiry, research.

پژوهیدن (*pezhuhidan*) to inquire, investigate.

پس (1) (*pas*) then, therefore.

پس (2) (*pas*) behind. پس از after.

پس انداز (*pas andāz*) savings. پس انداز کردن to save.

پست (*past*) low, base, humble.

پست (*post*) F. post.

پستان (*pestān*) breast, nipple.

پستان دار (*pestān dār*) mammal.

پستچی (*postchi*) postman.

پستخانه (*postkhāneh*) post office.

پسته (*pesteh*) pistachio.

پستی (*pasti*) lowness, meanness.

پستی (*posti*) postal.

پس دادن (*pas dādan*) to give back.

پسر (*pesar*) son, boy.

پس زدن (*pas zadan*) to reject.

پس فردا (*pas fardā*) the day after to-morrow.

پس گرفتن (*pas gereftan*) to take back.

پسند (*pasand*) approval.

پسندیدن (*pasandidan*) to like, to choose, to approve, to admire.

پشت (*posht*) back.

پشتوانه (*poshtvāneh*) cover, security.

پشته (*poshteh*) mound.

پشتی (*poshti*) cushion ; support.

پشتیبان (*poshtibān*) support(er).

پشتیبانی (*poshtibāni*) support.

پشم (*pashm*) wool.

پشمی (*pashmi*), پشمین (*pashmin*) woollen.

پشه (*pasheh*) gnat, mosquito.

پشه بند (*pasheh band*) mosquito net.

پشیمان (*pashimān*) remorseful, penitent. پشیمان شدن to repent.

پشیمانی (*pashimāni*) remorse, penitence.

پگاه (*pagāh*) dawn.

پل (*pol*) bridge.

پلک (*pelk*) eyelid.

پلکان (*pellegān*) stairs, staircase. (*Pl. of* پله).

پلنگ (*palang*) leopard.

پلو (*polou*) pilaw.

پله (*pelleh*) stair, step.

پلید (*palid*) unclean.

پلیس (*polis*) F. police.

پمپ (*pomp*) F. pump.

پناه (*panāh*) refuge. به — پناه بردن to take refuge in —.

پناهگاه (*panāhgāh*) asylum, shelter.

پناهنده (*panāhandeh*) refugee, fugitive.

پنبه (*panbeh*) cotton.

پنبه ای (*panbeh i*) pertaining to cotton.

پنج (*panj*) five.

پنجاب (*panjāb*) Punjab.

پنجاه (*panjāh*) fifty.

پنجره (*panjereh*) window.

پنجشنبه (*panjshanbeh*) Thursday.

پنجم (*panjom*), پنجمین (*panjomin*) fifth.

پنجه (*panjeh*) claw, talon.

پند (*pand*) advice.

پندار (*pendār*) fancy, conceit.

پنداشتن (*pendāshtan*) to think, suppose.

پنهان (*panhān*) hidden. پنهان کردن to hide.

پنیر (*panir*) cheese.

پوچ (*puch*) vain, futile, absurd.

پود (*pud*) woof.

پودر (*pudr*) F. powder.

پور (*pur*) son.

پوز (*puz*) snout.

پوزش (*puzesh*) excuse, apology.

پوزه بند (*puzeh band*) muzzle.

پوست (*pust*) skin ; hide ; bark ; shell.

پوستین (*pustin*) pelisse.

پوسیدن (*pusidan*) to rot, decay.

پوش (*push*) covering, tarpaulin ; covered stand.

پوشاک (*pushāk*) clothing.

پوشال (*pushāl*) packing, stuffing.

پوشانیدن (*pushānidan*) to clothe ; to conceal.

پوشش (*pushesh*) covering.

پوشیدن (*pushidan*) to put on, to wear ; to cover.

پوک (*puk*) hollow.

پول (*pul*) money.

پولدار (*puldār*) rich (man), capitalist.

پولک (*pulak*) fish-scale.

پولی (*puli*) monetary, pecuniary.

پوند (*pound*) E. pound.

پوئیدن (*pu'idan*) to run; to search.

پهلو (*pahlu*) side.

پهلوان (*pahlavān*) athlete, champion, hero.

پهن (*pahn*) wide, broad.

پهنا (*pahnā*) width, breadth.

پهناور (*pahnāvar*) wide, spacious.

پی (*pei*) trace, track; nerve, sinew. پی در پی successively. پی بردن to trace, discover. پیِ — گشتن to look for —.

پیاپی (*peyāpei*) successively.

پیاده (*piādeh*) on foot; pedestrian, footman; pawn. پیاده شدن to dismount, to disembark (*intr.*) پیاده کردن to dismount, to disembark (*tr.*).

پیاده رو (*piādeh rou*) pavement.

پیاز (*piāz*) onion, bulb.

پیاله (*piāleh*) cup, goblet.

پیام (*payām*) message.

پیپ (*pip*) cask.

پیچ (*pich*) twist; screw.

پیچیدن (*pichidan*) to wind, wrap, twist; to roll up.

پیچیده (*pichideh*) complicated.

پیدا (*peidā*) visible, apparent. پیدا کردن to find; to earn.

پیدایش (*peidāyesh*) genesis.

پیر (*pir*) old.

پیرار سال (*pirār sāl*) the year before last.

پیراستن (*pirāstan*) to adorn, embellish.

پیرامون (*pirāmun*) environs; skirt. در پیرامونِ about.

پیراهن (*pirāhan*) shirt.

پیرایش (*pirāyesh*) adornment, decoration.

پیرو (*peirou*) follower, following.

پیروز (*piruz*) victorious.

پیروزمند (*piruzmand*) victorious.

پیروزی (*piruzi*) victory.

پیروی (*peiravi*) (act of) following, continuation.

پیری (*piri*) old age.

پیریزی (*peirizi*) foundation.

پیش (*pish*) before; ago; forward. پیش از before.

پیشاب (*pishāb*) urine.

پیش آمد (*pish āmad*) occurrence, emergency.

پیشانی (*pishāni*) forehead.

پیشاهنگ (*pishāhang*) file-leader; boy scout.

پیش بین (*pish bin*) provident.

پیشبینی (*pishbini*) foresight, anticipation. پیشبینی کردن to foresee, anticipate, provide for.

پیشتر (*pishtar*) former(ly).

پیشترین (*pishtarin*) foremost.

پیشخدمت (*pishkhedmat*) a. waiter, attendant, servant, butler.

پیش دامن (*pish dāman*) apron.

پیشدستی (*pishdasti*) anticipation.

پیشرفت (*pishraft*) advance, progress.

پیشرو (*pishrou*) precursor, leader.

پیشقدم (*pishqadam*) *a.* initiator, pioneer.

پیش کار (*pish kār*) agent.

پیشکش (*pishkash*) present.

پیشکی (*pishaki*) in advance.

پیشگاه (*pishgāh*) front, presence.

پیش نماز (*pish namāz*) chaplain.

پیشنهاد (*pishnehād*) proposal, tender.

پیشوا (*pishvā*) leader.

پیشواز (*pishvāz*) (act of) going out to meet.

پیشه (*pisheh*) profession, trade. وزارتِ پیشه و هنر Ministry of Industry.

پیشین (*pishin*) former, ancient.

پیشینه (*pishineh*) record, antecedents.

پیغام (*peighām*) message.

پیغمبر (*peighambar*) prophet.

پیک (*peik*) messenger; courier.

پیکار (*peikār*) battle, fight.

پیکان (*peikān*) point of an arrow.

پیکر (*peikar*) image, picture; figure.

پیل (*pil*) elephant.

پیله (*pileh*) cocoon.

پیله ور (*pileh var*) peddler.

پیمان (*peimān*) treaty.

پیمانه (*peimāneh*) measure; cup.

پیمودن (*peimudan*) to measure; to traverse.

پینه (*pineh*) callosity; patch. پینه کردن to patch, repair.

پیوستن (*peivastan*) to join.

پیوسته (*peivasteh*) continually, always.

پیوند (*peivand*) grafting; joint.

پیه (*pih*) tallow, fat.

ت

تا (1) (*tā*) until, to.

تا (2) (*tā*) fold. دو تا قلم two pens.

تاب (*tāb*) glow; twist; endurance.

تابان (*tābān*) shining.

تابستان (*tābestān*) summer.

تابش (*tābesh*) brightness, heat.

تابع (*tābe'*) A. follower; subject.

تابعیت (*tābe'iyyat*) A. nationality.

تابلو (*tāblo*) F. picture; placard.

تابنده (*tābandeh*) shining.

تابوت (*tābut*) A. coffin, bier.

تابه (*tābeh*) frying-pan.

تابیدن (1) (*tābidan*) to twist.

تابیدن (2) (*tābidan*) to shine.

تآتر (*teātr*) F. theatre.

تاتوله (*tātuleh*) datura, thorn-apple.

تأثر (*ta'aṣṣor*) A. (state of) being touched, impressed.

تأثیر (*ta'ṣir*) A. impression, effect.

تاج (*tāj*) A. crown.

تاجدار (*tājdār*) *a.* crowned; sovereign.

تاجر (*tājer*) A. merchant.

تاجگذاری (*tājgozāri*) *a.* coronation.

تاجور (*tājvar*) *a.* wearing a crown; sovereign.

تاخت (*tākht*) assault. تاخت و تاز inroad, invasion.

تاختن (*tākhtan*) to rush, make an assault.

تأخير (*ta'khir*) A. delay, postponement.

تأديب (*ta'dib*) A. chastisement.

تار (1) (*tār*) warp.

تار (2) (*tār*) dark, dim.

تاراج (*tārāj*) pillage, plunder.

تارك (*tārak*) head, crown.

تارى (*tāri*) darkness, dimness.

تاريخ (*tārikh*) A. history; date.

تاريخى (*tārikhi*) A. historical.

تاريك (*tārik*) dark.

تاريكى (*tāriki*) darkness.

تاز (*tāz*) attack, assault.

تازگى (*tāzegi*) freshness, novelty.

تازه (*tāzeh*) new, fresh.

تازى (*tāzi*) Arab(ic); greyhound.

تازيانه (*tāziāneh*) whip.

تأسف (*ta'assof*) A. regret.

تأسى (*ta'assi*) A. imitation.

تأسيس (*ta'sis*) A. establishment, foundation. تأسيس كردن to establish.

تافتن (1) (*tāftan*) to twist, turn away.

تافتن (2) (*tāftan*) to shine.

تاك (*tāk*) vine.

تاكستان (*tākestān*) vineyard.

تاكسى (*tāksi*) F. taxi.

تأكيد (*ta'kid*) A. emphasis, strict injunction.

تالار (*tālār*) hall.

تألم (*ta'allom*) A. (suffering) pain.

تأليف (*ta'lif*) A. compilation, literary work.

تام (*tāmm*) A. complete, perfect.

تامل (*ta'ammol*) A. deliberation, reflection.

تأمين (*ta'min*) A. (act of) securing, safeguarding. تأمين كردن to secure, safeguard.

تانك (*tānk*) F. tank.

تأنى (*ta'anni*) A. slowness, delay.

تاو (*tāv*) endurance, power.

تاوان (*tāvān*) fine, indemnity.

تاول (*tāvel*) blister.

تأويل (*ta'vil*) A. commentary, interpretation, paraphrase.

تأهل (*ta'ahhol*) A. marriage.

تائيد (*ta'id*) A. confirmation. تائيد كردن to confirm.

تب (*tab*) fever. تب كردن to be attacked by fever.

تبادل (*tabādol*) A. exchange.

تبار (*tabār*) race, family.

تبانى (*tabāni*) A. collusion.

تباه (*tabāh*) ruined, spoiled.

تباهى (*tabāhi*) corruption, ruin.

تبت (*tabbat*) Tibet.

تبخير (*tabkhir*) A. evaporation.

تبديل (*tabdil*) A. change, alteration. تبديل دادن to change.

تبر (*tabar*) axe.

تبريد (*tabrid*) A. cooling, refrigeration.

تبريزى (*tabrizi*) native of Tabriz; poplar.

تبرئه (*tabre'eh*) A. acquittal, exoneration.

تبسم (*tabassom*) A. smile.

تبصره (*tabṣereh*) A. note.

تبعید (*tab'id*) A. banishment. تبعید کردن to banish.

تبعیض (*tab'iẓ*) A. (unjust) discrimination.

تبلیغ (*tabligh*) A. communication; propagation.

تبلیغات (*tablighāt*) A. propaganda.

تبهکار (*tabahkār*) criminal.

تبیره (*tabireh*) drum.

تپه (*tappeh*) T. hill.

تتار (*tatār*) Tartar.

تتبع (*tatabbo'*) A. research.

تتق (*totoq*) curtain, veil.

تتمه (*tatemmeh*) A. remainder, balance; supplement.

تثبیت (*taṣbit*) A. fixing, stabilization.

تجار (*tojjār*) A. merchants. (*Pl. of* تاجر.)

تجارب (*tajāreb*) A. experiences, experiments. (*Pl. of* تجربه.)

تجارت (*tejārat*) A. trade, commerce.

تجارتی (*tejārati*) *a.* commercial.

تجاسر (*tajāsor*) A. boldness; insurgence.

تجاوز (*tajāvoz*) A. transgression, encroachment, aggression.

تجاهل (*tajāhol*) A. (act of) feigning ignorance.

تجدید (*tajdid*) A. renewal. تجدید کردن to renew. تجدیدِ نظر revision, review.

تجربه (*tajrebeh*) A. experience.

تجزیه (*tajzieh*) A. analysis; decomposition.

تجسس (*tajassos*) A. search, research; espionage.

تجسم (*tajassom*) A. embodiment, personification.

تجلیل (*tajlil*) A. (act of) honouring, glorification.

تجویز (*tajviz*) A. (act of) declaring lawful; recommendation.

تحت (*taḥt*) A. underneath. تحتِ under.

تحت البحری (*taḥto'l-baḥri*) *a.* submarine.

تحت الحمایه (*taḥto'l-ḥemāyeh*) A. protected; protectorate.

تحتانی (*taḥtāni*) A. lower.

تحریر (*taḥrir*) A. writing.

تحریراً (*taḥriran*) A. in writing.

تحریف (*taḥrif*) A. alteration; corruption.

تحریک (*taḥrik*) A. incitement. تحریک کردن to incite.

تحریکات (*taḥrikāt*) A. subversive activities.

تحریک آمیز (*taḥrik āmiz*) *a.* provocative, inflammatory.

تحریم (*taḥrim*) A. deprivation; prohibition; boycott(ing). تحریم کردن to deprive; to prohibit; to boycott.

تحسین (*taḥsin*) A. applause, admiration. تحسین کردن to applaud, to admire.

تحصن (*taḥaṣṣon*) A. (act of) taking refuge.

تحصیل (*taḥṣil*) A. acquisition; collection; study.

تحصیلدار (*taḥṣildār*) A. tax-collector.

تحف (*toḥaf*) A. rareties, gifts. (*Pl. of* تحفه.)

تحفه (*toḥfeh*) A. gift, curiosity.

تحقیق (*taḥqiq*) A. enquiry.

تحکم (*taḥakkom*) A. command(ing), domineering.

تحلیل (*taḥlil*) A. assimilation, digestion; analysis; rendering lawful.

تحمل (*taḥammol*) A. endurance, forbearance. تحمل کردن to endure.

تحمیل (*taḥmil*) A. imposition. تحمیل کردن to impose.

تحول (*taḥavvol*) A. transformation.

تحویل (*taḥvil*) A. delivery. تحویل دادن to deliver. تحویل گرفتن to take delivery of.

تحویلدار (*taḥvildār*) *a.* cashier.

تخت (*takht*) throne.

تختگاه (*takhtgāh*) place where a throne stands.

تخته (*takhteh*) board, plank.

تخریب (*takhrib*) A. destruction.

تخصیص (*takhṣiṣ*) A. appropriation, allotment.

تخفیف (*takhfif*) A. reduction.

تخلیه (*takhlieh*) A. evacuation. تخلیه کردن to evacuate.

تخم (*tokhm*) seed, egg.

تخمیر (*takhmir*) A. fermentation.

تخمین (*takhmin*) A. estimation, appraisal. تخمین کردن, تخمین زدن to estimate.

تخمیناً (*takhminan*) A. approximately.

تدابیر (*tadābir*) A. plans, devices. (*Pl. of* تدبیر).

تدارک (*tadārok*) A. preparation, provision. تدارک دیدن to prepare, provide.

تدبیر (*tadbir*) A. plan, device; management, administration.

تدریج (*tadrij*) A. graduation.

تدریجاً (*tadrijan*) A. gradually.

تدریجی (*tadriji*) A. gradual.

تدریس (*tadris*) A. teaching, instruction.

تدمیر (*tadmir*) A. destruction.

تدوین (*tadvin*) A. collection (*of poems*); codification.

تذرو (*tazarv*) pheasant.

تذکره (*tazkereh*) A. passport.

تر (*tar*) moist, wet; fresh.

تراجم (*tarājem*) A. translations. (*Pl. of* ترجمه.)

تراخم (*trākhom*) F. trachoma.

ترازو (*tarāzu*) scales, balance.

تراشیدن (*tarāshidan*) to cut; to shave.

تراکتور (*trāktor*) F. tractor.

تراکم (*tarākom*) A. accumulation.

تراکمه (*tarākemeh*) A. Turcomans.

ترانزیت (*trānzit*) F. transit.

ترانه (*tarāneh*) melody.

تراوش (*tarāvesh*) exudation.

ترب (*torob*) radish.

تربت (*torbat*) A. earth; tomb.

تربچه (*torobcheh*) radish.

تربیت (*tarbiat*) A. education, training,

culture. تربیت کردن to educate, to rear.

ترتیب (*tartib*) A. arrangement.

ترجمان (*tarjomān*) A. interpreter.

ترجمه (*tarjomeh*) A. translation. ترجمه کردن to translate.

ترجیح (*tarjiḥ*) A. preference. ترجیح دادن to prefer.

ترحم (*taraḥḥom*) A. pity, compassion.

ترد (*tord*) brittle.

تردید (*tardid*) A., hesitation, doubt.

ترس (*tars*) fear.

ترسناک (*tarsnāk*) terrible, frightful.

ترسو (*tarsu*) timid.

ترسیدن (*tarsidan*) to fear.

ترش (*torsh*) sour.

ترشرو (*torshru*) peevish.

ترشی (*torshi*) sourness; pickles.

ترعه (*tor'eh*) A. canal.

ترغیب (*targhib*) A. persuasion, encouragement. ترغیب کردن to persuade, encourage.

ترفیع (*tarfi'*) A. elevation, promotion.

ترقه (*taraqqeh*) fire-cracker.

ترقی (*taraqqi*) A. progress.

ترقیخواه (*taraqqikhvāh*) *a.* progressive.

ترک (*tark*) A. (act of) leaving. ترک کردن to leave.

ترک (*tork*) Turk.

ترکتاز (*torktāz*) plundering.

ترکتازی (*torktāzi*) depredation, raid.

ترکستان (*torkestān*) Turkestan.

ترکمان (*torkmān*) Turcoman.

ترکیب (*tarkib*) A. composition, compound.

ترکیدن (*tarakidan*) to burst; to explode.

ترکیه (*torkiyyeh*) A. Turkey.

ترگ (*targ*) helmet.

ترمز (*tormoz*) R. brake.

ترمومتر (*termometr*) F. thermometer.

ترمیم (*tarmim*) A. amendment; reparation; reshuffling (*of a cabinet*).

ترن (*tran*) F. train.

ترنج (*toronj*) citron.

ترنم (*tarannom*) A. (act of) singing.

تروریست (*terorist*) F. terrorist.

ترویج (*tarvij*) A. propagation; circulation.

تره (*tareh*) leek.

تری (*tari*) moisture; freshness.

تریاک (*teryāk*) opium.

تز (*tez*) F. thesis.

تزاید (*tazāyod*) A. increase.

تزریق (*tazriq*) A. injection.

تزلزل (*tazalzol*) A. agitation, commotion.

تزویر (*tazvir*) A. dissimulation, hypocrisy.

تزیید (*tazyid*) A. (act of) increasing.

تزیین (*tazyin*) A. decoration.

تسامح (*tasāmoḥ*) A. negligence.

تساوی (*tasāvi*) A. equality.

تسبیح (*tasbiḥ*) A. rosary.

تسخیر (*taskhir*) A. subjugation.

تسریع (*tasri'*) A. hastening, acceleration. تسریع کردن to hasten, expedite.

تسطیح (*tasṭiḥ*) A. (act of) levelling.

تسعیر (*tas'ir*) A. conversion; evaluation.

تسکین (*taskin*) A. (act of) quieting, soothing. تسکین دادن to quiet, soothe.

تسلسل (*tasalsol*) A. concatenation; series.

تسلط (*tasalloṭ*) A. domination.

تسلی (*tasalli*) A., تسلیت (*tasliat*) A. consolation.

تسلیح (*tasliḥ*) A. arming, armament.

تسلیم (*taslim*) A. surrender(ing). تسلیم کردن to surrender.

تسمه (*tasmeh*) strap, thong.

تسنن (*tasannon*) A. (adhesion to) the Sunna sect.

تسویه (*tasvieh*) A. liquidation, settlement.

تسهیل (*tas-hil*) A. facilitation.

تسهیلات (*tas-hilāt*) A. facilities.

تشبیه (*tashbih*) A. comparison, simile. تشبیه کردن to compare.

تشتت (*tashattot*) A. dispersion; confusion; diversity.

تشخیص (*tashkhiṣ*) A. distinction; diagnosis. تشخیص دادن to distinguish; to diagnose.

تشدد (*tashaddod*) A. rigor, violence.

تشدید (*tashdid*) A. strengthening, corroboration; *name of the sign used to indicate that a consonant is doubled.*

تشریح (*tashriḥ*) A. description, explanation; dissection, anatomy.

تشریف (*tashrif*) A. (act of) honouring. تشریف آوردن *polite for* آمدن. تشریف بردن *polite for* رفتن.

تشریفات (*tashrifāt*) A. ceremonies; formalities.

تشکر (*tashakkor*) A. thanks. از — تشکر کردن to thank —.

تشکیل (*tashkil*) A. formation, organization. تشکیل دادن to form, to organize; to hold (*as a meeting*).

تشنج (*tashannoj*) A. convulsion, spasm.

تشنگی (*teshnegi*) thirst.

تشنه (*teshneh*) thirsty.

تشویش (*tashvish*) A. anxiety, disturbance, confusion.

تشویق (*tashviq*) A. encouragement. تشویق کردن to encourage.

تشیع (*tashayyo'*) A. (adhesion to) the Shia sect.

تشییع (*tashyi'*) A. (act of) escorting (*a funeral*).

تصاحب (*taṣāḥob*) A. (act of) taking possession of. تصاحب کردن to take possession of.

تصادف (*taṣādof*) A. encounter; coincidence.

تصادم (*taṣādom*) A. collision.

تصانیف (*taṣānif*) A. compositions. (*Pl. of* تصنیف.)

تصحیح (*taṣḥiḥ*) A. correction.

تصدی (*taṣaddi*) A. incumbency.

تصدیق (*taṣdiq*) A. confirmation, certification; certificate. تصدیق کردن to confirm, to admit as true.

تصرف (*taṣarrof*) A. possession, seizure.

تصريح (*taṣriḥ*) A. making clear, stipulation. تصريح كردن to make clear, to stipulate.

تصفيه (*taṣfieh*) A. (act of) filtering, refining; clearing, settling; liquidation.

تصميم (*taṣmim*) A. decision.

تصنع (*taṣanno'*) A. affectation, artifice.

تصنيف (*taṣnif*) A. composition. تصنيف كردن to compose.

تصور (*taṣavvor*) A. imagination, thought. تصور كردن to imagine, think.

تصوف (*taṣavvof*) A. Sufism.

تصويب (*taṣvib*) A. approval. تصويب كردن to approve.

تصويب نامه (*taṣvib nāmeh*) *a.* decree.

تصوير (*taṣvir*) A. picture.

تضرع (*taẓarro'*) A. supplication, lamentation.

تضعيف (*taẓ'if*) A. (act of) doubling; weakening.

تضمين (*taẓmin*) A. guarantee. تضمين كردن to guarantee.

تضييق (*taẓyiq*) A. (act of) restraining

تضييقات (*taẓyiqāt*) A. restraints, sanctions; difficulties.

تطابق (*taṭāboq*) A. conformity.

تطبيق (*taṭbiq*) A. (act of) comparing, checking; adaptation. تطبيق كردن to compare, check; to adapt.

تطهير (*taṭhir*) A. purification.

تظاهر (*taẓāhor*) A. appearance; affectation; demonstration.

تظلم (*taẓallom*) A. complaint of injustice.

تعادل (*ta'ādol*) A. equilibrium.

تعارف (*ta'ārof*) A. compliment(s). تعارف كردن to offer (as a compliment).

تعاطى (*ta'āṭi*) A. exchange.

تعاقب (*ta'āqob*) A. pursuit.

تعالى (*ta'āli*) A. elevation.

تعاون (*ta'āvon*) A. mutual aid.

تعبير (*ta'bir*) A. explanation, interpretation.

تعجب (*ta'ajjob*) A. wonder, surprise. تعجب كردن to be surprised.

تعجيل (*ta'jil*) A. hurry, haste.

تعداد (*ta'dād*) A. number; calculation.

تعدى (*ta'addi*) A. encroachment; oppression.

تعديل (*ta'dil*) A. adjustment.

تعرض (*ta'arroẓ*) A. opposition; molestation; aggression.

تعرضى (*ta'arroẓi*) A. aggressive.

تعرفه (*ta'refeh*) A. tariff.

تعريف (*ta'rif*) A. definition; commendation. تعريف كردن to define; to commend.

تعزيت (*ta'ziat*) A. condolence, mourning.

تعزيه (*ta'zieh*) A. passion-play.

تعصب (*ta'aṣṣob*) A. fanaticism.

تعطيل (*ta'ṭil*) A. cessation of work, standstill; holiday. تعطيل كردن to stop, suspend; to stop work.

تعظیم (*ta'ẓim*) A. homage, bowing down.

تعقل (*ta'aqqol*) A. (act of) reasoning.

تعقیب (*ta'qib*) A. pursuit. تعقیب کردن to pursue.

تعقیم (*ta'qim*) A. sterilization.

تعلق (*ta'alloq*) A. belonging, attachment. تعلق داشتن to belong.

تعلل (*ta'allol*) A. (act of) making excuses.

تعلیف (*ta'lif*) A. (act of) putting to grass.

تعلیم (*ta'lim*) A. instruction.

تعمید (*ta'mid*) A. baptism. تعمید دادن to baptize.

تعمیر (*ta'mir*) A. repair.

تعمیم (*ta'mim*) A. generalization, propagation.

تعویض (*ta'viẓ*) A. compensation, replacement.

تعویق (*ta'viq*) A. delay, postponement. بتعویق انداختن to put off, postpone.

تعهد (*ta'ahhod*) A. obligation, undertaking.

تعیین (*ta'yin*) A. appointment, fixing. تعیین کردن to appoint, to fix.

تغار (*taghār*) earthen trough.

تغذیه (*taghẕieh*) A. nourishment. تغذیه کردن to feed.

تغیر (*taghayyor*) A. (state of) getting angry.

تغییر (*taghyir*) A. change. تغییر دادن to change.

تغییر پذیر (*taghyir paẕir*) *a.* changeable.

تغییر نا پذیر (*taghyir nā paẕir*) *a.* unchangeable.

تف (*taf*) heat.

تف (*tof*) spittle. تف انداختن to spit.

تفاخر (*tafākhor*) A. boasting, self-glorification.

تفأل (*tafa''ol*) A. augury.

تفاوت (*tafāvot*) A. difference. با — تفاوت داشتن to be different from —.

تفاهم (*tafāhom*) A. mutual understanding.

تفتیش (*taftish*) A. inspection.

تفحص (*tafaḥḥoṣ*) A. inquiry, investigation.

تفرج (*tafarroj*) A. recreation, walk (*for pleasure*).

تفرجگاه (*tafarrojgāh*) *a.* public walk, promenade.

تفرقه (*tafreqeh*) A. dispersion, separation.

تفریح (*tafriḥ*) A. recreation, amusement, fun. تفریح کردن to take recreation, to act in fun.

تفریط (*tafriṭ*) A. dissipation, wasting.

تفریق (*tafriq*) A. subtraction.

تفسیدن (*tafsidan*) to grow hot.

تفسیر (*tafsir*) A. commentary.

تفصیل (*tafṣil*) A. detail.

تفضیح (*tafẓiḥ*) A. (act of) disgracing.

تفقد (*tafaqqod*) A. commiseration.

تفکیک (*tafkik*) A. separation, segregation.

تفنگ (*tofang*) T. rifle, gun.

تفنگچی (*tofangchi*) T. rifleman.

تفنن (*tafannon*) A. diversion, amusement.

تفو (*tofu*) fy !

تفوق (*tafavvoq*) A. superiority, supremacy.

تفویض (*tafviẓ*) A. (act of) entrusting, handing over.

تفهیم (*tafhim*) A. (act of) giving to understand, explaining.

تقاضا (*taqāẓā*) A. request. تقاضا کردن to request.

تقاعد (*taqā'od*) A. pension.

تقدس (*taqaddos*) A. holiness.

تقدم (*taqaddom*) A. precedence, priority.

تقدیر (*taqdir*) A. destiny ; appreciation.

تقدیس (*taqdis*) A. sanctification.

تقدیم (*taqdim*) A. presentation. تقدیم کردن to present.

تقریب (*taqrib*) A. approximation.

تقریباً (*taqriban*) A. approximately.

تقسیم (*taqsim*) A. distribution, division.

تقصیر (*taqṣir*) A. offence, fault.

تقطیر (*taqṭir*) A. distillation.

تقلب (*taqallob*) A. trickery, fraud ; falsification.

تقلید (*taqlid*) A. imitation.

تقلیل (*taqlil*) A. diminution, reduction. تقلیل دادن to diminish, reduce.

تقوا (*taqvā*) A. piety, virtue.

تقویت (*taqviat*) A. strengthening, reinforcement.

تقویم (*taqvim*) A. evaluation ; calendar, almanach.

تقی (*taqi*) A. *masc. proper name.*

تک (*tak*) T. single.

تکاپو (*takāpu*) search.

تکاثف (*takāṣof*) A. density.

تکافو (*takāfu*) A. equality.

تکالیف (*takālif*) A. duties. (*Pl. of* تکلیف.)

تکامل (*takāmol*) A. development, evolution.

تکان (*takān*) shake, jerk. تکان دادن to shake.

تکانیدن (*takānidan*) to shake.

تکبر (*takabbor*) A. pride, arrogance.

تکثیر (*takṣir*) A. (act of) increasing, multiplying.

تکثیف (*takṣif*) A. condensation.

تکدر (*takaddor*) A. annoyance.

تکدیر (*takdir*) A. (act of) making turbid ; disturbing, annoying.

تکذیب (*takẕib*) A. denial. تکذیب کردن to deny.

تکرار (*takrār*) A. repetition. تکرار کردن to repeat.

تکریم (*takrim*) A. (act of) honouring, respecting.

تکفیر (*takfir*) A. excommunication.

تکلم (*takallom*) A. speech, speaking. تکلم کردن to speak.

تکلیف (*taklif*) A. duty ; the thing to be done.

تکمه (*tokmeh*) T. button.

تکمیل (*takmil*) A. completion.

تکوین (*takvin*) A. creation, genesis.

تکه (*tekkeh*) piece. تکه تکه torn to pieces.

تکیه (*takyeh*) A. (act of) leaning; support, prop. تکیه کردن to lean.

تکیه گاه (*takyeh gāh*) *a.* resting-place; base.

تگ (*tag*) race.

تگرگ (*tagarg*) hail.

تل ابیب (*tall abib*) A. Tel Aviv.

تلاش (*talāsh*) search; bustling about; making an effort.

تلافی (*talāfi*) A. retaliation; recompense; revenge.

تلخ (*talkh*) bitter.

تلخی (*talkhi*) bitterness.

تلف (*talaf*) A. destruction, loss. تلف شدن to perish.

تلفظ (*talaffoẓ*) A. pronunciation. تلفظ کردن to pronounce.

تلفن (*telefon*) F. telephone. تلفن کردن to telephone.

تلقی (*talaqqi*) A. reception. تلقی کردن to receive; to regard, consider.

تلقیح (*talqiḥ*) A. fertilization; inoculation.

تلقین (*talqin*) A. instruction, inspiration, suggestion. تلقین کردن to instruct, to inspire, to suggest.

تلگراف (*telegrāf*) F. telegram. تلگراف کردن to telegraph.

تلگرافاً (*telegrāfan*) *a.* by telegram.

تلگرافچی (*telegrāfchi*) telegraphist.

تلگرافی (*telegrāfi*) telegraphic.

تلمیذ (*telmiẕ*) A. student, scholar.

تلنبه (*tolonbeh*) T. pump.

تلو تلو (*telou telou*) (act of) staggering, tottering.

تلون (*talavvon*) A. versatility; inconstancy.

تله (*taleh*) trap.

تم (*tamma*) A. finis.

تماس (*tamās*) A. contact.

تماشا (*tamāshā*) A. spectacle; sightseeing; something worth watching; interest. تماشا کردن to watch.

تماشاچی (*tamāshāchi*) *a.* spectator.

تماشا گاه (*tamāshā gāh*) *a.* theatre.

تمام (*tamām*) A. whole. تمام کردن to finish.

تمامیت (*tamāmiyyat*) A. integrity.

تمایل (*tamāyol*) A. wish, inclination.

تمبر (*tambr*) F. stamp.

تمتع (*tamatto'*) A. enjoyment.

تمثال (*temṣāl*) A. image, portrait.

تمثیل (*tamṣil*) A. allegory, parable.

تمجید (*tamjid*) A. praise. تمجید کردن to praise.

تمدد (*tamaddod*) A. tension.

تمدن (*tamaddon*) A. civilization.

تمدید (*tamdid*) A. prolongation, extension.

تمرکز (*tamarkoz*) A. concentration. تمرکز دادن to concentrate.

تمرین (*tamrin*) A. exercise; training.

تمساح (*temsāḥ*) A. crocodile.

تمسخر (*tamaskhor*) A. buffoonery; ridicule.

تمشک (*temeshk*) raspberry.

تمکین (*tamkin*) A. condescension; gravity.

تملق (*tamalloq*) A. flattery.

تملک (*tamallok*) A. (act of) taking possession.

تموج (*tamavvoj*) A. fluctuation, undulation.

تمول (*tamavvol*) A. riches, wealth.

تمیز (1) (*tamiz*) *a.* discernment, distinction. تمیز دادن to distinguish.

تمیز (2) (*tamiz*) *a.* neat, clean.

تن (*tan*) body; person. تن دادن to yield, submit.

تنازع (*tanāzo'*) A. dispute.

تن آسا (*tan āsā*) self-indulgent.

تن آسائی (*tan āsā'i*) self-indulgence.

تناسب (*tanāsob*) A. proportion, symmetry.

تناسل (*tanāsol*) A. generation, reproduction.

تناقض (*tanāqoẓ*) A. contradiction.

تناوب (*tanāvob*) A. alternation.

تناول (*tanāvol*) A. (act of) eating; taking, receiving. تناول کردن to eat; to take, receive.

تنباکو (*tanbāku*) tobacco (*for the hookah*).

تنبل (*tanbal*) lazy.

تنبلی (*tanbali*) laziness, idleness.

تنبیه (*tanbih*) A. punishment, correction, reprimand; note.

تند (*tond*) swift; sharp; violent.

تند خو (*tond khu*) hot-tempered, hasty.

تند خوئی (*tond khu'i*) hot temper.

تندر (*tondar*) thunder.

تندرست (*tandorost*) healthy.

تندرستی (*tandorosti*) health.

تند نویسی (*tond nevisi*) stenography.

تندی (*tondi*) rapidity; harshness; violence.

تنزل (*tanazzol*) A. descent, fall.

تنزیل (*tanzil*) A. interest, usury.

تنطور (*tanṭur*) F. tincture.

تنظیم (*tanẓim*) A. arrangement, organization; composition (*of verse*).

تنعم (*tana''om*) A. ease; affluence.

تنفر (*tanaffor*) A. aversion, loathing.

تنفر آمیز (*tanaffor āmiz*) *a.* repulsive.

تنفس (*tanaffos*) A. respiration; recess. تنفس کردن to breathe; to go into recess.

تنک (*tonok*) thin, sparse, scanty.

تنک آب (*tonok āb*) shallow.

تنگ (1) (*tang*) narrow, tight.

تنگ (2) (*tang*) girth; mountain-pass.

تنگ (*tong*) water-bottle.

تنگه (*tangeh*) mountain-pass; strait.

تنگی (*tangi*) narrowness, tightness.

تنور (*tanur*) oven, furnace.

تنوع (*tanavvo'*) A. variety.

تنومند (*tanumand*) corpulent.

تنویر (*tanvir*) A. illumination, enlightenment.

تنه (*taneh*) trunk; jostling. تنه زدن to jostle.

تنها (*tanhā*) alone, only.

تنهائی (*tanhā'i*) solitude.

تنیدن (*tanidan*) to spin, weave.

تو (*to*) thou.

تو (*tu*) in ; within.

توابع (*tavābe'*) A. dependencies. (*Pl. of* تابع.)

تواتر (*tavātor*) A. hearsay ; rumour.

تواريخ (*tavārikh*) A. histories ; dates. (*Pl. of* تاريخ.)

توازن (*tavāzon*) A. equilibrium.

تواضع (*tavāẓo'*) A. humility.

توافق (*tavāfoq*) A. agreement, concord.

توالد (*tavālod*) A. reproduction.

توالى (*tavāli*) A. succession.

توأم (*tou'am*) A. twin.

توانا (*tavānā*) powerful, able.

توانائى (*tavānā'i*) power, ability.

توانستن (*tavānestan*) to be able.

توانگر (*tavāngar*) rich (man).

توبه (*toubeh*) A. repentance.

توبيخ (*toubikh*) A. reprimand.

توپ (*tup*) T. cannon, gun.

توپخانه (*tupkhāneh*) artillery.

توت (*tut*) mulberry.

توتون (*tutun*) T. tobacco.

توجه (*tavajjoh*) A. care, attention.

توجيه (*toujih*) A. explanation.

توحش (*tavaḥḥosh*) A. wildness, savagery ; horror.

توحيد (*touḥid*) A. monotheism.

توده (*tudeh*) heap, pile ; mass ; rabble.

توديع (*toudi'*) A. farewell, valediction.

تور (*tur*) net.

تورم (*tavarrom*) A. swelling, inflammation ; inflation.

تورى (*turi*) lace.

توزيع (*touzi'*) A. distribution.

تو سرخ (*tu sorkh*) shaddock.

تو سرى (*tu sari*) blow on the head.

توسط (*tavassoṭ*) A. intermediation, agency. توسطِ ,بتوسطِ through, by ; care of.

توسعه (*touse'eh*) A. extent ; expansion.

توسعه طلب (*touse'eh ṭalab*) *a.* expansionist.

توسل (*tavassol*) A. (act of) resorting. توسل جستن to resort.

توسن (*tousan*) (unbroken) horse.

توشه (*tusheh*) (travelling) provisions.

توصيف (*touṣif*) A. description ; praise.

توصيه (*touṣieh*) A. recommendation ; appointment as heir.

توضيح (*touẓih*) A. explanation.

توطئه (*touṭe'eh*) A. plot.

توفق (*tavaffoq*) A. success.

توفيق (*toufiq*) A. grace, favour ; success.

توقر (*tavaqqor*) A. gravity, dignity.

توقع (*tavaqqo'*) A. expectation. توقع داشتن to expect.

توقف (*tavaqqof*) A. (act of) staying توقف كردن to stay.

توقيف (*touqif*) A. arrest, detention, seizure. توقيف كردن to arrest, ban, suspend.

توكل (*tavakkol*) A. trust, reliance.

تولد (*tavallod*) A. birth.

توله (*tuleh*) cub, whelp.

تولید (*toulid*) A. procreation; production. تولید کردن to beget; to produce.

تومان (*tomān*) T. *Persian money of account = 10 rials.*

تون (*tun*) stove, furnace.

تونس (*tunes*) A. Tunis.

توهین (*touhin*) A. insult.

توئی (*tu'i*) inner.

ته (*tah*) bottom.

تهاتر (*tahātor*) A. compensation, set-off.

تهاجم (*tahājom*) A. invasion, inroad, attack, aggression.

تهدید (*tahdid*) A. threat. تهدید کردن to threaten.

تهذیب (*tahzib*) A. (act of) refining; education.

تهران (*tehrān*) Tehran. (*The older spelling is* طهران.)

تهلکه (*tahlekeh*) A. perdition; danger.

تهلیل (*tahlil*) A. praising God.

تهمت (*tohmat*) A. accusation.

تهنیت (*tahniat*) A. congratulation. تهنیت گفتن to congratulate.

تهور (*tahavvor*) A. rashness, impetuosity.

تهوع (*tahavvo'*) A. nausea.

تهی (*tohi*) empty.

تهیه (*tahiyyeh*) A. preparation. تهیه کردن to prepare.

تیاتر (*tiātr*) F. theatre.

تیار (*tiār*) ready.

تیپ (*tip*) brigade.

تیر (1) (*tir*) arrow; shot.

تیر (2) (*tir*) *name of the fourth month of the Persian year.*

تیر (3) (*tir*) Mercury.

تیر اندازی (*tir andāzi*), تیرباران (*tir bārān*) (act of) shooting. تیرباران کردن to shoot.

تیر زن (*tir zan*) archer, shooter.

تیرگی (*tiregi*) darkness.

تیره (1) (*tireh*) dark, dull; turbid.

تیره (2) (*tireh*) sept.

تیز (1) (*tiz*) sharp, keen; swift.

تیز (2) (*tiz*) *crepitus ventris.*

تیزاب (*tizāb*) nitric acid.

تیز رو (*tiz rou*) quick.

تیزک (*tizak*) cress.

تیزی (*tizi*) sharpness; pungency; swiftness.

تیشه (*tisheh*) adze.

تیغ (*tigh*) sword; razor; thorn.

تیغه (*tigheh*) blade.

تیفوس (*tifus*) F. typhus.

تیله (*tileh*) (a) marble.

تیم (*tim*) E. team.

تیماج (*timāj*) goat leather.

تیمار (*timār*) care, attendance, grooming. تیمار کردن to groom.

تیمار گاه (*timār gāh*) relief post.

تیمسار (*timsār*) *title used in addressing officers.*

تیهو (*tihu*) grey partridge.

تیول (*toyul*) fief.

ث

ثابت (*ṣābet*) A. fixed; proved. ثابت کردن to prove.

ثالث (*ṣāleṣ*) A. third.

ثالثاً (*ṣāleṣan*) A. thirdly.

ثانوی (*ṣānavi*) A., ثانی (*ṣāni*) A. second.

ثانیاً (*ṣanian*) A. secondly.

ثانیه (*ṣānieh*) A. second (*in time*).

ثبات (*ṣabāt*) A. firmness, stability.

ثبات (*ṣabbāt*) A. registrar.

ثبت (*ṣabt*) A. registration; registered.

ثبوت (*ṣobut*) A. demonstration.

ثروت (*ṣarvat*) A. wealth, riches.

ثروتمند (*ṣarvatmand*) *a.* rich, wealthy.

ثریا (*ṣorayyā*) A. Pleiades.

ثغر (*ṣaghr*) A. frontier.

ثغور (*ṣoghur*) A. frontiers. (*Pl. of* ثغر.)

ثقل (*ṣeql*) A. weight.

ثقیل (*ṣaqil*) A. heavy.

ثلاث (*ṣalāṣ*) A., ثلاثه (*ṣalāṣeh*) A. three.

ثلث (*ṣolṣ*) A. third.

ثمر (*ṣamar*) A., ثمره (*ṣamareh*) A. fruit.

ثنا (*ṣanā*) A. praise.

ثواب (*ṣavāb*) A. reward.

ثور (*ṣour*) A. Taurus.

ج

جا (*jā*) place. بجا opportune, proper. بجایِ instead of. بجا آوردن to do; to comply with.

جابر (*jāber*) A. oppressing, oppressor.

جادار (*jādār*) roomy, spacious.

جادو (*jādu*) magic, sorcery.

جادوگر (*jādugar*) magician, sorcerer.

جاده (*jāddeh*) A. road.

جاذب (*jāẕeb*) A. attractive.

جاذبه (*jāẕebeh*) A. attraction.

جار (*jār*) T. proclamation. جار زدن to proclaim.

جارچی (*jārchi*) T. town-crier, herald.

جاروب (*jārub*) broom. جاروب کردن to sweep.

جاروب کش (*jārub kash*) sweeper.

جاری (*jāri*) A. flowing; current.

جاسوس (*jāsus*) A. spy.

جاسوسی (*jāsusi*) *a.* espionage.

جالب (*jāleb*) A. attracting, attractive. جالبِ توجه interesting.

جالیز (*jāliz*) kitchen garden.

جام (*jām*) cup, goblet.

جامد (*jāmed*) A. solid.

جامع (*jāme'*) A. comprehensive, universal; mosque.

جامعه (*jāme'eh*) A. community, society; university.

جامگی (*jāmegi*) allowance.

جامه (*jāmeh*) garment.

جامه دان (*jāmeh dān*) wardrobe; trunk.

جان (*jān*) soul, life. جانِ من my dear.

جانان (*jānān*) sweetheart.

جانانه (*jānāneh*) lovely.

جانب (*jāneb*) A. side, direction. اینجانب I.

جانخراش (*jānkharāsh*) vexing, tormenting.

جاندار (*jāndār*) animate; animal.

جانشین (*jāneshin*) successor; deputy.

جانور (*jānvar*) animal.

جانور شناسی (*jānvār shenāsi*) zoology.

جانی (*jāni*) A. criminal.

جاوه (*jāveh*) Java.

جاوید (*jāvid*), جاویدان (*jāvidān*) eternal, immortal.

جاه (*jāh*) rank, dignity.

جاهد (*jāhed*) A. diligent, industrious.

جاهل (*jāhel*) A. ignorant.

جایز (*jāyez*) A. allowable, permissible.

جایزه (*jāyezeh*) A. prize.

جایگاه (*jāygāh*) place, station.

جای گزین (*jāy gozin*) superseding.

جایگیر (*jāygir*) fixed; succeeding, successor.

جبار (*jabbār*) A. tyrannical, tyrant.

جبال (*jebāl*) A. mountains. (*Pl. of* جبل)

جبر (*jabr*) A. compulsion. جبر ومقابله algebra.

جبراً (*jabran*) A. forcibly.

جبران (*jobrān*) A. compensation.

جبران نا پذیر (*jobrān nā pazir*) *a.* irreparable.

جبل (*jabal*) A. mountain.

جبل الطارق (*jabalo'-ṭ-ṭāreq*) A. Gibraltar.

جبلت (*jebellat*) A. nature, disposition.

جبلی (*jebelli*) A. natural, innate.

جبهه (*jabheh*) A. forehead; front.

جبین (*jabin*) A. forehead.

جثه (*joṣṣeh*) A. body, corpulence.

جد (*jadd*) A. grandfather, ancestor.

جد (*jedd*) A. effort, exertion; seriousness.

جدا (*jodā*) separate.

جداً (*jeddan*) A. earnestly, seriously.

جداگانه (*jodāgāneh*) separate(ly).

جدال (*jedāl*) A. dispute.

جدائی (*jodā'i*) separation.

جدل (*jadal*) A. contest, dispute.

جدول (*jadval*) A. table, schedule.

جدّه (*jaddeh*) A. grandmother.

جدی (*jady*) A. Capricorn.

جدی (*jeddi*) A. serious; energetic.

جدید (*jadid*) A. new.

جدیداً (*jadidan*) A. recently.

جدید الورود (*jadido'l-vorud*) A. newly arrived.

جذاب (*jaẕẕāb*) A. attractive.

جذب (*jaẕb*) A. attraction. جذب کردن to attract.

جر (*jarr*) A. (act of) pulling.

جرأت (*jor'at*) A. daring, courage. جرأت کردن to dare.

جراح (*jarrāḥ*) A. surgeon.

جراحت (*jerāḥat*) A. wound; pus, matter.

جراحی (*jarrāḥi*) *a.* surgery.

جراید (*jarāyed*) A. newspapers. (*Pl. of* جریده.)

جرح (*jarḥ*) A. wound. جرح و تعدیل adaptation.

جرعه (*jor'eh*) A. draught, drink.

جرگه (*jergeh*) T. circle, ring.

جرم (*jorm*) A. crime.

جرم (*jerm*) A. body.

جری (*jari*) A. bold, courageous.

جریان (*jarayān*) A. course, flow, circulation.

جریب (*jarib*) A. *a measure of land.*

جریده (*jarideh*) A. newspaper.

جریمه (*jarimeh*) A. fine, penalty.

جز (*joz*) except.

جزء (*joz'*) A. part.

جزا (*jazā*) A. reward, compensation, punishment.

جزایر (*jazāyer*) A. islands. (*Pl. of* جزیره.)

جزر (*jazr*) A. ebb.

جزوه (*jozveh*) *a.* pamphlet; paragraph.

جزیره (*jazireh*) A. island.

جزیه (*jezyeh*) A. tribute, poll-tax.

جسارت (*jasārat*) A. boldness, daring.

جستجو (*jostoju*) search. جستجو کردن to search.

جستن (*jastan*) to leap.

جستن (*jostan*) to seek.

جست و خیز (*jast o khiz*) (act of) leaping. جست و خیز کردن to leap.

جسد (*jasad*) A. body.

جسم (*jesm*) A. body.

جسمانی (*jesmāni*) A. corporeal, worldly.

جسور (*jasur*) A. bold, insolent.

جشن (*jashn*) festival.

جعبه (*ja'beh*) A. box, case.

جعفر (*ja'far*) A. *masc. proper noun.*

جعفری (*ja'fari*) A. parsley.

جعل (*ja'l*) A. forgery.

جعلی (*ja'li*) A. counterfeit.

جغد (*joghd*) owl.

جغرافی (*joghrāfi*) A. geography.

جغرافیا (*joghrāfiā*) A. geography.

جغرافیائی (*joghrāfiā'i*) *a.* geographical.

جفا (*jafā*) A. oppression, cruelty.

جفت (*joft*) pair.

جفنگ (*jafang*) nonsense; absurd.

جگر (*jegar*) liver.

جقه (*jeqqeh*) tuft, crest, aigrette.

جل (*joll*) A. horse-cloth; dish-cloth; rag.

جلا (1) (*jalā*) A. exile, emigration.

جلا (2) (*jalā*) A. lustre, polish. جلا دادن to polish.

جلاد (*jallād*) A. executioner.

جلال (*jalāl*) A. glory.

جلب (*jalb*) A. attraction. جلب کردن to attract.

جلب (*jalab*) false, counterfeit.

جلد (*jald*) quick, nimble.

جلد (*jeld*) A. skin, hide; binding; volume.

جلدی (*jaldi*) quickness, agility.

جلسه (*jalseh*) A. session, meeting.

جلف (*jelf*) A. frivolous.

جلگه (*jolgeh*) plain.

جلو (*jelou*) M. front; bridle. جلوِ in front of. جلوِ — گرفتن to restrain —.

جلودار (*jeloudār*) postillion.

جلوس (*jolus*) A. accession (to the throne).

جلوگیری (*jelougiri*) prevention. جلوگیری کردن to prevent.

جلوه (*jelveh*) A. manifestation; splendour. جلوه دادن to show off, to display.

جلیل (*jalil*) A. glorious.

جماد (*jamād*) A. inorganic substance, mineral.

جمادی (*jamādi*) A. inorganic; solid.

جمادی الآخره (*jomādio'l-ākhereh*) A. *sixth month of the Arabic lunar year.*

جمادی الاولی (*jomādio'l-ulā*) A. *fifth month of the Arabic lunar year.*

جماع (*jemā'*) A. copulation, coitus.

جماعت (*jamā'at*) A. assembly.

جمال (*jamāl*) A. beauty, elegance.

جماهیر (*jamāhir*) A. republics. (*Pl. of* جمهور.)

جمجمه (*jomjomeh*) A. skull.

جمشید (*jamshid*) *name of a legendary king of Persia. Masc. proper name.* تختِ جمشید Persepolis.

جمع (*jam'*) A. company, crowd; addition; plural. جمع کردن to collect, assemble; to add.

جمع آوری (*jam' āvari*) *a.* (act of) collecting.

جمعه (*jom'eh*) A. Friday.

جمعیت (*jam'iyyat*) A. population.

جملگی (*jomlegi*) *a.* all; totality.

جمله (*jomleh*) A. sentence; whole, total. از جملهٔ among.

جمهور (*jomhur*) A. republic.

جمهوری (*jomhuri*) A. republic(an).

جمهوریخواه (*jomhurikhvāh*) *a.* republican.

جمیع (*jami'*) A. the whole, all.

جمیعاً (*jami'an*) A. altogether.

جمیل (*jamil*) A. beautiful, excellent.

جن (*jenn*) A. hobgoblin, jinnee.

جناب (*janāb*) A. honour, excellency.

جنابعالی (*janābe'āli*) *a.* Your Excellency.

جناح (*jenāḥ*) A. wing.

جنازه (*janāzeh*) A. funeral; corpse.

جنان (*jenān*) A. gardens; Paradise. (*Pl. of* جنت.)

جنایت (*jenāyat*) A. crime.

جنایتکار (*jenāyatkār*) *a.* criminal.

جنب (*janb*) A. side, flank.

جنبش (*jonbesh*) movement.

جنبه (*janbeh*) A. side; aspect.

جنبیدن (*jonbidan*) to move, to shake.

جنت (*jannat*) A. garden, paradise.

جنجال (*janjāl*) tumult, brawl.

جنده (*jendeh*) prostitute.

جنس (*jens*) A. species, sort, kind; gender, sex; goods, merchandise.

جنسیت (*jensiyyat*) A. race, homogeneity.

جنگ (*jang*) war.

جنگاور (*jangāvar*) warrior.

جنگجو (*jangju*) warlike.

جنگل (*jangal*) forest, wood.

جنگلی (*jangali*) pertaining to the forest; wild, savage.

جنگی (*jangi*) pertaining to war.

جنگیدن (*jangidan*) to fight.

جنوب (*janub*) A. south.

جنوباً (*januban*) A. on the south.

جنوبی (*janubi*) A. southern.

جنون (*jonun*) A. insanity.

جنین (*janin*) A. fœtus, embryo.

جو (*jou*) barley.

جو (*ju*) stream.

جوّ (*javv*) A. atmosphere.

جواب (*javāb*) A. answer, reply. جواب دادن to answer, reply.

جواز (*javāz*) A. permit, license.

جوال (*jovāl*) sack.

جوالدوز (*jovālduz*) packing needle.

جوان (*javān*) young (man), youth.

جوانمرد (*javānmard*) brave and generous youth, hero.

جوانمردی (*javānmardi*) generosity, chivalry.

جوانی (*javāni*) youth.

جواهر (*javāher*) A. jewel(s).

جوائز (*javā'ez*) A. prizes. (*Pl. of* جایزه.)

جوجه (*jujeh*) chick(en).

جود (*jud*) A. generosity.

جور (*jur*) sort, kind.

جور (*jour*) A. tyranny, oppression.

جوراب (*jurāb*) stocking, sock.

جوز (*jouz*) A. nut; walnut.

جوزا (*jouzā*) A. Gemini.

جوش (*jush*) ebullition, boiling; welding. جوش دادن to weld, solder.

جوشانده (*jushāndeh*) decoction.

جوشانیدن (*jushānidan*) to boil (*tr.*).

جو شناسی (*javv shenāsi*) *a.* meteorology.

جوشیدن (*jushidan*) to boil (*intr.*).

جوف (*jouf*) A. cavity; inside, interior.

جوفاً (*joufan*) A. enclosed.

جولان (*joulān*) A. career(ing).

جوهر (*jouhar*) A. essence, substance.

جوهری (*jouhari*) A. essential; dyed; jeweller.

جوی (*juy*) stream.

جوّی (*javvi*) A. atmospheric.

جویا (*juyā*) seeking.

جویدن (*javidan*) to chew, to gnaw.

جوینده (*juyandeh*) seeking, seeker.

جهاد (*jehād*) A. holy war.

جهاز (*jahāz*) A. ship; trousseau.

جهالت (*jahālat*) A. ignorance.

جهان (*jahān*) world.

جهانبانی (*jahānbāni*) government of the world.

جهانگیر (*jahāngir*) world conqueror.

جهانگیری (*jahāngiri*) world conquest, imperialism.

جهانی (*jahāni*) inhabitant of the world.

جهت (*jehat*) A. cause, reason. جهتِ for.

جهد (*jahd*) A. effort, endeavour.

جهل (*jahl*) A. ignorance.

جهنم (*jahannam*) A. hell.

جهود (*johud*) Jew.

جهیز (*jahiz*) A. trousseau.

جیب (*jib*) A. pocket; collar.

جیب بر (*jib bor*) *a.* pickpocket.

جیب بری (*jib bori*) *a.* pickpocket's business.

جیحون (*jeiḥun*) A. Oxus.

جیره (*jireh*) ration.

جیره بندی (*jireh bandi*) rationing.

جیش (*jeish*) A. army.

جیفه (*jifeh*) A. carrion, carcase.

جیوه (*jiveh*) quicksilver, mercury.

چ

چابک (*chābok*) nimble, agile.

چاپ (*chāp*) print(ing). چاپ کردن to print.

چاپار (*chāpār*) T. courier.

چاپخانه (*chāpkhāneh*) printing-house.

چاپلوس (*chāplus*) flatterer.

چاپلوسی (*chāplusi*) flattery.

چادر (*chādor*) tent; veil.

چادر نشین (*chādor neshin*) nomad.

چارپا (*chārpā*) quadruped.

چاره (*chāreh*) remedy, cure.

چاره پذیر (*chāreh paẕir*) curable, remediable.

چاشت (*chāsht*) noon; lunch.

چاشنی (1) (*chāshni*) sauce, relish; taste.

چاشنی (2) (*chāshni*) percussion cap, detonator.

چاق (*chāq*) T. fat; healthy.

چاقو (*chāqu*) T. knife.

چاقی (*chāqi*) plumpness, fatness.

چاک (*chāk*) fissure, rent. چاک کردن to rend.

چاکر (*chākar*) servant; *polite substitute for* من, I.

چال (*chāl*) hole, pit.

چانه (*chāneh*) chin. چانه زدن to haggle.

چاوش (*chāvosh*) T. herald; leader of a caravan.

چاه (*chāh*) well, pit.

چای (*chāy*) tea.

چبوق (*chobuq*) T. pipe.

چپ (*chap*) left.

چپاول (*chapāvol*) T. raid, plunder, pillage. چپاول کردن to plunder, loot.

چپ دست (*chap dast*) left-handed.

چتائی (*chatā'i*) H. mat.

چتر (*chatr*) umbrella, parasol; parachute.

چترباز (*chatrbāz*) parachutist.

چدن (*chodan*) cast iron.

چرا (*cherā*) why ?

چراغ (*cherāgh*) lamp.

چراگاه (*charāgāh*) pasture.

چرانیدن (*charānidan*) to graze (*tr.*).

چرب (*charb*) fat, greasy.

چربی (*charbi*) fat, grease.

چرخ (*charkh*) wheel. چرخ زدن to spin, turn.

چرخاندن (*charkhāndan*) to spin, whirl, rotate (*tr.*).

چرک (*cherk*) dirt(y).

چرکین (*cherkin*) dirty, filthy.

چرم (*charm*) leather, hide.

چرم ساز (*charm sāz*) currier.

چروک (*choruk*) wrinkle.

چریدن (*charidan*) to graze (*intr.*).

چریک (*charik*) T. irregular troops, guerrillas.

چسبنده (*chasbandeh*) adhesive.

چسبیدن (*chasbidan*) to stick ; to cling.

چست (*chost*) nimble.

چشم (*cheshm*) eye.

چشمه (*chashmeh*) spring, fountain.

چشیدن (*chashidan*) to taste.

چطور (*cheṭour*) *a.* how ?

چغندر (*choghondar*) beet.

چقدر (*cheqadr*) *a.* how much ?

چقماق (*chaqmāq*) T. flint.

چک (*chek*) E. cheque.

چکار (*chekār*) what ?

چکش (*chakkosh*) hammer.

چکیدن (*chakidan*) to trickle, drip.

چکمه (*chakmeh*) T. high boot.

چگونگی (*chegunegi*) quality, nature.

چگونه (*cheguneh*) how ?

چلاندن (*chelāndan*) to squeeze, press.

چلتوک (*chaltuk*) T. paddy.

چلچله (*chelcheleh*) swallow.

چلیک (*chalik*) cask, barrel.

چنار (*chanār*) plane-tree.

چنان (*chonān*) such.

چنانچه (*chonāncheh*) if ; as.

چنانکه (*chonānkeh*) as.

چنبر (*chanbar*) hoop, ring, circle.

چند (*chand*) some, several ; how much ? ; how many ?

چندان (*chandān*) so ; so many, so much.

چندی (*chandi*) a little while. از چندی باین طرف for some time past.

چندین (*chandin*) several.

چنگ (*chang*) claw ; clutch (*of a motor car*).

چنگال (*changāl*) claw, talon ; fork.

چنین (*chonin*) such.

چوب (*chub*) wood.

چوبدار (*chubdār*) mace-bearer ; cattle-dealer.

چوبی (*chubi*) wooden.

چوپان (*chupān*) shepherd.

چوگان (*chougān*) bat ; polo, hockey.

چون (*chun*) as, since.

چونکه (*chunkeh*) because.

چه (*cheh*) what ? — چه — وچه both — and —.

چهار (*chahār*) four.

چهارده (*chahārdah*) fourteen.

چهاردهم (*chahārdahom*) fourteenth.

چهار شنبه (*chahār shanbeh*) Wednesday.

چهارم (*chahārom*) fourth.

چهره (*chehreh*) face.

چهل (*chehel*) forty.

چهلم (*chehelom*) fortieth.

چیت (*chit*) chintz.

چیدن (*chidan*) to pluck, pick.

چیره (*chireh*) victorious; rude, violent.

چیز (*chiz*) thing. چیزی something.

چین (1) (*chin*) China.

چین (2) (*chin*) wrinkle, fold.

چینه (*chineh*) clay-wall.

چینی (*chini*) Chinese; chinaware.

ح

حاج (*ḥājj*) A. pilgrim.

حاجب (*ḥājeb*) A. doorkeeper, chamberlain.

حاجت (*ḥājat*) A. need, requirement.

حاجتمند (*ḥājatmand*) *a.* needy.

حاجی (*ḥāji*) *a.* pilgrim.

حاجی ترخان (*ḥāji tarkhān*) *a.* Astrakhan.

حادثه (*ḥādeṣeh*) A. event, calamity.

حاذق (*ḥāẕeq*) A. skilful.

حار (*ḥārr*) A. hot, torrid.

حاسد (*ḥāsed*) A. envious.

حاسه (*ḥāsseh*) A. sense.

حاشا (*ḥāshā*) A. God forbid!

حاشیه (*ḥāshieh*) A. margin, edge; note, annotation.

حاصل (*ḥāṣel*) A. produce, product; crop. حاصل کردن to acquire.

حاصل خیز (*ḥāṣel khiz*) *a.* fertile.

حاضر (*ḥāẓer*) A. ready; present.

حافظ (*ḥāfeẓ*) A. guardian, protector; one who knows the Koran by heart.

حافظه (*ḥāfeẓeh*) A. memory.

حاکم (*ḥākem*) A. governor; dominant.

حاکمیت (*ḥākemiyyat*) A. sovereignty; jurisdiction.

حاکی (*ḥāki*) A. telling, stating.

حال (*ḥāl*) A. condition, state; now. حال آنکه whereas.

حالا (*ḥālā*) A. now, at present.

حالت (*ḥālat*) A. state, condition.

حالیه (*ḥāliyyeh*) A. at (of) the present time.

حامل (*ḥāmel*) A. carrying.

حامله (*ḥāmeleh*) A. pregnant.

حامی (*ḥāmi*) A. protector.

حاوی (*ḥāvi*) A. containing.

حائز (*ḥa'ez*) A. possessing, holding. حائز شدن to (come) to hold.

حائل (*ḥā'el*) A. intervening.

حب (*ḥabb*) A. pill; grain; berry.

حب (*ḥobb*) A. love.

حباب (*ḥobāb*) A. bubble.

حبس (*ḥabs*) A. imprisonment; prison. حبس کردن to imprison.

حبسی (*ḥabsi*) A. prisoner.

حبشه (*ḥabasheh*) A. Abyssinia.

حبل (*ḥabl*) A. rope; vein.

حبل الورید (*ḥablo'l-varid*) A. jugular vein.

حبوب (*ḥobub*) A. grains; berries; pills. (*Pl. of* حب.)

حبوبات (*ḥobubāt*) A. cereals.

حبه (*ḥabbeh*) A. grain, seed, berry.

حبیب (*ḥabib*) A. beloved, friend.

حتم (*ḥatm*) A. resolution; certain, sure.

حتماً (*ḥatman*) A. certainly.

حتمی (*ḥatmi*) A. certain.

حتمی الوقوع (*ḥatmiyyo'l-voqu'*) A. inevitable.

حتی (*ḥattā*) A. even.

حتی الامکان (*ḥatta'l-emkān*) A. as far as possible.

حج (*ḥajj*) A. pilgrimage.

حجاب (*ḥejāb*) A. veil.

حجاج (*ḥojjāj*) A. pilgrims. (*Pl. of* حاج.)

حجاز (*ḥejāz*) A. Hejaz.

حجامت (*ḥajāmat*) A. cupping.

حجت (*ḥojjat*) A. argument.

حجر (*ḥajar*) A. stone.

حجره (*ḥojreh*) A. cell, chamber.

حجله (*ḥajleh*) A. bridal chamber.

حجم (*ḥajm*) A. volume, bulk.

حد (*ḥadd*) A. boundary, limit; extent. حدِ اکثر to the utmost.

حدس (*ḥads*) A. guess, surmise. حدس زدن to guess.

حدسیات (*ḥadsiyyāt*) A. guesses, conjectures. (*Used as pl. of* حدس.)

حدقه (*ḥadaqeh*) A. pupil of the eye.

حدوث (*ḥoduṣ*) A. occurrence.

حدود (*ḥodud*) A. boundaries, limits. (*Pl. of* حد.) در حدودِ about.

حدیث (*ḥadiṣ*) A. tradition.

حدیقه (*ḥadiqeh*) A. garden.

حذر (*ḥaẕar*) A. caution. حذر کردن to beware.

حذف (*ḥaẕf*) A. omission, elision. حذف کردن to omit, elide.

حراج (*ḥarāj*) A. sale by auction.

حرارت (*ḥarārat*) A. heat.

حراست (*ḥarāsat*) A. custody, preservation.

حرام (*ḥarām*) A. unlawful, forbidden.

حرامزاده (*ḥarāmzādeh*) *a.* illegitimate, bastard; rogue.

حرامی (*ḥarāmi*) A. robber.

حرب (*ḥarb*) A. fight, battle, war.

حربه (*ḥarbeh*) A. arms, weapons.

حرص (*ḥerṣ*) A. greed.

حرف (*ḥarf*) A. letter. حرف زدن to speak.

حرف (*ḥeraf*) A. crafts, trades. (*Pl. of* حرفه.)

حرفه (*ḥerfeh*) A. craft, trade.

حرکت (*ḥarakat*) A. motion; act; start. حرکت کردن to move; to act; to start.

حرم (*ḥaram*) A. harem; the temple in Mecca.

حرمت (*ḥormat*) A. respect.

حروف (*ḥoruf*) A. letters. (*Pl. of* حرف).

حریت (*ḥorriyyat*) A. liberty, freedom.

حریر (*ḥarir*) A. silk.

حریره (*ḥarireh*) A. pap made of flour and milk.

حریص (*ḥariṣ*) A. greedy.

حریق (*ḥariq*) A. conflagration.

حریم (*ḥarim*) A. harem.

حزب (*ḥezb*) A. party.

حزبی (*ḥezbi*) A. sectarian.

حزن (*ḥozn*) A. grief.

حزین (*ḥazin*) A. sad.

حس (*ḥess*) A. sense, feeling.

حس کردن to feel.

حساب (*ḥesāb*) A. reckoning, account.

حسابدار (*ḥesābdār*) *a.* accountant.

حسابداری (*ḥesābdāri*) *a.* accounts.

حسابی (*ḥesābi*) *a.* arithmetical; logical; accurate.

حساس (*ḥassās*) A. sensitive.

حسب (*ḥasab*) A. sufficiency, measure.

(بر) حسبِ according to.

حسب الامر (*ḥasabo'l-amr*) A. according to instructions.

حسد (*ḥasad*) A. envy.

حسرت (*ḥasrat*) A. regret.

حسن (*ḥosn*) A. beauty, goodness.

حسنِ نیت good will.

حسن (*ḥasan*) A. beautiful, good; *masc. proper name.*

حسود (*ḥasud*) A. envious.

حسی (*ḥessi*) *a.* tangible; sentimental.

حسیات (*ḥessiyyāt*) A. feelings, sentiments.

حسین (*ḥosein*) A. *masc. proper name.*

حشره (*ḥashareh*) A. insect.

حشره شناس (*ḥashareh shenās*) *a.* entomologist.

حشره شناسی (*ḥashareh shenāsi*) *a.* entomology.

حشم (*ḥasham*) A. retinue; household; animal.

حشمت (*ḥeshmat*) A. pomp.

حشو (*ḥashv*) A. padding; redundancy; marginal note.

حصاد (*ḥaṣād*) A. harvest.

حصار (*ḥeṣār*) A. castle, fortress; fence, wall.

حصبه (*ḥaṣbeh*) A. typhoid.

حصر (*ḥaṣr*) A. restriction.

حصن (*ḥeṣn*) A. fortress.

حصول (*ḥoṣul*) A. acquisition, attainment.

حصه (*ḥeṣṣeh*) A. share, portion.

حصیر (*ḥaṣir*) A. mat.

حضار (*ḥoẓẓār*) A. those present. (*Pl. of* حاضر)

حضارت (*ḥaẓārat*) A. civilization.

حضرت (*ḥaẓrat*) A. presence; Majesty, Highness, Excellency.

حضور (*ḥoẓur*) A. presence.

حظ (*ḥaẓẓ*) A. delight, enjoyment.

حفاظت (*ḥefāẓat*) A. protection, custody.

حفر (*ḥafr*) A. digging, excavation.

حفر کردن to dig, excavate.

حفریات (*ḥafriyyāt*) A. excavations.

حفظ (*ḥefẓ*) A. preservation, protection. حفظ کردن to preserve, protect; to memorize.

حفظ الصحه (*ḥefẓo'ṣ-ṣeḥḥeh*) A. hygiene.

حق (*ḥaqq*) A. right; truth; God.

حقارت (*ḥaqārat*) A. contempt.

حقوق (*ḥoquq*) A. rights; law; pay. (*Pl. of* حق.)

حقوقی (*ḥoquqi*) *a.* legal.

حقه (*ḥoqqeh*) A. casket; hookah; calyx; trick(ery).

حقه باز (*ḥoqqeh bāz*) *a.* juggler.

حقیر (*ḥaqir*) A. humble, base; *polite substitute for* من.

حقیقت (*ḥaqiqat*) A. truth.

حقیقةً (*ḥaqiqatan*) A. truly, indeed.

حقیقی (*ḥaqiqi*) A. real, true.

حک (*ḥakk*) A. erasure, abrasion.

حکاک (*ḥakkāk*) A. engraver.

حکاکی (*ḥakkaki*) *a.* engraving.

حکایت (*ḥekāyat*) A. story.

حکم (*ḥakam*) A. arbitrator.

حکم (*ḥokm*) A. order; sentence. بحکمِ because of, through.

حکما (*ḥokamā*) A. doctors, philosophers. (*Pl. of* حکیم.).

حکمت (*ḥekmat*) A. wisdom, philosophy.

حکمران (*ḥokmrān*) *a.* governor.

حکمفرما (*ḥokmfarmā*) *a.* prevailing.

حکمیت (*ḥakamiyyat*) A. arbitration.

حکومت (*ḥokumat*) A. government.

حکه (*ḥakkeh*) A. itch(ing).

حکیم (*ḥakim*) A. doctor, philosopher.

حل (*ḥall*) A. solution. حل کردن to solve; to dissolve.

حلاج (*ḥallāj*) A. cotton carder.

حلال (*ḥalāl*) A. lawful.

حلاوت (*ḥalāvat*) A. sweetness.

حلب (*ḥalab*) A. Aleppo.

حلزون (*ḥalzun*) A. snail.

حلق (*ḥalq*) A. throat.

حلقوم (*ḥolqum*) A. larynx.

حلقه (*ḥalqeh*) A. ring, circle.

حلقی (*ḥalqi*) A. guttural.

حلم (*ḥelm*) A. meekness.

حلوا (*ḥalvā*) A. sweetmeat.

حلول (*ḥolul*) A. transmigration, incarnation.

حله (*ḥolleh*) A. robe.

حلیم (*ḥalim*) A. meek.

حما (*ḥommā*) A. fever.

حماقت (*ḥamāqat*) A. stupidity, folly.

حمال (*ḥammāl*) A. porter.

حمام (*ḥammām*) A. bath.

حمامی (*ḥammāmi*) *a.* bathkeeper.

حمایت (*ḥemāyat*) A. protection.

حمایل (*ḥamāyel*) A. shoulder-belt, baldrick.

حمد (*ḥamd*) A. praise.

حمل (*ḥaml*) A. shipment, transportation; pregnancy, gestation. حمل کردن to ship, forward. حمل و نقل transport.

حمل (*ḥamal*) A. Aries.

حمله (*ḥamleh*) A. attack. حمله کردن to attack.

حمله ور (*ḥamleh var*) *a.* attacking.

حنا (*ḥannā*) A. henna.

حنجره (*ḥanjareh*) A. larynx.

حوا (*ḥavvā*) A. Eve.

حوادث (*ḥavādeṣ*) A. events, calamities. (*Pl. of* حادثه).

حوارى (*ḥavāri*) A. apostle, disciple (of Jesus Christ).

حواس (*ḥavāss*) A. senses. (*Pl. of* حاسه).

حواشى (*ḥavāshi*) A. notes, annotations. (*Pl. of* حاشيه).

حواله (*ḥavāleh*) A. assignment; draft.

حوالى (*ḥavāli*) A. environs; suburbs.

حوائج (*ḥavā'ej*) A. needs. (*Pl. of* حاجت).

حوت (*ḥut*) A. large fish; Pisces.

حور (*ḥur*) A. houri(s).

حورى (*ḥuri*) *a.* houri.

حوزه (*ḥouzeh*) A. sphere, domain, range.

حوصله (*ḥouseleh*) A. crop (of a bird); patience. حوصله اش تنگ شد he lost patience.

حوض (*ḥouẓ*) A. tank, pond; basin; dock.

حوضه (*ḥouẓeh*) A. river-basin.

حوله (*ḥouleh*) A. towel.

حومه (*ḥoumeh*) A. suburbs.

حى (*ḥayy*) A. alive.

حيا (*ḥayā*) A. modesty, shame.

حيات (*ḥayāt*) A. life.

حياتى (*ḥayāti*) *a.* vital.

حياط (*ḥayāṭ*) A. courtyard.

حيث (*ḥeiṣ*) A. respect. از حيثِ with respect to.

حيثيت (*ḥeiṣiyyat*) A. prestige.

حيدر (*ḥeidar*) A. ***masc. proper name.***

حيدر آباد (*ḥeidar ābād*) *a.* Hyderabad.

حيران (*ḥeirān*) A. amazed.

حيرت (*ḥeirat*) A. amazement.

حيض (*ḥeiẓ*) A. menses.

حيطه (*ḥiṭeh*) A. enclosure; compass, reach.

حيف (*ḥeif*) A. what a pity!

حيفا (*ḥeifā*) A. Haifa.

حيله (*ḥileh*) A. trick; deceit, fraud.

حيوان (*ḥeivān*) A. animal.

حيوان شناس (*ḥeivān shenās*) *a.* zoologist.

حيوان شناسى (*ḥeivān shenāsi*) *a.* zoology.

خ

خاتم (*khātam*) A. seal, signet; mosaic.

خاتمه (*khātemeh*) A. completion, conclusion. خاتمه دادن to complete.

خاتون (*khātun*) T. lady.

خاج (*khāj*) AR. cross.

خادم (*khādem*) A. servant.

خار (*khār*) thorn.

خارا (*khārā*) hard (stone); granite.

خار پشت (*khār posht*) porcupine, hedgehog.

خارج (*khārej*) A. external, outside. خارج شدن to come out.

خارجه (*khārejeh*) A. *fem. of* خارج. (*See* امور.)

خارجی (*khāreji*) A. foreign.

خاردار (*khārdār*) thorny; barbed.

خارش (*khāresh*) itch(ing). خارش کردن to itch.

خارق العاده (*khāreqo'l-'ādeh*) A. extraordinary, unusual.

خاریدن (*khāridan*) to itch.

خاستن (*khāstan*) to rise.

خاشاک (*khāshāk*) chips, shavings; rubbish.

خاشع (*khāshe'*) A. humble.

خاص (*khāṣṣ*) A. special, particular; private. خاصان men of rank.

خاصره (*khāṣereh*) A. waist, flank.

خاصه (*khāṣṣeh*) A. especially.

خاصیت (*khāṣṣiyyat*) A. property, virtue.

خاطر (*khāṭer*) A. mind, memory.

خاطر جمع (*khāṭer jam'*) *a.* calm, collected; certain, sure.

خاطر جمعی (*khāter jam'i*) *a.* calmness, composure; certainty.

خاطر خواه (*khāṭer khvāh*) *a.* lover.

خاطرنشان (*khāṭerneshān*) *a.* impressed in the mind. خاطرنشان کردن to point out.

خاطره (*khāṭereh*) A. memory.

خاک (*khāk*) dust; earth, soil; territory.

خاک انداز (*khāk andāz*) shovel.

خاکبیز (*khākbiz*) sieve.

خاکستر (*khākestar*) ashes, cinders.

خاکستری (*khākestari*) ash-coloured, grey.

خاکی (*khāki*) earthly, terrestrial; dusty; khaki.

خال (1) (*khāl*) mole.

خال (2) (*khāl*) A. maternal uncle.

خالص (*khāleṣ*) A. pure, sincere; net.

خالصه (*khāleṣeh*) A. public domain.

خالق (*khāleq*) A. creator.

خالی (*khāli*) A. empty, void.

خام (*khām*) raw.

خامس (*khāmes*) A. fifth.

خامساً (*khāmesan*) A. fifthly.

خاموش (*khāmush*) silent. خاموش کردن to silence, to extinguish.

خاموشی (*khāmushi*) silence.

خامه (*khāmeh*) pen.

خان (*khān*) T. khan.

خانقاه (*khāneqāh*) *a.* monastery.

خانگی (*khānegi*) domestic.

خانمان (*khānemān*) house and household goods.

خانم (*khānom*) T. lady.

خانوادگی (*khānevādegi*) (pertaining to a) family, domestic.

خانواده (*khānevādeh*) family.

خانه (*khāneh*) house.

خانه دار (*khāneh dār*) thrifty.

خانه داری (*khāneh dāri*) housekeeping.

خاور (*khāvar*) east.

خاور شناس (*khāvar shenās*) orientalist.

خاوری (*khāvari*) eastern.

خاویار (*khāviār*) T. caviare.

خائف (*khā'ef*) A. fearful, timid.

خائن (*khā'en*) A. treacherous; traitor.

خایه (*khāyeh*) testicle(s).

خباز (*khabbāz*) A. baker.

خبازی (*khabbāzi*) *a.* bakery.

خبر (*khabar*) A. news, report.

خبر دار (*khabar dār*) *a.* informed, aware.

خبر گزاری (*khabar gozāri*) *a.* news agency.

خبر نگار (*khabar negār*) *a.* newspaper correspondent.

خبره (*khebreh*) A. expert.

خبیث (*khabiṣ*) A. malicious, evil, impure.

ختم (*khatm*) A. (act of) finishing. ختم کردن to finish.

ختنه (*khatneh*) A. circumcision.

خجالت (*khajālat*) A. shame. خجالت کشیدن to be ashamed.

خجسته (*khojasteh*) blest, fortunate.

خجل (*khajel*) A. ashamed.

خدا (*khodā*) God. خدا حافظ good-bye!

خدا ترس (*khodā tars*) God-fearing.

خدا حافظی (*khodā ḥāfezi*) *a.* farewell, valediction.

خدا نشناس (*khodā nashnās*) impious.

خداوند (*khodāvand*) lord; God.

خدعه (*khod'eh*) A. deceit.

خدمت (*khedmat*) A. service.

خدمتگار (*khedmatgār*) *a.* servant.

خدیجه (*khadijeh*) A. *fem. proper name.*

خر (*khar*) donkey.

خراب (*kharāb*) A. ruin, destruction; ruined, spoiled. خراب کردن to ruin, to spoil.

خرابه (*kharābeh*) *a.* ruin.

خرابی (*kharābi*) *a.* ruined condition, badness.

خراج (*kharāj*) A. tribute, tax.

خرازی (*kharrāzi*) *a.* haberdashery.

خراشیدن (*kharāshidan*) to scratch, scrape.

خراط (*kharrāṭ*) A. turner.

خرافات (*khorāfāt*) A. mythological tales; nonsense.

خرامیدن (*kherāmidan*) to walk gracefully.

خربزه (*kharbozeh*) melon.

خرج (*kharj*) A. expense; tax.

خر چنگ (*khar chang*) crab, lobster.

خرد (*kherad*) wisdom, intellect.

خرد (*khord*) small; broken to pieces. خرد کردن to break to pieces.

خرداد (*khordād*) *name of the third month of the Persian year.*

خردل (*khardal*) A. mustard.

خردمند (*kheradmand*) wise, intelligent.

خرده (*khordeh*) bit, fragment. خرده گرفتن to find fault.

خردی (*khordi*) smallness, infancy.

خر زهره (*khar zahreh*) *a.* oleander; rhododendron; colocynth.

خرس (*khers*) bear.

خرسند (*khorsand*) content, glad.

خرسندی (*khorsandi*) contentment, gladness.

خرطوم (*khorṭum*) A. trunk, proboscis.

خرقه (*kherqeh*) A. cloak.

خرگاه (*khargāh*) tent, pavilion.

خر گوش (*khar gush*) hare, rabbit.

خرم (*khorram*) fresh, pleasant, cheerful.

خرما (*khormā*) date(s).

خرمائی (*khormā'i*) reddish brown.

خرمن (*kharman*) stack, heap; harvest. خرمن کردن to stack.

خر مهره (*khar mohreh*) glass beads, shells.

خروار (*kharvār*) *name of a dry measure* = *100 maunds.*

خروج (*khoruj*) A. exit, departure.

خروس (*khorus*) cock.

خروش (*khorush*) roar, cry.

خروشیدن (*khorushidan*) to roar, cry.

خرید (*kharid*) purchase.

خریدار (*kharidār*) buyer.

خریداری (*kharidāri*) purchase. خریداری کردن to buy.

خریدن (*kharidan*) to buy.

خریطه (*khariṭeh*) A. map, chart.

خز (*khazz*) A. fur of the marten.

خزان (*khazān*) autumn.

خزانه (*khazāneh*) A. treasure, treasury.

خزانه دار (*khazāneh dār*) *a.* treasurer.

خزانه داری (*khazāneh dāri*) *a.* treasury.

خزر (*khazar*) *name of a tribe formerly inhabiting the shores of the Caspian.* بحرِ خزر the Caspian Sea.

خزنده (*khazandeh*) creeping; reptile.

خس (*khas*) mean, vile.

خسارت (*khasārat*) A. loss, damage.

خسبیدن (*khosbidan*) to sleep.

خستگی (*khastegi*) fatigue; wound.

خستن (*khastan*) to tire; to wound.

خسته (*khasteh*) tired; wounded.

خسرو (*khosrou*) Chosroes; *masc. proper name.*

خسوف (*khosuf*) A. eclipse of the moon.

خسیس (*khasis*) A. miser(ly).

خشت (*khesht*) sun-dried brick.

خشخاش (*khashkhāsh*) poppy.

خشک (*khoshk*) dry.

خشکبار (*khoshkbār*) dried fruit.

خشکی (*khoshki*) dryness; (dry) land.

خشکیدن (*khoshkidan*) to dry up, wither.

خشم (*kheshm*) anger.

خشمگین (*kheshmgin*), خشمناک (*kheshmnāk*) angry, furious.

خشن (*khashen*) A. rough, coarse.

خشنود (*khoshnud*) pleased, happy.

خشونت (*khoshunat*) A. roughness, harshness.

خصال (*kheṣāl*) A. qualities, habits. (*Pl. of* خصلت).

خصائص (*khaṣā'es*) A. properties, virtues.

خصلت (*kheṣlat*) A. quality, habit.

خصم (*khaṣm*) A. enemy.

خصوص (*khoṣuṣ*) A. matter, concern. در خصوصِ concerning.

خصوصاً (*khoṣuṣan*) A. especially.

خصوصی (*khoṣuṣi*) A. special; private.

خصومت (*khoṣumat*) A. enmity.

خضاب (*kheẓāb*) A. hair dye.
خط (*khaṭṭ*) A. line ; writing, letter.
خطا (*khaṭā*) A. sin, error, mistake. خطا کردن to sin, to make a mistake, to miss.
خطاب (*kheṭāb*) A. address. خطاب به addressed to.
خطابه (*kheṭābeh*) A. oration.
خطاط (*khaṭṭāṭ*) A. calligraphist.
خطبه (*khoṭbeh*) A. (Friday) sermon ; speech.
خطر (*khaṭar*) A. danger.
خطرناک (*khaṭarnāk*) *a.* dangerous.
خطکش (*khaṭṭkash*) *a.* ruler.
خطور (*khoṭur*) A. occurring (to the mind).
خطوط (*khoṭuṭ*) A. lines ; letters. (*Pl. of* خط.)
خطیب (*khaṭib*) A. preacher, orator.
خطیر (*khaṭir*) A. dangerous ; important.
خفا (*khafā*) A. concealment.
خفاش (*khoffāsh*) A. bat (*animal*).
خفت (*kheffat*) A. lightness ; disgrace.
خفتن (*khoftan*) to sleep.
خفگی (*khafegi*) closeness, stuffiness.
خفه (*khafeh*) strangled ; close, stuffy. خفه کردن to strangle.
خفی (*khafi*) A. concealed, secret.
خفیف (*khafif*) A. light.
خفیه (*khofyeh*) A. concealment, secrecy.
خلا (*khalā*) A. vacuum ; water-closet.
خلاص (*khalāṣ*) A. deliverance, salvation. خلاص کردن to rescue, save.
خلاصه (*kholāṣeh*) A. summary ; in short.
خلاصی (*khalāṣi*) *a.* deliverance, liberation.
خلاف (*khelāf*) A. offence ; contradiction.
خلاق (*khallāq*) A. creator.
خلال (*khelāl*) A. interval, lacuna ; toothpick.
خلائق (*khalā'eq*) A. creatures, people.
خلبان (*khalabān*) (air) pilot.
خلخال (*khalkhāl*) A. anklet.
خلد (*khold*) A. eternity ; paradise.
خلع (*khal'*) A. deposal, dismissal. خلع کردن to depose, dismiss. خلعِ سلاح disarmament.
خلف (*khalaf*) A. successor ; dutiful (son).
خلفا (*kholafā*) A. caliphs. (*Pl. of* خلیفه.)
خلق (*khalq*) A. creation ; creatures, people.
خلق (*kholq*) A. disposition, temper.
خلق الساعه (*khalqo's-sā'eh*) A. spontaneous generation.
خلقت (*khelqat*) A. creation ; nature.
خلل (*khalal*) A. disorder ; injury.
خلوت (*khalvat*) A., place of retirement.
خلوص (*kholuṣ*) A. purity, sincerity.
خلیج (*khalij*) A. gulf.
خلیفه (*khalifeh*) A. caliph ; monitor.

خم (*kham*) bent, curved; curve. خم کردن to bend.

خم (*khom*) jar, vat, cask.

خمار (*khomār*) A. drunken headache.

خمپاره (*khompāreh*) mortar, shell.

خمخانه (*khomkhāneh*) tavern.

خمر (*khamr*) A. wine.

خمس (*khoms*) A. fifth (part).

خمسه (*khamseh*) A. five.

خموش (*khamush*) *i.q.* خاموش

خمی (*khami*) curvature, crookedness.

خمیازه (*khamyāzeh*) (act of) gaping, yawning. خمیازه کشیدن to gape, yawn.

خمیدن (*khamidan*) to bend.

خمیده (*khamideh*) bent, crooked.

خمیر (*khamir*) A. dough. خمیر کردن to knead.

خنثی (*khonṣā*) A. hermaphrodite; neutral. خنثی کردن to neutralize.

خنجر (*khanjar*) A. dagger.

خندان (*khandān*) smiling.

خندق (*khandaq*) A. moat, ditch.

خنده (*khandeh*) laughter, laugh.

خندیدن (*khandidan*) to laugh.

خنصر (*khonṣor*) A. little finger.

خنق (*khanq*) A. strangling, asphyxia.

خنک (*khonok*) happy, blest; cool, fresh.

خنگ (*kheng*) grey (horse).

خو (*khu*) disposition, character.

خواب (*khvāb*) sleep; dream. خواب دیدن to dream.

خواب آلود (*khvāb ālud*) sleepy, drowsy.

خواباندن (*khvābāndan*), خوابانیدن (*khvābānidan*) to put to sleep.

خوابیدن (*khvābidan*) to sleep; to lie down.

خوابگاه (*khvābgāh*) bedroom, dormitory.

خواجه (*khvājeh*) master, teacher; eunuch.

خوار (*khvār*) contemptible, abject.

خواربار (*khvārbār*) provisions.

خواری (*khvāri*) abjectness.

خواستار (*khvāstār*) wishing; asking.

خواستگار (*khvāstegār*) suitor.

خواستگاری (*khvāstegāri*) solicitation; wooing.

خواستن (*khvāstan*) to wish, ask for.

خوالیگر (*khvāligar*) cook; table-decker.

خوان (*khvān*) table; tray.

خواندن (*khvāndan*) to read; to sing; to study; to call, invite.

خوانین (*khavānin*) A. khans. (*Pl. of* خان.)

خواه (*khvāh*) whether. خواه — خواه — whether — or —.

خواهر (*khvāhar*) sister.

خواهش (*khvāhesh*) desire, request.

خواهشمند (*khvāheshmand*) desirous.

خوب (*khub*) good, pleasant, beautiful.

خوبی (*khubi*) goodness. بخوبی well.

خود (*khod*) self. خود بخود spontaneously.

خود (*khud*) helmet.

خود بین (*khod bin*) conceited, vain.

خود پرست (*khod parast*) egoist(ic).

خود پسند (*khod pasand*) selfish, conceited.

خود پسندی (*khod pasandi*) selfishness, conceit.

خود خواه (*khod khvāh*) selfish.

خود داری (*khod dāri*) self-control, restraint. خود داری کردن to refrain.

خود رأی (*khod ra'y*) *a.* wilful.

خود رو (*khod rou*) spontaneous; arbitrary; automobile.

خود سر (*khod sar*) obstinate, stubborn.

خود کار (*khod kār*) automatic.

خود کشی (*khod koshi*) suicide.

خود مختار (*khod mokhtār*) *a.* autonomous.

خور (*khor*) eating, food.

خوراک (*khorāk*) food.

خوراکی (*khorāki*) edible; food.

خوراندن (*khorāndan*), خورانیدن (*khorānidan*) to feed.

خورجین (*khorjin*) saddle-bag, wallet.

خوردن (*khordan*) to eat, drink. به— خوردن to strike, touch —; to fit, match —.

خورش (*khoresh*) sauce, stew.

خورشید (*khorshid*) sun.

خوش (*khosh*) good, pleasant. از— خوشم می آید I like —.

خوشا (*khoshā*) blessed (is).

خوشبخت (*khoshbakht*) fortunate.

خوشبختانه (*khoshbakhtāneh*) fortunately.

خوشبختی (*khoshbakhti*) good fortune, happiness.

خوشبو (*khoshbu*) sweet-smelling, fragrant.

خوشبین (*khoshbin*) optimistic.

خوشحال (*khoshḥāl*) *a.* happy, glad.

خوشخو (*khoshkhu*) goodnatured.

خوشرو (*khoshru*) cheerful, smiling; beautiful.

خوشروئی (*khoshru'i*) cheerfulness; beauty.

خوشگل (*khoshgel*) beautiful.

خوشمزه (*khoshmazeh*) delicious (to the taste).

خوشنوا (*khoshnavā*) melodious.

خوشنود (*khoshnud*) pleased.

خوشوقت (*khoshvaqt*) *a.* pleased.

خوشه (*khusheh*) ear (of corn); bunch, cluster.

خوف (*khouf*) A. fear.

خوفناک (*khoufnāk*) *a.* dreadful, terrible.

خوک (*khuk*) pig.

خوگر (*khugar*) accustomed, familiar(ized); tame.

خون (*khun*) blood.

خونخوار (*khunkhvār*) bloodthirsty, cruel.

خونریزی (*khunrizi*) bleeding, bloodshed.

خونی (*khuni*) bloody; murderer.

خونین (*khunin*) bloody.

خوی (*khoy*) sweat.

خویش (*khvish*) self; kinsman.

خویشتن (*khvishtan*) self.

خویشی (*khvishi*) relationship.

خیابان (*khiābān*) avenue, street.

خیار (*khiār*) cucumber.

خیاط (*khayyāṭ*) A. tailor.
خیاطی (*khayyāṭi*) *a.* (profession of) tailoring.
خیال (*khiāl*) A. thought, imagination. خیال کردن to think. بخیال افتادن to occur to the mind.
خیالبافی (*khiālbāfi*) *a.* day-dream(ing).
خیالی (*khiāli*) *a.* imaginary.
خیام (*khayyām*) A. tent-maker.
خیانت (*khiānat*) A. treachery.
خیانتکار (*khiānatkār*) *a.* traitor.
خیر (*kheir*) A. good, welfare, charity; no!
خیر خواه (*kheir khvāh*) *a.* benevolent.
خیر خواهی (*kheir khvāhi*) *a.* benevolence.
خیره (*khireh*) dazzled; staring; impudent; astounded.
خیزران (*kheizorān*) A. bamboo.
خیس (*khis*) drenched, soaked.
خیساندن (*khisāndan*), خیسانیدن (*khisānidan*) to soak (*tr.*).
خیسیدن (*khisidan*) to soak (*intr.*).
خیش (*khish*) plough(share).
خیل (*kheil*) A. horses; horsemen; tribe.
خیلی (*kheili*) *a.* much, many; very.
خیمه (*kheimeh*) A. tent.

د

داخل (*dākhel*) A. internal, interior, inside; entering. داخلِ جنگ شدن to enter the war.
داخله (*dākheleh*) A. internal, interior. وزارتِ داخله Ministry of the Interior.
داخلی (*dākheli*) A. internal. جنگِ داخلی civil war.
داد (1) (*dād*) justice; shout, cry.
داد (2) (*dād*) (act of) giving. داد و ستد trade, barter.
داد خواست (*dād khvāst*) petition.
داد خوانده (*dād khvāndeh*) defendant.
داد خواه (*dād khvāh*) plaintiff.
داد رس (*dād ras*) judge.
داد رسی (*dād rasi*) trial.
داد ستان (*dād setān*) public prosecutor, attorney-general.
داد سرا (*dād sarā*) office of the public prosecutor.
دادگاه (*dādgāh*) court, tribunal.
دادگستری (*dādgostari*) (administration of) justice.
دادن (*dādan*) to give.
دادیار (*dādyār*) barrister.
دار (1) (*dār*) tree; gallows.
دار (2) (*dār*) A. house, abode.
دارا (*dārā*) possessing.
دارابی (*dārābi*) *name of a fruit resembling the shaddock.*
دار الانشا (*dāro'l-enshā*) A. secretariat.
دار الخلافه (*dāro'l-khelāfeh*) A. capital.
دار الفنون (*dāro'l-fonun*) A. university.

دارائی (*dārā'i*) wealth ; finance. وزارتِ دارائی Ministry of Finance.

دارچین (*dārchin*) cinnamon.

دارو (*dāru*) drug.

داروئی (*dāru'i*) pertaining to drugs.

داس (*dās*) sickle, scythe.

داستان (*dāstān*) story.

داشتن (*dāshtan*) to have.

داغ (*dāgh*) scar, mark, brand ; hot.

دافع (*dāfe'*) A. repelling ; repellent.

دال (*dāll*) A. indicating, denoting.

دالان (*dālān*) hall, vestibule, corridor.

دام (1) (*dām*) net, snare.

دام (2) (*dām*) domesticated animals.

داماد (*dāmād*) bridegroom ; son-in-law.

دام پزشک (*dām pezeshk*) veterinary surgeon.

دامدار (*dāmdār*) stock-breeder.

دامن (*dāman*) skirt, lap.

دامنگیر (*dāmangir*) attaching oneself to ; chronic.

دامنه (*dāmaneh*) skirt ; slope, foot ; extent.

دانا (*dānā*) learned, wise.

دانائی (*dānā'i*) learning, wisdom.

دانستن (*dānestan*) to know (*savoir*) ; to consider.

دانش (*dānesh*) knowledge.

دانشجو (*dāneshju*) student.

دانش سرا (*dānesh sarā*) normal school.

دانشکده (*dāneshkadeh*) faculty, institute, academy, college.

دانشگاه (*dāneshgāh*) university.

دانشمند (*dāneshmand*) learned (man), scientist.

دانشنامه (*dāneshnāmeh*) diploma.

دانشیار (*dāneshyār*) lecturer.

دانگ (*dāng*) sixth part (*of real estate*).

دانمارک (*dānmārk*) F. Denmark.

دانه (*dāneh*) grain, pip, berry.

داود (*dāvud*) A. David.

داور (*dāvar*) judge, arbitrator.

داوری (*dāvari*) judgment, arbitration.

داو طلب (*dāv ṭalab*) *a.* candidate.

دایر (*dāyer*) A. running, going. دایر کردن to set up. دایر بر regarding, concerning.

دایره (*dāyereh*) A. circle, cycle.

دائم (*dā'em*) A. perpetual, permanent.

دائماً (*dā'eman*) A. always.

دائمی (*dā'emi*) A. perpetual, permanent.

دایه (*dāyeh*) nurse.

دباغ (*dabbāgh*) A. tanner.

دباغی (*dabbāghi*) *a.* tanning. دباغی کردن to tan.

دبستان (*dabestān*) elementary school.

دبه (*dabbeh*) trying to go back on a bargain.

دبیر (*dabir*) secretary ; teacher in a secondary school.

دبیر خانه (*dabir khāneh*) secretariat.

دبیرستان (*dabirestān*) secondary school.

دجله (*dejleh*) A. Tigris.

دچار (*dochār*) meeting. دچارِ اشکالات شدن to encounter difficulties.

دخالت (*dekhālat*) A. interference.

دخانیات (*dokhāniyyāt*) A. tobacco (products).

دخت (*dokht*) daughter.

دختر (*dokhtar*) daughter; girl.

دخل (*dakhl*) A. income; concern, connection.

دخمه (*dakhmeh*) tower of silence.

دخول (*dokhul*) A. entry.

دخیل (*dakhil*) A. interfering, involved; material, important.

دد (*dad*) wild animals.

در (1) (*dar*) in, into.

در (2) (*dar*) door; topic.

در (*dorr*) A. pearl.

دراز (*derāz*) long. دراز کردن to lengthen, to stretch.

درام (*drām*) F. drama, play.

در آمد (*dar āmad*) income.

در آمدن (*dar āmadan*) to come in (out); to prove to be; to appear.

در آوردن (*dar āvardan*) to bring out, produce; to put forth.

درب (*darb*) A. door, gate.

دربار (*darbār*) court.

دربان (*darbān*) doorkeeper.

دربدر (*darbedar*) vagrant, vagabond.

دربند (*darband*) pass, defile; bolt, bar.

درج (*darj*) A. insertion, publication.

درجه (*darajeh*) A. degree, rank.

درجه بندی (*darajeh bandi*) *a.* classification.

درخت (*derakht*) tree.

درخشان (*derakhshān*) bright, shining, brilliant.

درخشنده (*derakhshandeh*) shining, bright, brilliant.

درخشیدن (*derakhshidan*) to shine.

درخواست (*darkhvāst*) request. درخواست کردن to request.

در خور (*dar khor*), در خورد (*dar khord*) suitable, fit.

درد (*dard*) pain. بدرد خوردن to be of use.

درد (*dord*) dregs, lees.

دردا (*dardā*) alas!

درد آلود (*dard ālud*) painful.

دردمند (*dardmand*) ill; painful; afflicted.

دردمندی (*dardmandi*) illness, affliction.

دردناک (*dardnāk*) painful.

درر (*dorar*) A. pearls. (*Pl. of* دُرّ.)

در ربودن (*dar robudan*) to seize.

در رسیدن (*dar rasidan*) to overtake.

در رفتن (*dar raftan*) to run away.

در رو (*dar rou*) outlet.

درز (*darz*) seam.

درس (*dars*) A. lesson. درس دادن to teach.

درست (*dorost*) right, correct; honest. درست کردن to make, fashion.

درستکار (*dorostkār*) honest, upright.

درستی (*dorosti*) honesty.

درشت (*dorosht*) rough, coarse.

درشتی (*doroshti*) roughness, harshness.

درشکه (*doroshkeh*) R. carriage, droshky.

درع (*der'*) A. coat of mail.
درفش (*derafsh*) flag, banner; awl.
درک (*darak*) A. hell.
درک (*dark*) A. perception. درک کردن to perceive.
درگاه (*dargāh*) palace, court.
در گذشتن (*dar goẕashtan*) to pass away.
در گرفتن (*dar gereftan*) to be kindled; to overspread.
درم (*deram*) drachma.
درمان (*darmān*) remedy, cure.
درمانگاه (*darmāngāh*) clinic.
در ماندگی (*dar māndegi*) distress.
در ماندن (*dar māndan*) to become helpless.
در مانده (*dar māndeh*) helpless, distressed.
درمنه (*dermaneh*) wormseed.
درنده (*darandeh*) fierce, rapacious (animal).
درنگ (*derang*) delay.
درو (*derou*) reaping, harvest. درو کردن to reap.
دروازه (*darvāzeh*) gate; goal.
دروازه بان (*darvāzeh bān*) gatekeeper; goalkeeper.
درود (1) (*dorud*) praise, blessing.
درود (2) (*dorud*) wood, timber.
درودگر (*dorudgar*) carpenter.
درودن (*dorudan*) to reap, mow.
دروس (*dorus*) A. lessons, lectures. (*Pl. of* درس.)
دروغ (*dorugh*) lie; false. دروغ گفتن to lie.
دروغگو (*dorughgu*) lying, liar.
درون (*darun*) inside.
درونی (*daruni*) inner, internal.
درویش (*darvish*) poor man; beggar; dervish.
دره (*darreh*) valley.
درهم (*darham*) confused.
درهم (*derham*) A. drachma.
دریا (*daryā*) sea.
دریابان (*daryābān*) vice-admiral.
دریاچه (*daryācheh*) lake.
دریا دار (*daryā dār*) rear-admiral.
دریا داری (*daryā dāri*) admiralty.
دریا سالار (*daryā sālār*) admiral.
در یافت (*dar yāft*) perception; receipt.
در یافتن (*dar yāftan*) to perceive, to guess.
دریا نورد (*daryā navard*) navigator.
دریائی (*daryā'i*) marine, naval.
دریچه (*daricheh*) shutter; wicket; valve.
دریدگی (*daridegi*) rent; impudence.
دریدن (*daridan*) to tear, rend.
دریغ (*darigh*) refusal, denial. دریغ داشتن to refuse, begrudge.
دریغا (*darighā*) alas!
دز (*dez*) fortress.
دزد (*dozd*) thief.
دزدی (*dozdi*) theft, stealing.
دزدیدن (*dozdidan*) to steal.
دژ (*dezh*) fortress.
دژبان (*dezhbān*) military police.
دژخیم (*dazhkhim*) ill-tempered; jailer, executioner.
دژم (*dezham*) sad, dejected; fierce, furious.

دسامبر (*desāmbr*) F. December.

دست (*dast*) hand; suit, set. از دست دادن to lose. بدست آوردن to acquire. دست دادن to shake hands; to take place. دست زدن to clap. از — دست کشیدن to leave off —; to forsake —. از دستم بر نمی‌آید I cannot do it. دستِ کم at least.

دستار (*dastār*) turban; handkerchief, napkin.

دست آموز (*dast āmuz*) pet, tame.

دستان (*dastān*) story, fable.

دست آویز (*dast āviz*) document; pretext.

دستبرد (*dastbord*) rapine.

دستخط (*dastkhaṭṭ*) *a.* handwriting.

دستخوش (*dastkhosh*) subject, exposed (*to disasters, etc.*).

دسترس (*dastras*) accessible; accessibility, reach.

دست فروش (*dast forush*) pedlar.

دستکش (*dastkash*) glove.

دستگاه (*dastgāh*) apparatus, machine.

دستگیر (1) (*dastgir*) helper.

دستگیر (2) (*dastgir*) captured, captive.

دستگیری (1) (*dastgiri*) help, aid.

دستگیری (2) (*dastgiri*) capture, arrest.

دستمال (*dastmāl*) handkerchief, towel.

دست نشانده (*dast neshāndeh*) creature, instrument.

دستور (*dastur*) instruction; minister; grammar.

دستور العمل (*dasturo'l-'amal*) A. prescription.

دسته (*dasteh*) handle; bunch, bundle; group; platoon.

دستی (*dasti*) handmade.

دستیار (*dastyār*) helper.

دستیاری (*dastyāri*) help.

دسیسه (*dasiseh*) A. intrigue.

دشت (*dasht*) plain, desert, field.

دشمن (*doshman*) enemy.

دشمنی (*doshmani*) enmity.

دشنام (*doshnām*) insult, abuse.

دشنه (*dashneh*) dagger.

دشوار (*doshvār*) difficult.

دشواری (*doshvāri*) difficulty.

دعا (*do'ā*) A. prayer. دعا کردن to pray, to bless.

دعوا (*da'vā*) A. quarrel, dispute; lawsuit.

دعوت (*da'vat*) A. invitation. دعوت کردن to invite.

دعوی (*da'vi*) A. claim, pretension.

دف (*daff*) A. tambourine.

دفاع (*defā'*) A. defence. دفاع کردن to defend.

دفاعی (*defā'i*) A. pertaining to defence.

دفتر (*daftar*) A. account-book; office.

دفع (*daf'*) A. (act of) warding off, repelling. دفع کردن to ward off, repel.

دفعه (*daf'eh*) A. time (*fois*). یکدفعه once.

دفن (*dafn*) A. burial, interment. دفن کردن to bury.

دق (*daqq*) A. (act of) knocking. دق کردن to knock.

دق (*deqq*) A. tuberculosis.

دقت (*deqqat*) A. care, precision.

دقیق (*daqiq*) A. minute, delicate.

دقیقه (*daqiqeh*) A. minute.

دکاکین (*dakākin*) A. shops. (*Pl. of* دکان.)

دکان (*dokkān*) A. shop.

دکتر (*doktor*) F. doctor.

دکترا (*doktorā*) F. doctorate.

دکمه (*dokmeh*) T. button.

دل (*del*) heart; stomach.

دلار (*dolār*) E. dollar.

دل آرام (*del ārām*) charming; sweet-heart.

دل آزرده (*del āzordeh*) displeased.

دلاک (*dallāk*) A. masseur; barber.

دلال (*dallāl*) A. broker.

دلالت (*dalālat*) A. indication.

دلاله (*dallāleh*) A. procuress.

دلاور (*delāvar*) brave.

دلاویز (*delāviz*) pleasant, desirable.

دلائل (*dalā'el*) A. proofs. (*Pl. of* دلیل.)

دلبر (*delbar*) charming; sweet-heart.

دلبسته (*delbasteh*) attached, devoted.

دلپذیر (*delpazir*) agreeable, pleasant.

دلتنگ (*deltang*) sad; displeased.

دلخراش (*delkharāsh*) harsh, grating; heart-rending.

دلخواه (*delkhvāh*) desire, wish.

دلدار (*deldār*) sweetheart.

دلداری (*deldāri*) consolation. دلداری دادن to console.

دلربا (*delrobā*) ravishing, charming.

دلشکسته (*delshekasteh*) broken-hearted, disappointed.

دلشکن (*delshekan*) disappointing.

دلگران (*delgerān*) despondent; displeased.

دلگشا (*delgoshā*) pleasant.

دلگیر (*delgir*) displeased.

دلو (*dalv*) A. bucket; Aquarius.

دلیر (*delir*) brave.

دلیرانه (*delirāneh*) brave(ly).

دلیری (*deliri*) bravery.

دلیل (*dalil*) A. guide; proof, reason.

دم (1) (*dam*) breath; moment. دم کردن to infuse. دم زدن to breathe. دمِ near.

دم (2) (*dam*) A. blood.

دُم (*dom*) tail.

دمار (*damār*) A. destruction, perdition.

دماغ (*demāgh*) A. brain; nose; vanity; talent.

دماغه (*demāgheh*) *a.* cape, promontory.

دم جنبانک (*dom jonbānak*) wagtail.

دمساز (*damsāz*) confidant, friend.

دمشق (*demeshq*) A. Damascus.

دمل (*dommal*) A. boil.

دموکرات (*demokrāt*) F. democrat.

دموکراسی (*demokrāsi*) F. democracy.

دموی (*damavi*) A. bloody; plethoric.

دمیدن (*damidan*) to blow.

دنائت (*denā'at*) A. meanness, baseness.

دنبال (*donbāl*) rear, back; trail. دنبال کردن to follow, track, pursue.

دنبه (*danbeh*) (fat of) sheep's tail.

دندان (*dandān*) tooth.

دندان ساز (*dandān sāz*) dentist.

دندان گرد (*dandān gerd*) covetous, greedy.

دنده (*dandeh*) rib.

دنی (*dani*) A. mean, base.
دنیا (*donyā*) A. world.
دو (*do*) two.
دوا (*davā*) A. medicine, drug.
دواب (*davābb*) A. beasts of burden.
دوات (*davāt*) A. inkstand.
دو آتشه (*do ātesheh*) overheated; double-dyed.
دوازده (*davāzdah*) twelve.
دوازدهم (*davāzdahom*) twelfth.
دوا ساز (*davā sāz*) *a.* druggist.
دوال (*davāl*) strap, thong.
دوام (*davām*) A. durability; endurance.
دوائر (*davā'er*) A. circles; departments. (*Pl. of* دایره.)
دو باره (*do bāreh*) twice; again.
دوچار (*dochār*) *i.q.* دچار.
دو چرخه (*do charkheh*) bicycle.
دوختن (*dukhtan*) to sew.
دود (*dud*) smoke.
دود کش (*dud kash*) chimney.
دو دل (*do del*) irresolute.
دودمان (*dudmān*) family, race.
دوده (*dudeh*) soot; family, tribe.
دور (*dur*) far, distant.
دور (*dour*) A. turn, cycle; age. دورِ around.
دوران (*dourān*) A. period.
دور اندیش (*dur andish*) farsighted.
دور بین (*dur bin*) telescope.
دور دست (*dur dast*) distant, remote.
دو رگ (*do rag*) mongrel.
دو رنگی (*do rangi*) hypocrisy.
دور نما (*dur nomā*) landscape, panorama.
دو روئی (*do ru'i*) hypocrisy.
دوره (*doureh*) A. period, age; course; cycle.
دوری (*douri*) *a.* tray.
دوری (*duri*) distance; avoidance. از — دوری کردن to avoid —.
دوزخ (*duzakh*) hell.
دو زیست (*do zist*) amphibious, amphibian.
دوست (*dust*) friend. دوست داشتن to love.
دوستانه (*dustāneh*) friendly.
دوستدار (*dustdār*) loving (friend).
دوستی (*dusti*) friendship.
دوسیه (*dosieh*) F. dossier.
دوش (1) (*dush*) shoulder.
دوش (2) (*dush*) last night.
دوش (3) (*dush*) F. shower-bath.
دو شاخه (*do shākheh*) bifurcate; pillory; pitchfork.
دوشک (*doshak*) T. mattress.
دو شنبه (*do shanbeh*) Monday.
دوشیدن (*dushidan*) to milk.
دوشیزه (*dushizeh*) maiden, virgin, girl.
دوغ (*dugh*) churned sour milk.
دوک (*duk*) spindle.
دول (*dul*) bucket.
دول (*doval*) A. governments, states. (*Pl. of* دولت.)
دولاب (*dulāb*) water-wheel; pantry.
دولار (*dolār*) E. dollar.
دولت (*doulat*) A. riches, wealth; government, state. دولتِ متبوعه state to which one belongs.
دولتمند (*doulatmand*) *a.* rich, wealthy.

دولتی (*doulati*) *a.* (belonging to the) state.

دولتین (*doulatein*) A. the two governments, states.

دوم (*dovvom*), دومین (*dovvomin*) second.

دون (*dun*) A. mean, base.

دویدن (*davidan*) to run.

دویست (*devist*) two hundred.

ده (*dah*) ten.

ده (*deh*) village. (*The* h *is pronounced.*)

دهاتی (*dehāti*) *a.* villager, peasant.

دهاقین (*dahāqin*) A. peasants. (*Pl. of* دهقان.)

دهان (*dahān*) mouth.

دهر (*dahr*) A. time, age; world; destiny.

دهری (*dahri*) A. materialist, atheist.

دهستان (*dehestān*) rural district.

دهش (*dehish*) bounty, munificence.

دهشت (*dehshat*) A. terror; amazement.

دهقان (*dehqān*) *a.* peasant, farmer.

دهکده (*dehkadeh*) hamlet.

دهل (*dohol*) drum.

دهلی (*dehli*) Delhi.

دهلیز (*dehliz*) vestibule, hall.

دهم (*dahom*) tenth.

دهن (*dahan*) mouth.

دهنه (*dahaneh*) bit (of bridle); opening; estuary.

دی (*dei*) *name of the tenth month of the Persian year.*

دیانت (*diānat*) A. piety, honesty.

دیباچه (*dibācheh*) preface.

دیپلومات (*diplomāt*) F. diplomat.

دیپلماسی (*diplomāsi*) F. diplomacy; diplomatic.

دیدار (*didār*) sight; visit; face.

دیدن (*didan*) to see; to suffer.

دیده (*dideh*) eye.

دیده بان (*dideh bān*) sentinel, lookout; observer.

دیر (*deir*) A. monastery.

دیر (*dir*) late.

دیرینه (*dirineh*) old, ancient.

دیروز (*diruz*) yesterday.

دیکتاتور (*diktātor*) F. dictator.

دیگ (*dig*) pot, cauldron.

دیگر (*digar*) other, again.

دیم (*deim*) A. dry farming.

دیمی (*deimi*) *a.* cultivated by dry farming; superficial.

دین (*dein*) A. debt.

دین (*din*) A. faith, religion.

دینار (*dinār*) A. *name of the 100th part of a* ریال.

دیندار (*dindār*) *a.* religious.

دینی (*dini*) A. religious.

دیو (*div*) demon, devil.

دیوار (*divār*) wall.

دیوان (*divān*) A. collection of poems; court, tribunal; council, divan.

دیوانخانه (*divānkhāneh*) *a.* law court.

دیوانگی (*divānegi*) madness.

دیوانه (*divāneh*) mad.

دیوث (*dayyuṣ*) A. cuckold.

دیون (*doyun*) A. debts. (*Pl. of* دَیْن.)

دیهیم (*deihim*) crown, diadem.

ذ

ذات (*ẕāt*) A. essence, nature; person.

ذات الجنب (*ẕāto'-l-janb*) A. pleurisy.

ذات الريه (*ẕāto'r-rieh*) A. pneumonia.

ذاتی (*ẕāti*) *a.* inherent, inborn, natural.

ذائقه (*ẕā'eqeh*) A. (sense of) taste.

ذبح (*ẕabḥ*) A. (act of) slaughtering.

ذخائر (*ẕakhā'er*) A. stores, treasures. (*Pl. of* ذخیره.)

ذخیره (*ẕakhireh*) A. store; treasure.

ذرت (*ẕorrat*) A. maize.

ذرع (*ẕar'*) A. *name of a unit of length* = 41 *inches.*

ذره (*ẕarreh*) A. molecule, atom, particle.

ذروه (*ẕorveh*) A. summit, apex.

ذغال (*ẕoghāl*) charcoal. ذغالِ سنگ coal.

ذکاوت (*ẕakāvat*) A. shrewdness.

ذکر (*ẕakar*) A. male; penis.

ذکر (*ẕekr*) A. mention. ذکر کردن to mention.

ذکور (*ẕokur*) A. males. (*Pl. of* ذَکَر.)

ذکی (*ẕaki*) A. shrewd.

ذلت (*ẕellat*) A. abjectness.

ذلیل (*ẕalil*) A. abject.

ذم (*ẕamm*) A. reproach; vilification.

ذمه (*ẕemmeh*) A. obligation.

ذوب (*ẕoub*) A. (process of) melting. ذوب شدن to melt.

ذو حیاتین (*ẕu ḥayātein*) A. amphibious, amphibian.

ذوق (*ẕouq*) A. taste.

ذهن (*ẕehn*) A. memory, mind.

ذهنی (*ẕehni*) A. mental.

ذی فقار (*ẕi faqār*) A. vertebrate. غیرِ ذی فقار invertebrate.

ذی الحجه (*ẕe 'l-ḥejjeh*) A. *name of the twelfth month of the Arabic lunar year.*

ذی القعده (*ẕe'l-qa'deh*) A. *name of the eleventh month of the Arabic lunar year.*

ذیل (*ẕeil*) A. skirt, train; appendix. از قرارِ ذیل as follows.

ذیلاً (*ẕeilan*) A. as follows.

ذینفع (*ẕinaf'*) A. interested (*party*).

ر

را (*rā*) *sign of the accusative.*

رابطه (*rābeṭeh*) A. tie, connection.

رابع (*rābe'*) A. fourth.

رابعاً (*rābe'an*) A. fourthly.

راپرت (*rāport*) F. report.

راجع (*rāje'*) A. referring. راجع به referring to, regarding.

راحت (*rāḥat*) A. rest, comfort; quiet, comfortable.

رادیو (*rādio*) F. radio, wireless.

راز (*rāz*) secret.
رأس (*ra's*) A. head, chief.
راست (*rāst*) right, straight, true.
راستگو (*rāstgu*) truthful.
راستی (*rāsti*) truth, honesty; indeed.
راسو (*rāsu*) weasel.
راشد (*rāshed*) A. orthodox.
راضی (*rāẕi*) A. pleased, content.
راغ (*rāgh*) meadow.
راقی (*rāqi*) A. sorcerer; progressive.
راکد (*rāked*) A. stagnant.
رام (*rām*) tame, obedient.
ران (*rān*) thigh.
راندن (*rāndan*) to drive; to utter, pronounce.
راننده (*rānandeh*) driver.
راوی (*rāvi*) A. narrator, historian.
راه (*rāh*) road, way. راه رفتن to walk. راهِ آهن railway.
راهب (*rāheb*) A. monk.
راهبر (*rāhbar*) guide.
راهدار (*rāhdār*) toll-gatherer.
راه راه (*rāh rāh*) striped.
راهرو (*rāhrou*) passage, corridor; traveller.
راهزن (*rāhzan*) highway robber.
راهزنی (*rāhzani*) highway robbery.
راه گذار (*rāh goẕār*) passer-by, traveller; event.
راهنما (*rāhnomā*) guide.
راهنمائی (*rāhnomā'i*) guidance. راهنمائی کردن to guide.
رأی (*ra'y*) A. opinion; vote. رأی دادن to vote.
رایت (*rāyat*) A. banner, flag.
رایج (*rāyej*) A. current.
رایحه (*rāyeḥeh*) A. odour, fragrance.
رای زن (*rāy zan*) *a.* counsellor.
رایگان (*rāyegān*) gratis.
رب (*rabb*) A. lord.
رباط (*rebāṭ*) A. inn, caravanserai; ligament.
رباعی (*robā'i*) A. quatrain.
رب النوع (*rabbo'n-nou'*) A. god.
ربح (*rebḥ*) A. interest, usury.
ربط (*rabṭ*) A. connection, coherence; concern.
ربع (*rob'*) A. quarter.
ربقه (*rebqeh*) A. noose.
ربودن (*robudan*) to seize, to rob.
ربیع الاول (*rabi'o 'l-avval*) A. *name of the third month of the Arabic lunar year.*
ربیع الثانی (*rabi'o 'ṣ-ṣāni*) A. *name of the fourth month of the Arabic lunar year.*
رتبه (*rotbeh*) A. rank, grade.
رجال (*rejāl*) A. distinguished men, leaders. (*Pl. of* رجل.)
رجب (*rajab*) A. *name of the seventh month of the Arabic lunar year.*
رجحان (*rejḥān*) A. preference.
رجل (*rajol*) A. man.
رجوع (*roju'*) A. return, reference, recourse. رجوع کردن to refer.
رحم (*raḥm*) A. compassion, mercy.
رحم (*raḥem*) A. womb.
رحمت (*raḥmat*) A. mercy.
رحمن (*raḥmān*) A., رحیم (*raḥim*) A. merciful, compassionate.
رخ (*rokh*) cheek, face. رخ دادن to happen.

رخام (*rokhām*) A. marble.

رخت (*rakht*) clothes; furniture; baggage.

رختخواب (*rakhtekhvāb*) bed clothes, bed.

رخت شوی (*rakht shuy*) launderer.

رخت شوی خانه (*rakht shuy khāneh*) laundry.

رخسار (*rokhsār*) face, cheek.

رخصت (*rokhṣat*) A. leave, permission.

رخنه (*rakhneh*) slit, crack; breach; leak.

رخوت (*rekhvat*) A. softness, laxity, slackness.

رد (*radd*) A. restitution; rejection. رد کردن to give back; to reject.

رده (*radeh*) row, line.

ردیف (*radif*) A. row, rank.

رز (*raz*) vine.

رزاز (*razzāz*) A. rice-seller.

رزق (*rezq*) A. daily bread.

رزم (*razm*) war, battle.

رزمناو (*razmnāv*) cruiser.

رزین (*rezin*) F. tyre.

رژه (*razheh*) review (*of troops*).

رژیم (*rezhim*) F. régime; regimen.

رسا (*rasā*) loud.

رساله (*resāleh*) A. letter; treatise.

رساندن (*rasāndan*) رسانیدن (*rasānidan*) to cause to arrive, to send.

رست (*rost*) firm, strong. خاکِ رست clay.

رستاخیز (*rastākhiz*), رستخیز (*rastekhiz*) Day of Resurrection.

رستگاری (*rastegāri*) freedom, salvtion.

رستم (*rostam*) Rustam; *masc. proper name.*

رستن (*rastan*) to escape.

رستن (*rostan*) to grow.

رستوران (*restorān*) F. restaurant.

رسدبان (*rasadbān*) police lieutenant.

رسل (*rosol*) A. messengers, prophets. (*Pl. of* رسول.)

رسم (*rasm*) A. custom, ceremony; mark, design.

رسماً (*rasman*) A. officially.

رسمی (*rasmi*) A. official (*adj.*).

رسوا (*rosvā*) disgraced, infamous.

رسوائی (*rosvā'i*) disgrace, infamy.

رسوب (*rosub*) A. sediment, dregs.

رسوخ (*rosukh*) A. firmness, stability.

رسول (*rasul*) A. messenger, prophet.

رسوم (*rosum*) A. customs, ceremonies. (*Pl. of* رسم.)

رسید (*rasid*) receipt.

رسیدگی (*rasidegi*) investigation.

رسیدن (*rasidan*) to arrive. تا چه رسد به — still less (more), let alone —.

رسیده (*rasideh*) arrived; ripe.

رشادت (*rashādat*) A. bravery.

رشته (*reshteh*) thread; series.

رشد (*roshd*) A. growth, adolescence; orthodoxy.

رشک (*rashk*) envy, jealousy.

رشوه (*roshveh*) A. bribe(ry); manure.

رشید (*rashid*) A. brave.

رصاد (*raṣṣād*) A. astronomer, astrologer.

رصد (*raṣad*) A. astronomical table; horoscope.

رصد خانه (*raṣad khāneh*) *a.* observatory.

رضا (*reẓā*) A. consent, acquiescence; *masc. proper name.*

رضایت (*reẓāyat*) A. satisfaction; consent.

رضایت بخش (*reẓāyat bakhsh*) *a.* satisfactory.

رضیع (*raẓiʻ*) A. suckling; fosterchild.

رطب (*roṭab*) A. fresh dates.

رطوبت (*roṭubat*) A. moisture, dampness.

رعایا (*raʻāyā*) A. subjects; peasants, farmers. (*Pl. of* رعیت.)

رعایت (*reʻāyat*) A. observance; favour.

رعد (*raʻd*) A. thunder.

رعنا (*raʻnā*) A. handsome.

رعیت (*raʻiyyat*) A. subject; peasant, farmer.

رغبت (*raghbat*) A. desire, liking.

رغم (*raghm*) A. spite. علی رغمِ in spite of.

رفاقت (*rafāqat*) A. companionship.

رفقا (*rofaqā*) A. companions. (*Pl. of* رفیق.)

رفاهیت (*refahiyyat*) A. welfare, comfort.

رفتار (*raftār*) gait; behaviour.

رفتن (*raftan*) to go.

رفتن (*roftan*) to sweep.

رفت و آمد (*raft o āmad*) coming and going, traffic.

رفته (*rafteh*) gone. رفته رفته gradually.

رفع (*rafʻ*) A. (act of) removing; meeting (*requirements*).

رفو (*rofu*) A. (act of) darning. رفو کردن to darn.

رفو گر (*rofu gar*) *a.* darner.

رفیق (*rafiq*) A. companion, friend.

رقابت (*raqābat*) A. rivalry.

رقاص (*raqqāṣ*) A. dancer.

رقاصه (*raqqāṣeh*) A. female dancer, dancing-girl, ballerina.

رقاصی (*raqqāṣi*) *a.* (profession of) dancing.

رقت (*reqqat*) A. thinness; delicacy; pity.

رقص (*raqṣ*) A. dance, dancing.

رقصیدن (*raqṣidan*) *a.* to dance.

رقعه (*roqʻeh*) A. patch; piece of paper; letter.

رقم (*raqam*) A. figure, character, number.

رقیب (*raqib*) A. rival.

رقیق (*raqiq*) A. thin, rarefied.

رقیمه (*raqimeh*) A. letter.

رقیه (*roqyeh*) A. spell.

رکاب (*rekāb*) A. stirrup; pedal; retinue.

رکعت (*rakʻat*) A. unit of prayer.

رکن (*rokn*) A. pillar; foundation.

رکیک (*rakik*) A. thin, weak; indecent.

رگ (*rag*) vein.

رل (*rol*) F. rôle.

رم (*ram*) shy(ing), fright.

رم (*rom*) F. Rome.

رمال (*rammāl*) A. geomancer.

رمز (*ramz*) A. mystery; cipher; allegory.

رمزی (*ramzi*) *a.* allegorical.

رمضان (*ramaẓān*) A. *name of the ninth month of the Arabic lunar year.*

رمق (*ramaq*) A. last breath of life.

رمل (*raml*) A. sand; gravel; geomancy.

رموز (*romuz*) A. mysteries, symbols. (*Pl. of* رمز.)

رمه (*rameh*) herd, flock.

رمیدن (*ramidan*) to shy.

رنج (*ranj*) toil, pain.

رنجاندن (*ranjāndan*), رنجانیدن (*ranjānidan*) to offend.

رنجبر (*ranjbar*) toiler, labourer, workman.

رنجش (*ranjesh*) offence, umbrage.

رنجور (*ranjur*) ill; distressed.

رنجه (*ranjeh*) troubled, pained.

رنجیدن (*ranjidan*) to be offended, annoyed.

رند (*rend*) rogue, knave; roguish, sly.

رنده (*randeh*) plane; grater.

رندیدن (*randidan*) to plane; to grate.

رنگ (*rang*) colour; dye. رنگ کردن to paint; to dye.

رنگارنگ (*rangārang*) many-coloured; various.

رنگرز (*rangraz*) dyer.

رنگین (*rangin*) coloured.

رنود (*ronud*) A. rogues, knaves. (*Pl. of* رند.)

رو (1) (*ru*), روی (*ruy*) face; surface. روی on. رو برو face to face; opposite. رو دادن to happen. روی هم in a lump. روی هم رفته on an average.

رو (2) (*ru*), روی (*ruy*) zinc.

روا (*ravā*) allowable, lawful; current.

روابط (*ravābeṭ*) A. connections, relations. (*Pl. of* رابطه.)

رواج (*ravāj*) currency; prevalence. رواج دادن to circulate; to propagate.

روادید (*ravādid*) visa.

روان (1) (*ravān*) soul.

روان (2) (*ravān*) flowing, fluent. روان کردن to learn.

روانامه (*ravānāmeh*) exequatur.

روان شناسی (*ravān shenāsi*) psychology.

روانه (*ravāneh*) going, travelling. روانه کردن to send.

روانی (*ravāni*) fluency; currency.

روایت (*revāyat*) A. narrative, tradition.

روبان (*rubān*) F. ribbon.

روباه (*rubāh*) fox.

روبیدن (*rubidan*) to sweep.

روپیه (*rupieh*) H. rupee.

روح (*ruḥ*) A. spirit, soul.

روح القدس (*ruḥo 'l-qodos*) A. Holy Ghost.

روحانی (*ruḥāni*) A. spiritual.

روحیه (*ruḥiyyeh*) A. morale.

رود (*rud*), رودخانه (*rudkhāneh*) river.

روده (*rudeh*) intestine, gut.

روز (*ruz*) day.

روزانه (*ruzāneh*) daily.

روزگار (*ruzgār*) time; world.

روز مره (*ruz marreh*) *a.* from day to day; daily.

روزن (*rouzan*) opening; loophole; window.

روزنامه (*ruznāmeh*) newspaper.

روزنامه نویس (*ruznāmeh nevis*), روزنامه نگار (*ruznāmeh negār*) journalist, reporter.

روزنه (*rouzaneh*) opening, aperture; loophole; window.

روزه (1) (*ruzeh*) fast(ing).

روزه (2) (*ruzeh*) (*in compounds*) —days'.

روزی (*ruzi*) daily bread.

روژ (*ruzh*) F. rouge.

روس (*rus*) Russia(n).

رؤسا (*ro'asā*) A. chiefs, directors. (*Pl. of* رئیس.)

روسپی (*ruspi*) prostitute.

روستا (*rustā*) village.

روستائی (*rustā'i*) villager; rural.

رو سفید (*ru sefid*) guiltless; acquitted.

روسی (*rusi*) Russian.

رو سیاه (*ru siāh*) disgraced, dishonoured; proved guilty.

روسیه (*rusiyyeh*) A. Russia.

روش (*ravesh*) manner, course, policy.

روشن (*roushan*) bright, clear, light(ed). روشن کردن to light.

روشنائی (*roushanā'i*) light.

روشنفکر (*roushanfekr*) *a.* enlightened.

روشنی (*roushani*) brightness.

روضه (*rouzeh*) A. garden.

روغن (*roughan*) oil, fat, clarified butter.

روغن داغکن (*roughan dāghkon*) saucepan.

روغنی (*roughani*) oily, greasy.

رؤف (*ra'uf*) A. kind.

رو کش (*ru kash*) plating; veneer(ing).

رومانی (*rumāni*) F. Roumania.

رونده (*ravandeh*) passer-by, traveller.

رونق (*rounaq*) A. brilliance, lustre; elegance, beauty.

رونوشت (*runevesht*) copy.

روه (*ruveh*) outside (*of cloth*).

رؤیا (*ro'yā*) A. dream.

رؤیت (*ro'yat*) A. sight.

رویه (*raviyyeh*) *a.* method, policy.

روئی (*ru'i*) upper; outer.

روئیدن (*ru'idan*) to grow.

رها (*rahā*) free, liberated. رها کردن to liberate, release.

رهانیدن (*rahānidan*) to rescue, free.

رهائی (*rahā'i*) deliverance, liberation.

رهبان (*rohbān*) A. monks. (*Pl. of* راهب.)

رهبر (*rahbar*) guide, leader.

رهبری (*rahbari*) guidance.

رهزن (*rahzan*) highway robber.

رهسپار (*rahsepār*) setting out. رهسپار شدن to set out.

رهگذر (*rahgozar*) passer-by, traveller; event.

رهن (*rahn*) A. mortgage, pledge.

رهنما (*rahnomā*) guide.

رهنمائی (*rahnomā'i*) guidance. رهنمائی کردن to guide.

رهنی (*rahni*) *a.* mortgaged, pawned.

رهین (*rahin*) A. indebted, obliged.

ریا (*riā*) A. hypocrisy.

رياست (*riāsat*) A. direction, management; directorship, presidency.

رياض (*riāẓ*) A. Riyadh.

رياضى (*riāẓi*) A. mathematical.

رياضيات (*riāẓiyyāt*) A. mathematics.

ريا كار (*riā kār*) *a.* hypocrite.

ريال (*riāl*) A. *name of the Persian monetary unit.*

ريتين (*riatein*) A. the lungs.

ريحان (*reiḥān*) A. sweet basil.

ريختن (*rikhtan*) to pour, spill.

ريدن (*ridan*) to defecate.

ريز (*riz*) minute, small, fine.

ريزه (*rizeh*) crumbs, chips.

ريستن (*ristan*) to spin, twist.

ريسمان (*rismān*) rope.

ريش (1) (*rish*) beard.

ريش (2) (*rish*) wound.

ريشخند (*rishkhand*) (act of) coaxing, wheedling.

ريش سفيد (*rish sefid*) grey-beard(ed); elder.

ريشه (*risheh*) root.

ريگ (*rig*) sand; gravel.

ريگ زار (*rig zār*) sandy region.

ريل (*reil*) E. rail.

ريم (*rim*) pus, matter.

ريوند (*rivand*) rhubarb.

ريه (*rieh*) A. lung.

رئيس (*ra'is*) A. chief, leader; director. رئيسِ كل Director-General. رئيسِ جمهورى President of the Republic.

رئيس الوزرا (*ra'iso'l-vozarā*) A. Prime Minister.

ز

ز (*ze*) *poetic form of* از.

زاج (*zāj*) vitriol.

زاد (*zād*) A. (travelling) provisions.

زادن (*zādan*) to bear, to give birth to; to appear.

زار (*zār*) sad, mournful.

زارع (*zāre'*) A. farmer.

زارى (*zāri*) lamentation.

زاغ (*zāgh*) crow, raven.

زاغى (*zāghi*) magpie.

زال (*zāl*) old woman.

زالو (*zālu*) leech.

زانو (*zānu*) knee. زانو زدن to kneel.

زانى (*zāni*) A. adulterer.

زانيه (*zānieh*) A. adulteress.

زاويه (*zāvieh*) A. corner; angle. زاويهٔ قائمه right angle. زاويهٔ حادّه acute angle. زاويهٔ منفرجه obtuse angle.

زاهد (*zāhed*) A. ascetic, hermit.

زايچه (*zāyecheh*) horoscope; birth certificate.

زايد (*zāyed*) A. superfluous, redundant; additional.

زائر (*zā'er*) A. pilgrim, visitor.

زايشگاه (*zāyeshgāh*) maternity hospital.

زایل (*zāyel*) A. disappearing, transitory.

زائیدن (*zā'idan*) to give birth to.

زبان (*zabān*) tongue; language.

زبان بسته (*zabān basteh*) dumb.

زبان دان (*zabān dān*) linguist.

زبانه (*zabāneh*) flame.

زبانی (*zabāni*) oral; linguistic.

زبده (*zobdeh*) A. the cream, best part; gist.

زبر (*zebr*) rough, coarse.

زبر (*zabar*) upper part; *name of the short vowel* ـَ.

زبرجد (*zabarjad*) emerald, chrysolite.

زبر دست (*zabar dast*) superior; skilful; overbearing.

زبور (*zabur*) A. Psalms.

زبون (*zabun*) humbled, vanquished; weak; vile.

زبیده (*zobeideh*) A. *fem. proper name.*

زجاج (*zojāj*) A. glass.

زجر (*zajr*) A. torment, vexation.

زحل (*zoḥal*) A. Saturn.

زحمت (*zaḥmat*) A. toil, trouble. زحمت دادن to trouble, inconvenience. زحمت کشیدن to take trouble.

زخم (*zakhm*) wound.

زخمی (*zakhmi*) wounded.

زدن (*zadan*) to strike, beat, hit.

زد و خورد (*zad o khord*) clash, skirmish.

زدودن (*zedudan*) to wipe, scour, polish.

زر (*zar*) gold.

زرادخانه (*zarrādkhāneh*) arsenal.

زراعت (*zerā'at*) A. agriculture.

زراعتی (*zerā'ati*) *a.* agricultural.

زرافه (*zarrāfeh*) A. giraffe.

زرد (*zard*) yellow.

زرداب (*zardāb*) bile, gall.

زرد آلو (*zard ālu*) apricot.

زرد چوبه (*zard chubeh*) turmeric.

زرده (*zardeh*) yolk of egg.

زردی (*zardi*) yellowness.

زرشک (*zereshk*) barberry.

زرع (*zar'*) A. cultivation.

زرگر (*zargar*) goldsmith.

زرنگ (*zerang*) clever.

زره (*zereh*) coat of mail. (*The* h *is pronounced.*)

زره پوش (*zereh push*) armoured (car).

زره دار (*zereh dār*) ironclad.

زرین (*zarrin*) golden.

زشت (*zesht*) ugly.

زشتی (*zeshti*) ugliness.

زعفران (*za'farān*) A. saffron.

زعم (*za'm*) A. opinion, belief.

زغال (*zoghāl*) charcoal. زغالِ سنگ coal.

زغن (*zaghan*) kite.

زفاف (*zefāf*) A. marriage procession; (consummation of) marriage.

زفیر (*zafir*) A. exhalation.

زکام (*zokām*) A. cold in the head.

زکوة (*zakāt*) A. alms, tithe.

زلال (*zolāl*) A. pure, limpid (water).

زلزله (*zelzeleh*) A. earthquake.

زلزله شناس (*zelzeleh shenās*) *a.* seismologist.

زلف (*zolf*) lock(s), hair.

زمام (*zemām*) A. reins, bridle.

زمامدار (*zemamdār*) *a.* one in authority; statesman.

زمامداری (*zemāmdāri*) *a.* control, authority; statesmanship.

زمان (*zamān*) A. time.

زمانه (*zamāneh*) *a.* time, age; fortune; world.

زمرد (*zomorrod*) emerald.

زمره (*zomreh*) A. class, group.

زمزمه (*zamzameh*) *a.* murmuring, humming (sound).

زمستان (*zamestān*) winter.

زمین (*zamin*) earth, ground. زمین خوردن to fall down. زمین گذاشتن to lay down.

زمین شناسی (*zamin shenāsi*) geology.

زمین لرزه (*zamin larzeh*) earthquake.

زمینه (*zamineh*) ground, background, basis.

زن (*zan*) woman, wife.

زنا (*zenā*) A. adultery.

زنانه (*zanāneh*) belonging to women, feminine; harem.

زناشوئی (*zanāshu'i*) matrimony.

زنبق (*zanbaq*) *a.* iris.

زنبور (*zanbur*) bee, wasp. زنبورِ عسل bee.

زنبیل (*zanbil*) basket.

زنجبیل (*zanjebil*) ginger.

زنجیر (*zanjir*) chain.

زنخ (*zanakh*), زنخدان (*zanakhdān*) chin.

زندان (*zendān*) prison.

زندانبان (*zendānbān*) jailer.

زندانی (*zendāni*) prisoner.

زندگانی (*zendegāni*) life, living, livelihood. زندگانی کردن to live.

زندگی (*zendegi*) life, living.

زندن (*zendan*) to live.

زندوست (*zandust*) fond of women, uxorious.

زنده (*zendeh*) alive, living.

زنده دل (*zendeh del*) pious; lively.

زنگ (1) (*zang*) rust. زنگ زدن to rust.

زنگ (2) (*zang*) bell.

زنگوله (*zanguleh*) little bell.

زنگبار (*zangebār*) Zanzibar.

زنگی (*zangi*) Ethiopian, negro.

زننده (*zanandeh*) striking; pungent; gaudy; striker, player.

زنهار (*zenhār*) caution; mercy; protection; beware!

زوار (*zovvār*) A. pilgrims. (*Pl. of* زائر.)

زوال (*zavāl*) A. decline.

زوج (*zouj*) A. pair, couple; husband.

زوجه (*zoujeh*) A. wife.

زود (*zud*) early; quick; soon.

زودی (*zudi*) earliness; quickness. بزودی soon.

زور (*zur*) strength, force, power; violence.

زور آزما (*zur āzmā*) athlete.

زور خانه (*zur khāneh*) gymnasium.

زورق (*zouraq*) A. boat.

زور گو (*zur gu*) tyrant, tyrannical.

زوزه (*zuzeh*) (act of) howling, wailing. زوزه کشیدن to howl, wail.

زه (*zeh*) bowstring. (*The* h *is pronounced.*)

زهار (*zehār*) A. pubes.

زهد (*zohd*) A. asceticism.

زهر (*zahr*) poison.

زهر دار (*zahr dār*) poisonous.

زهره (*zahreh*) gall ; gall-bladder.

زهره (*zohreh*) A. Venus.

زه کشی (*zeh kashi*) drainage. زه کشی کردن to drain. (*The* h *is pronounced.*)

زیاد (*ziād*) *a.* many, much ; very ; too.

زیادت (*ziādat*) A. increase.

زیادی (*ziādi*) *a.* extra, superfluous ; excess, surplus.

زیارت (*ziārat*) A. pilgrimage ; visit.

زیان (*ziān*) loss, injury.

زیب (*zib*) ornament.

زیبا (*zibā*) beautiful.

زیبائی (*zibā'i*) beauty.

زیبق (*zeibaq*) A. mercury.

زیبیدن (*zibidan*) to adorn ; to become, suit.

زیت (*zeit*) A. olive-oil.

زیتون (*zeitun*) A. olive.

زیر (*zir*) underneath ; *name of the short vowel* —ِ. زیرِ under.

زیرا (*zirā*) because.

زیر پوش (*zir push*) underwear.

زیر دریائی (*zir daryā'i*) submarine.

زیردست (*zirdast*) inferior.

زیر زمین (*zir zamin*), underground, subterranean ; cellar.

زیرک (*zirak*) clever.

زیرکی (*ziraki*) cleverness.

زیره (1) (*zireh*) cumin(-seed).

زیره (2) (*zireh*) (shoe) sole.

زیست (*zist*) subsistence, livelihood, existence. زیست کردن to live.

زیستن (*zistan*) to live.

زین (*zin*) saddle.

زین (*zein*) A. ornament.

زینت (*zinat*) A. decoration, adornment. زینت دادن to decorate, adorn.

زین ساز (*zin sāz*) saddler.

زینهار (*zinhār*) *i.q.* زنهار.

زیور (*zivar*) ornament, jewels.

ژ

ژاپن (*zhāpon*) F. Japan.

ژپنی (*zhāponi*) Japanese.

ژاژ (*zhāzh*) idle talk.

ژاژ خا (*zhāzh khā*) babbler.

ژاله (*zhāleh*) dew.

ژاندارم (*zhāndārm*) F. gendarme.

ژاندارمری (*zhāndārmeri*) F. gendarmerie.

ژانویه (*zhānvieh*) F. January.

ژرف (*zharf*) deep.

ژرفی (*zharfi*) depth.
ژن (*zhen*) F. Genoa.
ژنده (1) (*zhandeh*) worn-out; patched; patched garment.
ژنده (2) (*zhandeh*) terrible, furious.
ژنرال (*zhenerāl*) F. general.
ژنرالیسیم (*zhenerālisim*) F. generalissimo.
ژنو (*zhenev*) F. Geneva.
ژولیده (*zhulideh*) dishevelled.
ژوئن (*zhu'an*) F. June.
ژوئیه (*zhu'ieh*) F. July.
ژیان (*zhiān*) furious; swift.
ژیمناستیک (*zhimnāstik*) F. gymnastics.

س

سابع (*sābe'*) A. seventh.
سابعاً (*sābe'an*) A. seventhly.
سابق (*sābeq*) A. former.
سابقاً (*sābeqan*) A. formerly.
سابقه (*sābeqeh*) A. antecedents, precedent.
ساج (1) (*sāj*) round iron plate for baking bread.
ساج (2) (*sāj*) teak.
ساجد (*sājed*) A. worshipper.
ساحت (*sāḥat*) A. court-yard.
ساحر (*sāḥer*) A. magician.
ساحل (*sāḥel*) A. shore, bank, coast.
ساختگی (*sākhtegi*) artificial.
ساختمان (*sākhtemān*) building, structure.
ساختن (*sākhtan*) to make, build; to suit. با — ساختن to put up with —.
ساخلو (*sākhlou*) T. garrison.
سادات (*sādāt*) A. descendants of the Prophet. (*Pl. of* سید.)
سادگی (*sādegi*) simplicity.
ساده (*sādeh*) simple.
ساده لوح (*sādeh louḥ*) *a.* simple-minded.
سار (*sār*) starling.
ساربان (*sārbān*) camel-driver.
سارق (*sāreq*) A. thief, robber.
ساروان (*sārvān*) camel-driver.
ساروج (*sāruj*) *a.* mortar, plaster.
ساز (*sāz*) string instrument; music; equipment; tool.
سازش (*sāzesh*) agreement.
سازمان (*sāzmān*) organization.
سازنده (*sāzandeh*) maker; player.
ساس (*sās*) bug.
ساسانی (*sāsāni*) Sassanide.
ساطور (*sāṭur*) A. cleaver, chopper.
ساعت (*sā'at*) A. hour; watch, clock.
ساعتِ ده ten o'clock.
ساعت ساز (*sā'at sāz*) *a.* watch-maker.
ساعد (*sā'ed*) A. forearm.
ساعی (*sā'i*) A. diligent, assiduous.
ساغر (*sāghar*) cup, goblet.
سافل (*sāfel*) A. low, humble.

ساق (*sāq*) A. foreleg.

ساقط (*sāqeṭ*) A. fallen.

ساقه (*sāqeh*) A. stem, stalk.

ساقی (*sāqi*) A. cupbearer.

ساکت (*sāket*) A. silent.

ساکن (*sāken*) A. still, motionless; resident, dwelling, inhabitant.

سال (*sāl*) year.

سالار (*sālār*) chief, leader, commander.

سالخورده (*sālkhordeh*) aged.

سالف (*sālef*) A. preceding; predecessor.

سالف الذکر (*sālefo'z-zekr*) A. above-mentioned.

سالگی (*sālegi*) (*preceded by numeral*) — years old.

سالم (*sālem*) A. safe, sound, healthy.

سالنامه (*sālnāmeh*) calendar, almanac.

ساله (*sāleh*) (*preceded by numeral*) — years old.

سالیانه (*sāliāneh*) yearly, annual.

سام (*sām*) A. Shem.

سامان (*sāmān*) house furniture, equipment; dynasty.

سامعه (*sāme'eh*) A. (sense of) hearing.

سامی (*sāmi*) A. Semitic.

سان (*sān*) parade, review. سان دیدن to review.

سانحه (*sāneḥeh*) A. accident.

سانسور (*sānsur*) F. censorship.

ساو (*sāv*) tribute.

سایر (*sāyer*) A. rest, remainder.

سائل (*sā'el*) A. beggar.

سایه (*sāyeh*) shadow, shade.

سائیدن (*sā'idan*) to pound, pulverize.

سبب (*sabab*) A. reason, cause.

سبت (*sabt*) A. Sabbath.

سبحان الله (*sobḥāna'llāh*) A. glory be to God!

سبد (*sabad*) basket.

سبز (*sabz*) green.

سبزی (*sabzi*) greenness; vegetable(s).

سبع (*sob'*) A. seventh (part).

سبع (*sabo'*) A. beast of prey.

سبقت (*sabqat*) A. precedence.

سبک (*sabk*) A. method, system; style.

سبک (*sabok*) light.

سبو (*sabu*) pitcher.

سبوس (*sabus*) bran, chaff.

سبیل (1) (*sabil*) A. road, way; gratuitously.

سبیل (2) (*sabil*) *a.* moustache.

سپاس (*sepās*) thanks.

سپاسگذاری (*sepāsgozāri*) thanksgiving.

سپاه (*sepāh*) army; corps.

سپاهی (*sepāhi*) soldier.

سپتامبر (*septāmbr*) F. September.

سپر (*separ*) shield.

سپردن (*sepordan*) to commit, entrust; to travel.

سپرز (*seporz*) spleen.

سپس (*sepas*) then.

سپنج (*sepanj*) transitory.

سپند (*sepand*) wild rue.

سپوختن (*sepukhtan*) to pierce.

سپهبد (*sepahbod*) field-marshal.

سپهر (*sepehr*) heavens.

سپهسالار (*sepahsālār*) commander-in-chief.

سپید (*sepid*) white.

سپیده دم (*sepideh dam*) dawn.

ستاد (*setād*) staff. ستادِ ارتش general staff.

ستار (*setār*) three-stringed guitar.

ستاره (*setāreh*) star.

ستام (*setām*) trappings of a horse.

ستاندن (*setāndan*) to take.

ستایش (*setāyesh*) praise, worship.

ستایش کردن to praise, to worship.

ستبر (*setabr*) big, coarse.

ستدن (*setadan*) to take.

ستر (*setr*) A. veil, screen, curtain.

ستردن (*sotordan*) to shave.

سترگ (*sotorg*) large, coarse.

سترون (*setarvān*) barren, sterile.

ستم (*setam*) oppression.

ستم کار (*setam kār*) oppressor.

ستوان (*setvān*) lieutenant (*in the army*).

ستودن (*sotudan*) to praise.

ستور (*sotur*) beast of burden.

ستون (*sotun*) column. ستونِ فقرات spinal column.

ستوه (*sotuh*) wearied, annoyed; weariness, annoyance. بستوه آوردن to annoy.

ستیزه (*setizeh*) quarrel.

سجاد (*sajjād*) A. worshipper.

سجاده (*sajjādeh*) A. prayer-carpet.

سجاف (*sejāf*) A. hem.

سجده (*sajdeh*) A. worship.

سجده کردن to worship.

سجع (*saj'*) A. rhyming prose.

سجل (*sejell*) A. register.

سجود (*sojud*) A. worship, prostration.

سحاب (*saḥāb*) A. cloud(s).

سحار (*saḥḥār*) A. magician.

سحر (*saḥar*) A. dawn.

سحر (*seḥr*) A. magic.

سخا (*sakhā*) A. سخاوت (*sakhāvat*) A. generosity, liberality.

سخت (*sakht*) hard, difficult, severe; very.

سختگیری (*sakhtgiri*) severity, rigour.

سختی (*sakhti*) hardness, difficulty.

سخن (*sokhan*) word. سخن از — راندن to speak of —.

سخن پراکنی (*sokhan parākani*) (wireless) broadcast(ing).

سخن چین (*sokhan chin*) tale-bearer.

سخنران (*sokhanrān*) orator, speaker, lecturer.

سخنرانی (*sokhanrāni*) oratory, speaking; speech, lecture.

سخنگو (*sokhangu*) spokesman.

سد (*sadd*) A. dam, dyke, barrier.

سدس (*sods*) A. sixth (part).

سده (*sadeh*) hundred (*centaine*); century.

سر (*sar*) head; top; beginning; end. سرِ on. بسر بردن to spend, pass; to live. از سر گرفتن to begin again. سر آمدن to come to an end; to excel, attain perfection. سر زدن to appear; to be committed (*said of a crime*); to behead.

سر (*serr*) A. secret.

سراب (*sarāb*) mirage.

سراج (*sarrāj*) A. saddler.

سرازیر (*sarāzir*) sloping. سرازیر شدن to slope.

سراسر (*sarāsar*) throughout, entirely.

سراسیمه (*sarāsimeh*) confused, amazed.

سراغ (*sorāgh*) T. trail, track. سراغ داشتن to know of. سراغ گرفتن to make inquiries.

سراندیب (*sarāndib*) Ceylon.

سرانگشت (*sar angosht*) finger-tip.

سرای (*sarāy*) house ; abode.

سرایت (*serāyat*) A. contagion ; penetration. سرایت کردن to spread (*as a contagion*) ; to penetrate.

سرایدار (*sarāydār*) janitor, hall-porter.

سرائیدن (*sarā'idan*) to sing.

سرب (*sorb*) lead.

سرباز (*sarbāz*) soldier.

سربازخانه (*sarbāzkhāneh*) barracks.

سرپرست (*sarparast*) guardian, warden.

سرپرستی (*sarparasti*) guardianship, protection, patronage.

سرتیپ (*sartip*) brigadier.

سرحد (*sarḥadd*) *a.* frontier.

سرخ (*sorkh*) red.

سرخاب (*sorkhāb*) rouge.

سرخجه (*sorkhjeh*) measles.

سر خوش (*sar khosh*) tipsy.

سرخی (*sorkhi*) redness.

سرد (*sard*) cold.

سرداب (*sardāb*) cellar.

سردار (*sardār*) commander.

سر درختی (*sar darakhti*) fruit (crop).

سردسیر (*sardsir*) cold region.

سردی (*sardi*) coldness.

سرزمین (*sar zamin*) region, territory.

سر زنش (*sar zanesh*) reproach.

سرسام (*sarsām*) delirium.

سرسره (*sorsoreh*) slide.

سرسری (*sarsari*) inconsiderate.

سرشار (*sarshār*) brimful.

سرشت (*seresht*) nature, temperament.

سرشتن (*sereshtan*) to mix, mould.

سرشك (*sereshk*) tear.

سر شماری (*sar shomāri*) census.

سر شیر (*sar shir*) cream.

سرطان (*saraṭān*) A. cancer ; sign of Cancer.

سرعت (*sor'at*) A. speed, rapidity.

سرفراز (*sar farāz*) exalted.

سرفه (*sorfeh*) cough.

سرفیدن (*sorfidan*) to cough.

سرقت (*serqat*) A. theft, robbery.

سرکار (*sarkār*) overseer ; *polite substitute for* شما.

سرکرده (*sar kardeh*) leader, commander.

سرکش (*sarkash*) rebel.

سرکشی (1) (*sarkashi*) rebellion, mutiny.

سرکشی (2) (*sarkashi*) inspection, visit.

سر کنسول (*sar konsul*) consul-general.

سر کوبی (*sar kubi*) suppression.

سرکه (*serkeh*) vinegar.

سرکه شیره (*serkeh shireh*) mixture of vinegar and grape syrup.

سر گذشت (*sar goẕasht*) adventure(s).

سرگرد (*sargord*) major.

سر گردان (*sar gardān*) wandering, errant; amazed.

سر گرم (*sar garm*) busy, occupied.

سرگین (*sargin*) dung.

سرلشگر (*sarlashgar*) general.

سرم (*serom*) F. serum.

سرما (*sarmā*) cold, chill.

سرمایه (*sarmāyeh*) capital.

سرمایه دار (*sarmāyeh dār*) capitalist.

سرمایه داری (*sarmāyeh dāri*) capitalism.

سرمد (*sarmad*) A. eternal; eternity.

سر مقاله (*sar maqāleh*) *a.* leading article.

سر مشق (*sar mashq*) *a.* copy, model.

سرمه (*sormeh*) collyrium.

سرنا (*sornā*) oboe.

سر نگون (*sar negun*) upside down; overthrown.

سر نیزه (*sar neizeh*) bayonet.

سرو (*sarv*) cypress.

سروان (*sarvān*) captain (*in the army*).

سرود (*sorud*) song, anthem.

سرودن (*sorudan*) to sing.

سرور (*sarvar*) chief, leader.

سرور (*sorur*) A. joy.

سروش (*sorush*) angel.

سرویس (*servis*) F. service.

سرهنگ (*sarhang*) colonel.

سری (*serri*) A. secret.

سریر (*sarir*) A. throne.

سریشم (*serishom*) glue.

سریع (*sari‘*) A. rapid, swift.

سریعاً (*sari‘an*) A. swiftly, speedily.

سریع الفساد (*sari‘o'l-fasād*) A. perishable.

سریع الهضم (*sari‘o'l-haẓm*) A. digestible.

سرین (*sorin*) buttocks.

سزا (*sazā*) reward, retribution; well-deserved.

سزاوار (*sazāvār*) worthy, deserving.

سزیدن (*sazidan*) to be worthy, suitable.

سست (*sost*) weak, feeble, slack.

سستی (*sosti*) weakness, slackness, negligence.

سطح (*saṭḥ*) A. surface.

سطحی (*saṭḥi*) A. superficial.

سطر (*saṭr*) A. line.

سطوح (*soṭuḥ*) A. surfaces. (*Pl. of* سطح.)

سطل (*saṭl*) A. pail.

سطور (*soṭur*) A. lines. (*Pl. of* سطر.)

سعادت (*sa‘ādat*) A. happiness, prosperity.

سعادتمند (*sa‘ādatmand*) *a.* happy, prosperous.

سعایت (*se‘āyat*) A. slander.

سعت (*sa‘at*) A. width, amplitude.

سعد (*sa‘d*) A. fortunate aspect of the stars.

سعر (*se‘r*) A. price, rate.

سعودی (*so‘udi*) A. Saudi.

سعی (*sa‘y*) A. endeavour, attempt. سعی کردن to try.

سعید (*sa‘id*) A. happy, prosperous.

سفارت (*sefārat*) A. legation. سفارتِ کبری embassy.
سفارتخانه (*sefāratkhāneh*) *a.* legation, embassy (building).
سفارش (*sefāresh*) recommendation; order (*for goods*); instruction, charge. سفارش کردن to recommend; to enjoin. سفارش دادن to order (*goods*).
سفال (*sofāl*) potsherd; earthenware.
سفاهت (*safāhat*) A. foolishness.
سفاین (*safāyen*) A. ships. (*Pl. of* سفینه.)
سفت (*seft*) tight; stiff; hard.
سفت (*soft*) shoulder.
سفتن (*softan*) to perforate.
سفر (*safar*) A. journey; travel.
سفره (*sofreh*) A. table-cloth; table.
سفسطه (*safsaṭeh*) A. sophism.
سفله (*sofleh*) A. rabble; low person; mean, base.
سفلی (*soflā*) A. lower, lowest.
سفلیس (*seflis*) F. syphilis.
سفلیسی (*seflisi*) syphilitic.
سفید (*sefid*) white.
سفیدار (*sefidār*) aspen.
سفیده (*sefideh*) white of the egg; dawn.
سفیر (*safir*) A. envoy, ambassador. سفیرِ کبیر ambassador.
سفینه (*safineh*) A. ship, vessel.
سفیه (*safih*) A. silly, stupid.
سقا (*saqqā*) A. water-carrier.
سقا خانه (*saqqā khāneh*) *a.* drinking fountain.
سقراط (*soqrāṭ*) A. Socrates.
سقط (*saqaṭ*) A. rubble; abuse; maimed.
سقط (*seqṭ*) A. abortion.
سقط فروش (*saqaṭ forush*) *a.* wholesale dealer.
سقف (*saqf*) A. ceiling, roof.
سقم (*saqam*) A. untruth.
سقوط (*soquṭ*) A. fall. سقوط کردن to fall.
سکته (*sakteh*) A. apoplexy.
سکنه (*sakaneh*) A. inhabitants. (*Pl. of* ساکن.)
سکنی (*soknā*) A. dwelling, abode.
سکوت (*sokut*) A. silence.
سکون (*sokun*) A. calm, repose.
سکونت (*sokunat*) A. dwelling, residence. سکونت کردن to dwell.
سکه (*sekkeh*) A. coin.
سگ (*sag*) dog. سگِ آبی beaver.
سگالش (*segālesh*) thought, intention.
سل (*sell*) A. consumption, tuberculosis.
سلاح (*selāḥ*) A. arms, armour.
سلاخ (*sallākh*) A. flayer, butcher.
سلاخ خانه (*sallākh khāneh*) *a.* slaughter-house, shambles.
سلاست (*salāsat*) A. ease, smoothness (*of style*).
سلاطین (*salāṭin*) A. sultans, kings. (*Pl. of* سلطان.)
سلام (*salām*) A. peace; salutation. سلام علیکم peace be upon you! (*Greeting.*) علیکم السلام upon you be peace! (*Reply to greeting.*)
سلامت (*salāmat*) A. health, safety; healthy, safe.

سلامتی (*salāmati*) *a.* health, safety.
سلب (*salb*) A. negation ; deprivation.
سلحشور (*selaḥshur*) *a.* skilled in the use of arms.
سلسله (*selseleh*) A. chain ; series ; dynasty.
سلطان (*solṭān*) A. sultan, king ; captain.
سلطنت (*salṭanat*) A. reign ; kingdom, monarchy ; government.
سلطنت طلب (*ṣalṭanat ṭalab*) *a.* monarchist.
سلطنتی (*salṭanati*) *a.* royal.
سلطه (*salṭeh*) A. rule, sovereignty.
سلف (*salaf*) A. predecessor, ancestor ; in advance.
سلک (*selk*) A. string, thread ; class, category.
سلم (*salam*) A. advance money ; in advance.
سلمانی (*salmāni*) *a.* hairdresser.
سلوک (*soluk*) A. behaviour.
سلول (*selul*) F. cell.
سلیس (*salis*) A. easy, fluent.
سلیطه (*saliṭeh*) A. shrew.
سلیقه (*saliqeh*) A. taste, tact.
سلیم (*salim*) A. sound, intact ; meek, humble.
سلیمان (*soleimān*) A. Solomon ; *masc. proper name.*
سلیمانی (*soleimāni*) *a.* onyx.
سم (*samm*) A. poison.
سم (*som*) hoof.
سما (*samā*) A. heaven.
سماجت (*samājat*) A. insistence, importunity.
سماع (*samā'*) A. (act of) hearing ; singing, music.
سمت (*samt*) A. direction.
سمت (*semat*) A. capacity, title, designation.
سمسار (*semsār*) second-hand dealer.
سمع (*sam'*) A. (act of) hearing ; ear.
سمک (*samak*) A. fish.
سمن (*saman*) jasmine.
سمنت (*sement*) E. cement.
سمند (*samand*) light bay (horse).
سمندر (*samandar*) salamander.
سمور (*samur*) sable.
سمی (*sammi*) A. poisonous.
سمیت (*sammiyyat*) A. poisonousness.
سن (*sen*) *name of an insect pest.*
سن (*senn*) A. age.
سنا (*senā*) F. senate.
سنان (*senān*) A. (point of a) spear.
سنبل (*sonbol*) A. hyacinth.
سنبله (*sonboleh*) A. ear of corn ; Virgo.
سنجاب (*sanjāb*) grey squirrel.
سنجاق (*sanjāq*) T. pin ; brooch.
سنجیدن (*sanjidan*) to weigh ; to measure.
سنخ (*senkh*) A. class, group.
سند (*sanad*) A. document.
سند (*send*) Indus.
سندان (*sendān*) A. anvil.
سندل (*sandal*) sandal-wood.
سندیکا (*sandikā*) F. syndicate ; trade union.
سنگ (*sang*) stone.
سنگ پشت (*sang posht*) tortoise.
سنگدان (*sangdān*) gizzard.

سنگدل (*sangdel*) hard-hearted.
سنگر (*sangar*) trench.
سنگربندی (*sangarbandi*) intrenchment. سنگربندی کردن to dig in, intrench oneself.
سنگسار (*sangsār*) (act of) stoning.
سنگک (*sangak*) (bread) baked on heated pebbles in a furnace.
سنگین (*sangin*) heavy.
سنگینی (*sangini*) heaviness, weight.
سنوات (*sanavāt*) A. years. (*Pl. of* سنه.)
سنوی (*sanavi*) A. annual.
سنه (*saneh*) A. year.
سنی (*sonni*) A. Sunnite.
سنین (*sanin*) A. years. (*Pl. of* سنه.)
سو (1) (*su*) direction. سوىِ *or* بسوىِ towards.
سو (2) (*su*) light; sight. کم سو short-sighted.
سؤ (*su'*) A. badness. سؤ تفاهم misunderstanding. سؤ استفاده misuse, abuse.
سوا (*sevā*) A. other, separate, different. سواىِ except.
سوابق (*savābeq*) A. antecedents, record. (*Pl. of* سابقه.)
سواحل (*savāḥel*) A. shores, coasts. (*Pl. of* ساحل.)
سواد (*savād*) A. environs; copy, draft; ability to read and write. با سواد literate. بی سواد illiterate.
سوار (*savār*) horseman; mounted, riding. سوار شدن to mount, to ride.
سواره (*savāreh*) on horseback; horseman.
سواری (1) (*savāri*) (act of) riding. سواری کردن to ride. سواری دادن to be capable of being ridden.
سواری (2) (*savāri*) pertaining to riding. اتومبیلِ سواری touring car.
سوانح (*savāneḥ*) A. accidents. (*Pl. of* سانحه.)
سوپاپ (*supāp*) F. valve.
سوت (*sut*) whistle.
سوخت (*sukht*) fuel.
سوخت آما (*sukht āmā*) carburettor.
سوختن (*sukhtan*) to burn (*intr.*).
سود (*sud*) profit; use; usury, interest.
سودا (1) (*soudā*) transaction, trade.
سودا (2) (*soudā*) A. black bile; melancholy.
سوداگر (*soudāgar*) merchant.
سودان (*sudān*) A. Sudan.
سودمند (*sudmand*) useful.
سودن (*sudan*) to rub, to grind.
سور (*sur*) banquet, feast.
سوراخ (*surākh*) hole.
سورتمه (*surtmeh*) T. sledge.
سوره (*sureh*) A. chapter of the Koran.
سوریه (*suriyyeh*) A. Syria.
سوز (*suz*) pain, grief.
سوزاک (*suzāk*) gonorrhœa.
سوزان (*suzān*) burning.
سوزاندن (*suzāndan*), سوزانیدن (*suzānidan*) to burn (*tr.*).
سوزش (*suzesh*) burning, inflammation.

سوزن (*suzan*) needle.

سوزناک (*suznāk*) plaintive, sad.

سوسک (*susk*) beetle.

سوسمار (*susmār*) lizard.

سوسن (*susan*) lily.

سوسیالیست (*sosiālist*) F. Socialist.

سوفار (*sufār*) notch (in an arrow).

سوق (*souq*) A. (act of) driving, leading. سوق دادن to drive, to lead.

سوق الجیش (*souqo'l-jeish*) A. strategy.

سوق الجیشی (*souqo'l-jeishi*) *a.* strategical.

سوگ (*sug*) sorrow, grief.

سوگلی (*sougoli*) T. favourite.

سوگند (*sougand*) oath.

سوگوار (*sugvār*) mournful, sad.

سوگواری (*sugvāri*) grief, lamentation.

سوم (*sevvom*), سومین (*sevvomin*) third.

سوهان (*suhān*) file, rasp.

سوئد (*su'ed*) F. Sweden.

سویس (*svis*) F. Switzerland.

سه (*seh*) three.

سهام (*sehām*) A. shares, bonds. (*Pl. of* سهم.)

سه تار (*seh tār*) guitar.

سهراب (*sohrāb*) *name of the son of Rustam ; masc. proper name.*

سه شنبه (*seh shanbeh*) Tuesday.

سه گوش (*seh gush*) triangular ; triangle.

سه گانه (*seh gāneh*) triple, tripartite.

سهل (*sahl*) A. easy.

سهل انگاری (*sahl engāri*) *a.* carelessness, nonchalance.

سهم (1) (*sahm*) A. share, bond.

سهم (2) (*sahm*) dread, terror.

سهمگین (*sahmgin*) fearful, terrible.

سهمیه (*sahmiyyeh*) A. quota.

سهو (*sahv*) A. error, blunder.

سهواً (*sahvan*) A. by mistake.

سهولت (*sohulat*) A. ease.

سهیم (*sahim*) A. sharing.

سی (*si*) thirty.

سیاح (*sayyāḥ*) A. traveller.

سیاحت (*siāḥat*) A. (act of) travelling. سیاحت کردن to travel.

سیار (*sayyār*) A. wandering, itinerant.

سیاره (*sayyāreh*) A. planet.

سیاست (*siāsat*) A. politics, policy ; diplomacy.

سیاستمدار (*siāsatmadār*) *a.* statesman.

سیاسی (*siāsi*) A. political ; diplomatic.

سیاسیون (*siāsiyyun*) A. statesmen, politicians.

سیاق (*siāq*) A. order, form ; *name of a method of notation and accounting.*

سی ام (*si om*) thirtieth.

سیاه (*siāh*) black.

سیاه سرفه (*siāh sorfeh*) whooping cough.

سیاه گوش (*siāh gush*) lynx.

سیاهه (*siāheh*) invoice, inventory.

سیاهی (*siāhi*) blackness.

سیب (*sib*) apple. سیبِ زمینی potato.

سیبری (*siberi*) F. Siberia.

سیحون (*seiḥun*) A. Jaxartes.

سیخ (*sikh*) spit ; skewer ; poker.

سید (*sayyed*) A. descendant of the Prophet.

سیر (*seir*) A. (act of) going, walking, travel; sightseeing.

سیر (1) (*sir*) satisfied, full, satiated.

سیر (2) (*sir*) garlic.

سیر (3) (*sir*) *name of a dry measure* = *approx.* $\frac{1}{6}$ *lb.*

سیرت (*sirat*) A. character, morals.

سیری (*siri*) satiety.

سیزده (*sizdah*) thirteen.

سیزدهم (*sizdahom*) thirteenth.

سیستم (*sistem*) F. system.

سیسیل (*sisil*) F. Sicily.

سیصد (*siṣad*) three hundred.

سیف (*seif*) A. sword.

سیگار (*sigār*) F. cigar, cigarette. سیگار کشیدن to smoke a cigar(ette).

سیگارت (*sigāret*) F. cigarette.

سیل (*seil*) A. flood.

سیلی (*sili*) slap.

سیم (*sim*) silver; wire.

سیما (*simā*) aspect, countenance.

سیمان (*simān*) F. cement.

سیمرغ (*simorgh*) *name of a fabulous bird.*

سیمین (*simin*) (of) silver; silvery.

سینما (*sinemā*) F. cinema.

سینه (*sineh*) breast; chest.

سینی (*sini*) tray.

ش

شاخ (*shākh*) branch; horn. شاخ زدن to butt.

شاخه (*shākheh*) branch.

شاد (*shād*) happy, glad.

شاداب (*shādāb*) juicy; moist; fresh.

شاد باش (*shād bāsh*) bravo! congratulation.

شادمان (*shādmān*) glad, joyful.

شادمانی (*shādmāni*) gladness, joy.

شادی (*shādi*) joy. شادی کردن to rejoice.

شاذ (*shāẕẕ*) A. rare, uncommon.

شارب (*shāreb*) A. long moustache.

شارژدافر (*shārzhedāfer*) F. chargé d'affaires.

شارع (*shāre'*) A. road, thoroughfare.

شاسی (*shāsi*) F. chassis; frame.

شاش (*shāsh*) urine.

شاشدان (*shāshdān*) bladder; chamber-pot.

شاشیدن (*shāshidan*) to urinate.

شاطر (*shāṭer*) A. nimble, clever; outrunner; baker.

شاعر (*shā'er*) A. poet.

شافع (*shāfe'*) A. mediator, intercessor.

شافی (*shāfi*) A. healing; categorical.

شاق (*shāqq*) A. difficult, onerous. اعمالِ شاقه hard labour.

شاقول (*shāqul*) A. plumb-line.

شاکر (*shāker*) A. thankful, grateful.

شاکی (*shāki*) A. complaining.

شاگرد (*shāgerd*) apprentice, pupil.

شاگردی (*shāgerdi*) apprenticeship, discipleship.

شال (*shāl*) sash, shawl.

شالوده (*shāludeh*) foundation.

شالی (*shāli*) paddy.

شام (*shām*) evening; supper.

شام (*shām*) A. Syria; Damascus.

شامخ (*shāmekh*) A. lofty.

شامل (*shāmel*) A. containing, including.

شامه (*shāmmeh*) A. (sense of) smell.

شأن (*sha'n*) A. rank, dignity; concern, affair.

شانزده (*shānzdah*) sixteen.

شانزدهم (*shānzdahom*) sixteenth.

شانس (*shāns*) F. luck.

شانه (1) (*shāneh*) comb. شانه زدن to comb.

شانه (2) (*shāneh*) shoulder(-blade). از — شانه خالی کردن to shirk —.

شاه (*shāh*) king, shah.

شاهانه (*shāhāneh*) royal.

شاه بلوط (*shāh baluṭ*) *a.* chestnut (tree).

شاه پرست (*shāh parast*) royalist.

شاهپور (*shāhpur*) prince.

شاهتوت (*shāhtut*) black mulberry.

شاهد (*shāhed*) A. witness.

شاهدانه (*shāhdāneh*) hemp-seed.

شاهراه (*shāhrāh*) highway.

شاهزاده (*shāhzādeh*) prince.

شاهکار (*shāhkār*) masterpiece.

شاه ماهی (*shāh māhi*) red mullet; herring.

شاهنشاه (*shāhenshāh*) king of kings, emperor.

شاهنشاهی (*shāhenshāhi*) imperial.

شاه نشین (*shāh neshin*) royal seat; balcony.

شاهی (*shāhi*) kingdom; kingship, sovereignty.

شاهین (*shāhin*) royal falcon.

شایان (*shāyān*) worthy, deserving.

شائبه (*shā'ebeh*) A. stain, blemish.

شاید (*shāyad*) perhaps.

شایستگی (*shāyestegi*) worthiness, suitability.

شایستن (*shāyestan*) to befit, to be worthy.

شایسته (*shāyesteh*) worthy, suitable.

شایع (*shāye'*) A. spread abroad; prevalent.

شایعه (*shāye'eh*) A. rumour.

شایق (*shāyeq*) A. eager, curious.

شایگان (*shāygān*) worthy; royal.

شب (*shab*) night.

شباب (*shabāb*) A. youth.

شبان (*shabān*) shepherd.

شبانگاه (*shabāngāh*), شبانگه (*shabāngah*) evening, night.

شبانه (*shabāneh*) nightly, by night. شبانه روز day and night.

شباهت (*shabāhat*) A. resemblance.

شب پره (*shab pareh*) bat.

شبح (*shabaḥ*) A. phantom; silhouette.

شبدر (*shabdar*) clover.

شبستان (*shabestān*) bedroom; harem.

شبکه (*shabakeh*) A. net(work).

شبگرد (*shabgard*) watchman.

شب نشینی (*shab neshini*) evening party.
شبنم (*shabnam*) dew.
شبو (*shabbu*) gilly-flower, wall-flower.
شبه (*shebh*) A. likeness, similarity. شبه جزیره peninsula.
شبهه (*shobheh*) A. doubt.
شبیخون (*shabikhun*) surprise attack by night.
شبیه (*shabih*) A. alike, resembling.
شپش (*shepesh*) louse.
شپشه (*shepesheh*) weevil.
شتاب (*shetāb*) haste.
شتابان (*shetābān*) hasty, hastily.
شتافتن (*shetāftan*) to hasten.
شتر (*shotor*) camel.
شتربان (*shotorbān*) camel-driver.
شتر مرغ (*shotor morgh*) ostrich.
شجاع (*shojā'*) A. brave.
شجاعت (*shajā'at*) A. bravery.
شجر (*shajar*) A. tree(s).
شجره (*shajareh*) A. tree; genealogical tree.
شحنه (*shaḥneh*) A. chief of police.
شخص (*shakhṣ*) A. person.
شخصا (*shakhṣan*) A. personally.
شخصی (*shakhṣi*) A. personal.
شخصیت (*shakhsiyyat*) A. personality.
شُخم (*shokhm*) plough(ing). شخم کردن to plough.
شخودن (*shakhudan*) to scratch.
شدائد (*shadā'ed*) A. hardships.
شدت (*sheddat*) A. violence, severity. شدت کردن to be intensified, aggravated.
شدن (*shodan*) to become.
شدنی (*shodani*) feasible.
شدید (*shadid*) A. violent.
شدیداً (*shadidan*) A. violently.
شر (*sharr*) A. evil, wickedness.
شراب (*sharāb*) A. wine.
شرارت (*sharārat*) A. revolt, rising.
شراع (*sherā'*) A. sail.
شرافت (*sharāfat*) A. nobility.
شراکت (*sherākat*) A. partnership.
شرایط (*sharāyeṭ*) A. conditions, terms. (*Pl. of* شرط.)
شرب (*shorb*) A. (act of) drinking.
شربت (*sharbat*) A. sherbet; syrup.
شرح (*sharḥ*) A. description, account, explanation. بشرح زیر as follows. شرح دادن to describe, explain.
شرحه (*sharḥeh*) A. slice.
شرزه (*sharzeh*) fierce.
شرط (*sharṭ*) A. condition, stipulation.
شرطی (*sharṭi*) A. conditional.
شرع (*shar'*) A. divine law.
شرعاً (*shar'an*) A. according to divine law.
شرعی (*shar'i*) A. (religiously) lawful.
شرف (*sharaf*) A. honour.
شرفیاب (*sharafyāb*) *a.* honoured. شرفیاب شدن to have the honour of meeting someone, to be received in audience.
شرفیابی (*sharafyābi*) *a.* honour of meeting someone, audience.
شرق (*sharq*) A. east.
شرقاً (*sharqan*) A. on the east.
شرقی (*sharqi*) A. eastern.
شرک (*sherk*) A. polytheism.

شرکت (*sherkat*) A. company, partnership; participation. شرکت کردن to go into partnership; to participate.

شرم (*sharm*) modesty, shame.

شرم آور (*sharm āvar*) shameful.

شرمسار (*sharmsār*) ashamed, disgraced.

شروع (*shoru'*) A. beginning, commencement. شروع به — کردن to begin to —.

شریان (*sharyān*) A. artery.

شریر (*sharir*) A. wicked.

شریعت (*shari'at*) A. religious law.

شریف (*sharif*) A. noble.

شریك (*sharik*) A. partner, participant.

شست (*shast*) thumb.

شستن (*shostan*) to wash.

شست و شو (*shost o shu*) (act of) washing.

شش (*shesh*) six.

شش (*shosh*) lungs.

ششلول (*sheshlul*) revolver.

ششم (*sheshom*) sixth.

شصت (*shaṣt*) sixty.

شطرنج (*shaṭranj*) A. chess.

شعار (*she'ār*) A. sign, mark, standard.

شعاع (*sho'ā'*) A. ray, sunbeam.

شعائر (*sha'ā'er*) A. rites.

شعب (*she'b*) A. mountain path, pass.

شعبان (*sha'bān*) A. *name of the eighth month of the Arabic lunar year.*

شعبده (*sho'badeh*) *a.* jugglery, sleight-of-hand.

شعبده باز (*sho'badeh bāz*) *a.* juggler, conjuror.

شعبه (*sho'beh*) A. branch.

شعر (*sha'r*) A. hair.

شعر (*she'r*) A. poetry, poem.

شعرا (*sho'arā*) A. poets. (*Pl. of* شاعر.)

شعله (*sho'leh*) A. flame.

شعله ور (*sho'leh var*) *a.* flaming.

شعور (*sho'ur*) A. common sense, intelligence.

شغال (*shaghāl*) jackal.

شغل (*shoghl*) A. business, occupation, profession.

شفا (*shefā*) A. (act of) healing, curing. شفا دادن to heal, cure.

شفاعت (*shafā'at*) A. intercession.

شفاف (*shaffāf*) A. transparent.

شفاهاً (*shefāhan*) A. orally.

شفاهی (*shefāhi*) A. oral.

شفتالو (*shaftālu*) peach.

شفق (*shafaq*) A. twilight.

شفقت (*shafaqat*) A. compassion.

شفیع (*shafi'*) A. mediator, intercessor.

شفیق (*shafiq*) A. compassionate.

شق (*sheqq*) A. alternative.

شقائق (*shaqā'eq*) A. peony, tulip.

شقاوت (*shaqāvat*) A. adversity, misfortune.

شقی (*shaqi*) A. wretched, miserable.

شقیقه (*shaqiqeh*) A. temple (of the head).

شك (*shakk*) A. doubt.

شكار (*shekār*) hunting, chase; game.

شكارچی (*shekārchi*) hunter.

شكاری (*shekāri*) pertaining to hunting. مرغِ شكاری bird of prey.

شكاف (*shekāf*) cleft, breach.
شكافتن (*shekāftan*) to split, rip.
شكايت (*shekāyat*) A. complaint.
شكر (*shakar*) (granulated) sugar.
شكر (*shukr*) A. thanks (to God). شكر كردن to thank (God).
شكرانه (*shokrāneh*) *a.* thankfulness.
شكرستان (*shakarestān*) sugar plantation.
شكست (*shekast*) defeat. شكست دادن to defeat.
شكستن (*shekastan*) to break.
شكسته (*shekasteh*) broken; *name of a kind of cursive handwriting.*
شكفتن (*shekoftan*) to open (*as a bud*).
شكل (*shakl*) A. shape, form ; picture.
شكم (*shekam*) belly.
شكمبه (*shekambeh*) (first) stomach (of ruminant).
شكم خوار (*shekam khvār*) glutton(ous).
شكن (*shekan*) fold, plait, curl.
شكنجه (*shekanjeh*) torture.
شكننده (*shekanandeh*) brittle, fragile.
شكوفه (*shokufeh*) blossom.
شكوه (*shokuh*) splendour, magnificence.
شكوه (*shakveh*) A. complaint.
شكيب (*shakib*), شكيبا (*shakibā*) patient.
شكيبيدن (*shakibidan*) to be patient.
شگرف (*shegarf*) wonderful ; excellent ; great.
شگفت (*shegeft*) wonder, surprise.
شگفت آميز (*shegeft āmiz*) surprising.
شگفتی (*shegefti*) wonder.
شگون (*shogun*) M. good omen.
شل (*shal*) lame.
شل (*shol*) loose, slack ; flabby, languid.
شلاق (*shallāq*) whip, scourge. شلاق زدن to whip. شلاق خوردن to be whipped.
شلتوك (*shaltuk*) T. paddy.
شلغم (*shalgham*) turnip.
شلوار (*shalvār*) trousers.
شلوق (*sholuq*) T. disorder, confusion ; noise.
شليك (*shalik*) discharge, volley.
شما (*shomā*) you.
شمار (*shomār*) (act of) counting, reckoning. بشمار رفتن to be reckoned.
شماره (*shomāreh*) number.
شماره گير (*shomāreh gir*) telephone dial.
شماع (*shammā'*) A. candle-maker.
شمال (*shemāl*) A. north. شمالِ شرقی north-east.
شمالاً (*shemālan*) A. on the north.
شمالی (*shemāli*) A. northern.
شمائل (*shamā'el*) A. good qualities.
شمردن (*shomordan*) to count, reckon.
شمس (*shams*) A. sun.
شمسی (*shamsi*) A. solar.
شمش (*shemsh*) ingot.
شمشاد (*shemshād*) box-tree.
شمشير (*shamshir*) sword.
شمع (*sham'*) A. candle ; prop.
شمعدان (*sham'dān*) *a.* candle-stick.

شمعدانی (*sham'dāni*) *a.* geranium.

شمول (*shomul*) A. comprehension, inclusion.

شن (*shen*) sand, gravel.

شنا (*shenā*) (act of) swimming. شنا کردن to swim.

شناختن (*shenākhtan*) to know, recognize. (*Connaître.*)

شناسا (*shenāsā*) knowing, acquainted; acquaintance.

شناسائی (*shenāsā'i*) acquaintance; recognition.

شناسنامه (*shenāsnāmeh*) identity book.

شناعت (*shenā'at*) A. abomination, obscenity.

شناور (*shenāvar*) swimmer.

شناوری (*shenāvari*) (art of) swimming.

شنبه (*shanbeh*) Saturday.

شنونده (*shenavandeh*) listener.

شنیدن (*shanidan*) to hear.

شنیع (*shani'*) A. shameful, obscene.

شو (*shu*) husband.

شوال (*shavvāl*) A. *name of the tenth month of the Arabic lunar year.*

شوخ (*shukh*) saucy, impudent.

شوخی (*shukhi*) impudence; joke.

شور (1) (*shur*) salt(y).

شور (2) (*shur*) zeal; agitation, anxiety.

شور (*shour*) A. consultation; reading (*in Parliament*).

شوربا (*shurbā*) pottage.

شورش (*shuresh*) revolution; turmoil.

شورشی (*shureshi*) insurgent, revolutionary.

شوروی (*shouravi*) A. Soviet.

شوره (*shureh*) saltpeter.

شوری (*shurā*) A. council.

شوریدن (*shuridan*) to revolt; to be frenzied.

شوریده (*shurideh*) frenzied.

شوسه (*shoseh*) F. metalled (road).

شوفور (*shofor*) F. chauffeur.

شوق (*shouq*) A. desire, yearning.

شوك (*shouk*) A. thorn, thistle.

شوکت (*shoukat*) A. glory, pomp, dignity.

شوم (*shum*) A. inauspicious(ness).

شوهر (*shouhar*) husband.

شهاب (*shehāb*) A. meteor.

شهادت (*shahādat*) A. testimony, evidence; martyrdom.

شهامت (*shahāmat*) A. bravery

شهپر (*shahpar*) large(st) feather; aileron.

شهپور (*shahpur*) prince.

شهد (*shahd*) A. honey.

شهدا (*shohadā*) A. martyrs. (*Pl. of* شهید.)

شهدخت (*shahdokht*) princess.

شهر (1) (*shahr*) town, city.

شهر (2) (*shahr*) A. (lunar) month.

شهربانی (*shahrbāni*) police.

شهرت (*shohrat*) A. fame, renown.

شهردار (*shahrdār*) mayor.

شهرداری (*shahrdāri*) municipality.

شهرستان (*shahrestān*) district, county.

شهری (*shahri*) pertaining to a town; civic.

شهریار (*shahriār*) monarch, sovereign.

شهریور (*shahrivar*) *name of the sixth month of the Persian year.*

شهوت (*shahvat*) A. lust, concupiscence.

شهوت پرست (*shahvat parast*) *a.* lascivious, lewd; libertine, debauchee.

شهود (*shohud*) A. witnesses. (*Pl. of* شاهد.)

شهید (*shahid*) A. martyr(ed). شهید شدن to suffer martyrdom, to die for one's country.

شهیر (*shahir*) A. famous.

شهیق (*shahiq*) A. inhalation

شیء (*shei'*) A. thing.

شیاد (*shayyād*) A. imposter, cheat.

شیار (*shiār*) ploughed land; furrow.

شیب (*shib*) slope.

شیپور (*sheipur*) trumpet.

شیخ (*sheikh*) A. sheikh; old man; learned man.

شیر (1) (*shir*) lion; tap.

شیر (2) (*shir*) milk.

شیر اوژن (*shir ouzhan*) brave, valiant.

شیر خوار (*shir khvār*) sucking, suckling.

شیره (*shireh*) juice, sap; syrup.

شیرین (*shirin*) sweet, melodious.

شیرینی (*shirini*) sweetness; sweetmeat.

شیشه (*shisheh*) glass; bottle.

شیشه گر (*shisheh gar*) glass-blower.

شیطان (*sheiṭān*) A. Satan; mischievous, naughty.

شیطانی (*sheiṭāni*) *a.* devilish; mischievous, naughty.

شیعه (*shi'eh*) A. Shiite.

شیفتن (*shiftan*) to charm, fascinate; to distract.

شیفته (*shifteh*) enamoured.

شیلات (*shilāt*) *a.* fisheries.

شیمه (*shimeh*) A. disposition, character.

شیمی (*shimi*) F. chemistry.

شیمیائی (*shimiā'i*) chemical.

شیوع (*shoyu'*) A. prevalence; spreading abroad. شیوع داشتن to be prevalent.

شئون (*sho'un*) A. affairs. (*Pl. of* شأن.)

شیون (*shivan*) wailing, lamentation.

شیوه (*shiveh*) way, manner coquetry; trick.

شیهه (*shiheh*) neighing.

ص

صابر (*ṣāber*) A. patient.

صابون (*ṣābun*) A. soap.

صاحب (*ṣāḥab*) A. owner, master.

صاحب منصب (*ṣāḥab manṣab*) *a.* officer.

صادر (*ṣāder*) A. emanating, coming forth; exported. صادر کردن to issue; to export.

صادرات (*ṣāderāt*) A. exports.

صادق (*ṣādeq*) A. truthful; loyal.

صاروج (*ṣāruj*) A. mortar, plaster.

صاعقه (*ṣā'eqeh*) A. thunderbolt.

صاف (*ṣāf*) A. clear; pure; smooth; even.

صافی (1) (*ṣāfi*) A. clear, pure.

صافی (2) (*ṣāfi*) *a.* clearness, purity.

صافی (3) (*ṣāfi*) A. filter, strainer.

صالح (*ṣāleḥ*) A. good, pious; fit, competent.

صامت (*ṣāmet*) A. silent, mute.

صانع (*ṣāne'*) A. Maker, Creator.

صائب (*ṣā'eb*) A. right, correct.

صبا (*ṣabā*) A. zephyr.

صباح (*ṣabāḥ*) A. morning.

صباغ (*ṣabbāgh*) A. dyer.

صباغی (*ṣabbāghi*) *a.* (act of) dyeing.

صبح (*ṣobḥ*) A. morning.

صبحدم (*ṣobḥdam*) *a.* (early) morning.

صبر (*ṣabr*) A. patience. صبر کردن to be patient; to wait.

صبوح (*ṣabuḥ*) A., صبوحی (*ṣabuḥi*) *a.* morning-draught.

صبور (*ṣabur*) A. patient.

صبی (*ṣabi*) A. lad, youth.

صبیه (*ṣabiyyeh*) A. girl, daughter.

صحاری (*ṣaḥāri*) A. deserts. (*Pl. of* صحرا.)

صحاف (*ṣaḥḥāf*) A. bookbinder.

صحبت (*ṣoḥbat*) A. intercourse; conversation. صحبت کردن to talk.

صحت (*ṣeḥḥat*) A. soundness, correctness, truth; health.

صحرا (*ṣaḥrā*) A. desert; plain.

صحرائی (*ṣaḥrā'i*) *a.* pertaining to the desert, wild; field (*e.g. artillery*).

صحف (*ṣoḥof*) A. leaves, sheets; books. (*Pl. of* صحیفه.)

صحن (*ṣaḥn*) A. open space, courtyard.

صحنه (*ṣaḥneh*) *a.* stage, scene.

صحه (*ṣaḥḥeh*) A. signature.

صحی (*ṣehhi*) A. pertaining to health, sanitary.

صحیح (*ṣaḥiḥ*) A. correct, true, proper, sound.

صحیحاً (*ṣaḥiḥan*) A. correctly, properly.

صحیفه (*ṣaḥifeh*) A. leaf, sheet, page; book.

صحیه (*ṣeḥḥiyyeh*) A. health department.

صخره (*ṣakhreh*) A. rock.

صد (*ṣad*) hundred.

صدا (*ṣedā*) A. voice; sound.

صدارت (*ṣadārat*) A. office of premier.

صداع (*ṣodā'*) A. headache.

صداقت (*ṣadāqat*) A. truth, sincerity.

صد پا (*ṣad pā*) centipede.

صدد (*ṣadad*) A. design. — در صددِ بودن to be about to —.

صدر (*ṣadr*) A. breast, chest; upper part; minister.

صدف (*ṣadaf*) A. shell.

صدق (*ṣedq*) A. truth.

صدقه (*ṣadaqeh*) A. alms.

صدمه (*ṣadameh*) A. shock, collision; injury. صدمه زدن to injure.

صدور (*ṣodur*) A. issue; export.

صدیق (*ṣadiq*) A. true, sincere (friend).

صراحت (*ṣarāḥat*) A. clearness, explicitness.

صراحةً (*ṣarāḥatan*) A. clearly, explicitly.

صراف (*ṣarrāf*) A. banker.

صرافت (*ṣarāfat*) A. thought, idea, intention.

صربستان (*ṣerbestān*) Serbia.

صرف (*ṣarf*) A. expenditure; consumption. صرف کردن to spend; to consume. از — صرفِ نظر کردن to dispense with —. صرفِ نظر از apart from. صرف و نحو grammar.

صرف (*ṣerf*) A. pure, mere.

صرفاً (*ṣerfan*) A. merely.

صرفه (*ṣarfeh*) A. profit; economy.

صرفه جو (*ṣarfeh ju*) *a.* economical.

صرفه جوئی (*ṣarfeh ju'i*) *a.* economy.

صریح (*ṣariḥ*) A. clear, explicit, categorical.

صریحاً (*ṣariḥan*) A. explicitly, categorically.

صعب (*ṣa'b*) A. difficult.

صعوبت (*ṣo'ubat*) A. difficulty.

صعود (*ṣo'ud*) A. ascent.

صغر (*ṣeghar*) A. infancy.

صغری (*ṣoghrā*) A. lesser, minor.

صغیر (*ṣaghir*) A. small, young, minor.

صف (*ṣaff*) A. row, rank, line. صف کشیدن to line up.

صفا (*ṣafā*) A. purity; pleasantness; delight.

صفاق (*ṣefāq*) A. peritoneum.

صفت (*ṣefat*) A. quality, attribute; adjective.

صفحه (*ṣafḥeh*) A. page; face, surface; tract.

صفر (*ṣafar*) A. *name of the second month of the Arabic lunar year.*

صفر (*ṣefr*) A. zero.

صفرا (*ṣafrā*) A. bile.

صفوف (*ṣofuf*) A. rows, ranks. (*Pl. of* صف.)

صفوی (*ṣafavi*) A. Safavide.

صفویه (*ṣafaviyyeh*) A. Safavide (dynasty).

صفه (*ṣoffeh*) A. sofa.

صفی (*ṣafi*) A. pure, clear.

صفیر (*ṣafir*) A. whistle.

صلابت (*ṣalābat*) A. hardness, rigidity, firmness.

صلات (*ṣalāt*) A. *i. q.* صلوة.

صلاح (*ṣalāḥ*) A. rectitude; interest, welfare; advisability; advisable.

صلاحیت (*ṣalāḥiyyat*) A. competence.

صلاحیت دار (*ṣalāḥiyyat dār*) *a.* competent.

صلب (*ṣolb*) A. spine; loins.

صلح (*ṣolḥ*) A. peace.

صلوات (*ṣalavāt*) A. prayers; blessing. (*Pl. of* صلوة)

صلوة (*ṣalāt*) A. prayer.

صله (*ṣeleh*) A. bond, tie; prize.

صليب (*ṣalib*) A. cross.

صمد (*ṣamad*) A. eternal.

صمغ (*ṣamgh*) A. gum.

صميم (*ṣamim*) A. pith, core; bottom.

صميمانه (*ṣamimāneh*) *a.* sincere, hearty; sincerely, heartily.

صميمى (*ṣamimi*) A. sincere.

صناعت (*ṣanā'at*) A. art, craft, industry.

صنايع (*ṣanāye'*) A. arts, industries. (*Pl. of* صنعت.)

صندلى (*ṣandali*) *a.* chair.

صندوق (*ṣanduq*) A. box, case.

صندوقخانه (*ṣanduqkhāneh*) *a.* wardrobe.

صنعت (*ṣan'at*) A. art, industry.

صنعتگر (*ṣan'atgar*) *a.* artisan, craftsman; industrialist.

صنعتى (*ṣan'ati*) *a.* industrial.

صنف (*ṣenf*) A. guild; class, sort.

صنم (*ṣanam*) A. idol.

صنوبر (*ṣanoubar*) A. fir.

صواب (*ṣavāb*) A. righteousness; righteous action.

صوابديد (*ṣavābdid*) *a.* approval; advisability.

صوب (*ṣoub*) A. side, direction.

صوت (*ṣout*) A. sound.

صور (*ṣur*) A. Tyre.

صورت (*ṣurat*) A. face; form, shape; list, inventory; case. در صورتِ in the case of. در صورتيكه in case; whereas.

صوفى (*ṣufi*) A. Sufi.

صوفيه (*ṣofieh*) Sofia.

صولت (*ṣoulat*) A. fury.

صوم (*ṣoum*) A. fast(ing).

صومعه (*ṣouma'eh*) A. cell, monastery.

صهيونى (*ṣahyuni*) A. Zionist.

صياد (*ṣayyād*) A. hunter.

صيام (*ṣiām*) A. fast(ing).

صيانت (*ṣiānat*) A. preservation.

صيت (*ṣit*) A. fame, renown.

صيحه (*ṣeiḥeh*) A. shout, cry.

صيد (*ṣeid*) A. hunting, fishing. صيد كردن to hunt; to catch.

صيغه (*ṣigheh*) A. mood, tense, voice; temporary marriage.

صيقل (*ṣeiqal*) A. polish.

صيقلى (*ṣeiqali*) *a.* polished.

ض

ضابط (*ẓābeṭ*) A. bailiff, manager.

ضامن (*ẓāmen*) A. guarantor, surety.

ضايع (*ẓāye'*) A. spoilt, damaged. ضايع كردن to spoil.

ضايعه (*ẓāye'eh*) A. loss.

ضباط (*ẓabbāṭ*) A. archivist.

ضبط (*ẓabṭ*) A. restraint; management; confiscation; files, archives;

orthography. ضبط کردن to confiscate; to file.

ضحاک (*ẓoḥāk*) A. *name of a mythical tyrant.*

ضخامت (*ẓakhāmat*) A. thickness, bulkiness.

ضخیم (*ẓakhim*) A. thick, bulky.

ضد (*ẓedd*) A. contrary, opposite; antagonist. ضدِ یهودی anti-Jewish. بر ضدِ against.

ضراب (*ẓarrāb*) A. coiner.

ضرابخانه (*ẓarrābkhāneh*) *a.* mint.

ضرب (*ẓarb*) A. blow; coining; multiplication.

ضرب الاجل (*ẓarbo'l-ajal*) A. period of grace.

ضرب المثل (*ẓarbo'l-maṣal*) A. proverb.

ضربت (*ẓarbat*) A. blow.

ضرر (*ẓarar*) A. loss, damage; injury, harm.

ضرور (*ẓarur*) A. necessary.

ضرورت (*ẓarurat*) A. necessity.

ضروری (*ẓaruri*) A. necessary.

ضعف (*ẓa'f*) A. weakness.

ضعفا (*ẓo'afā*) A. the weak. (*Pl. of* ضعیف.)

ضعیف (*ẓa'if*) A. weak.

ضلالت (*ẓalālat*) A. aberration; ruin.

ضلع (*ẓel'*) A. rib.

ضم (*ẓamm*) A. connection, annexation.

ضماد (*ẓemād*) A. poultice.

ضمانت (*ẓamānat*) A. surety, guarantee.

ضمن (*ẓemn*) A. contents; middle; meantime. ضمنِ in the course of.

ضمناً (*ẓemnan*) A. meanwhile; incidentally.

ضمیر (*ẓamir*) A. heart, mind, secret thought; pronoun.

ضمیمه (*ẓamimeh*) A. annex, appendix.

ضیا (*ẓiā*) A. light.

ضیافت (*ẓiāfat*) A. banquet.

ضیف (*ẓeif*) A. guest; stranger.

ضیق (*ẓiq*) A. narrowness, straits.

ط

طاس (*ṭās*) bowl, cup; dice.

طاعون (*ṭā'un*) A. plague.

طاغی (*ṭāghi*) A. rebel(lious).

طاق (1) (*ṭāq*) A. arch, vault.

طاق (2) (*ṭāq*) odd.

طاقت (*ṭāqat*) A. endurance.

طاقت فرسا (*ṭāqat farsā*) *a.* onerous, insupportable.

طاقچه (*ṭāqcheh*) *a.* shelf, niche.

طالب (*ṭāleb*) A. seeking, demanding; demand.

طالع (*ṭāle'*) A. horoscope, fortune.

طاووس (*ṭā'us*) A. peacock.

طاهر (*ṭāher*) A. clean, chaste.

طایر (*ṭāyer*) A. bird.

طائفه (*ṭā'efeh*) A. tribe.

طب (*ṭebb*) A. medicine.

طبابت (*ṭabābat*) A. medical profession.

طباخ (*ṭabbākh*) A. cook.

طباشیر (*ṭabāshir*) A. chalk.

طبال (*ṭabbāl*) A. drummer.

طبخ (*ṭabkh*) A. cooking, cookery.

طبرق (*ṭobroq*) A. Tobruk.

طبع (*ṭab'*) A. nature; impression, print(ing). طبع کردن to print.

طبعاً (*ṭab'an*) A. naturally.

طبق (*ṭabaq*) A. tray.

طبق (*ṭebq*) A. conformity. طبقِ according to.

طبقه (*ṭabaqeh*) A. layer; class; storey.

طبقه بندی (*ṭabaqeh bandi*) *a.* classification.

طبل (*ṭabl*) A. drum.

طبی (*ṭebbi*) A. medical.

طبیب (*ṭabib*) A. doctor.

طبیعت (*ṭabi'at*) A. nature.

طبیعی (*ṭabi'i*) A. natural, normal; physical.

طبیعیات (*ṭabi'iyyāt*) A. physics.

طپانچه (*ṭapāncheh*) T. pistol.

طپیدن (*ṭapidan*) to palpitate.

طرابلس (*ṭarābolos*) A. Tripoli.

طرابوزن (*ṭarābuzan*) A. Trebizond.

طراح (*ṭarrāḥ*) A. draughtsman.

طراوت (*ṭarāvat*) A. freshness.

طرب (*ṭarab*) A. joy, mirth.

طرح (*ṭarḥ*) A. design, sketch, plan, project.

طرخون (*ṭarkhun*) A. tarragon.

طرد (*ṭard*) A. (act of) driving away, banishing.

طرز (*ṭarz*) A. manner, method.

طرف (*ṭaraf*) A. side; end; party; opponent. بطرفِ towards, to. از طرفِ on the part of, by. بر طرف کردن to do away with.

طرفدار (*ṭarafdār*) *a.* partial; partisan.

طرفه (*ṭorfeh*) A. something rare, novelty.

طرفة العین (*ṭarfato'l-'ein*) A. twinkling of the eye.

طرفین (*ṭarafein*) A. the two parties. (*Dual of* طرف.)

طرق (*ṭoroq*) A. ways, roads; means (*Pl. of* طریق.)

طره (*ṭorreh*) A. ringlet.

طریق (*ṭariq*) A. way, road; means.

طریقه (*ṭariqeh*) A. way, road; manner, fashion.

طشت (*ṭasht*) tub, wash-basin.

طعام (*ṭa'ām*) A. food.

طعم (*ṭa'm*) A. taste, flavour.

طعمه (*ṭo'meh*) A. bait; prey.

طعن (*ṭa'n*) A. (act of) taunting.

طعنه (*ṭa'neh*) A. sarcasm, irony.

طعنه آمیز (*ṭa'neh āmiz*) *a.* sarcastic, ironical.

طغرا (*ṭoghrā*) T. royal signature.

طغیان (*ṭoghyān*) A. rebellion; overflowing, flood.

طفره (*ṭafreh*) A. evasion. طفره زدن to evade.

طفل (*ṭefl*) A. child.

طفلانه (*ṭeflāneh*) *a.* childish(ly).

طفولیت (*ṭofuliyyat*) A. childhood, infancy.

طفیل (*ṭofeil*) A. uninvited guest, parasite.

طفیلی (*ṭofeili*) *a.* parasitic, parasite.

طلا (*ṭelā*) gold. طلای سفید platinum.

طلاب (*ṭollāb*) A. (theological) students (*Pl. of* طالب.)

طلاق (*ṭalāq*) A. divorce. طلاق دادن to divorce.

طلایه (*ṭalāyeh*) *a.* vanguard.

طلائی (*ṭelā'i*) (of) gold, golden.

طلب (*ṭalab*) A. demand, request; search; claim.

طلب گار (*ṭalab gār*) *a.* seeking, seeker; creditor.

طلبیدن (*ṭalabidan*) *a.* to seek.

طلسم (*ṭelesm*) A. talisman.

طلعت (*ṭal'at*) A. countenance, mien; *fem. proper name.*

طلوع (*ṭolu'*) A. rising (of the sun).

طماع (*ṭammā'*) A. greedy.

طمع (*ṭama'*) A. covetousness, greed.

طناب (*ṭanāb*) A. rope, cord.

طنجه (*ṭanjeh*) A. Tangiers.

طنز (*ṭanz*) A. ridicule.

طنین (*ṭanin*) A. buzz, tinkling.

طواف (*ṭavāf*) A. circumambulation.

طواف (*ṭavvāf*) A. peddling fruit-seller.

طوائف (*ṭavā'ef*) A. tribes. (*Pl. of* طائفه.)

طور (*ṭour*) A. manner, way. چه طور how? این طور thus; such. بطوری in such a manner, so. بطوریکه as.

طوطی (*ṭuṭi*) parrot.

طوفان (*ṭufān*) A. flood; storm.

طوق (*ṭouq*) A. necklace.

طول (*ṭul*) A. length, longitude. بطول انجامیدن, طول کشیدن to last.

طولانی (*ṭulāni*) A. long.

طومار (*ṭumār*) A. roll, scroll.

طویل (*ṭavil*) A. long.

طویله (*ṭavileh*) A. stable.

طهارت (*ṭahārat*) A. cleanliness, purity.

طهران (*ṭehrān*) Tehran. (*The new spelling is* تهران.)

طی (*ṭei*) A. (act of) traversing. (در) طیِ in the course of.

طیار (*ṭayyār*) A. flying, volatile.

طیاره (*ṭayyāreh*) A. aeroplane.

طیب (*ṭib*) A. sweet smell.

طیب (*ṭayyeb*) A. good, pleasant.

طیبت (*ṭibat*) A. goodness.

طیر (*ṭeir*) A. bird(s).

طیران (*ṭayarān*) A. flight, flying.

طیف (*ṭeif*) A. spectre; spectrum.

طیف بین (*ṭeif bin*) *a.* spectroscope.

طیور (*ṭoyur*) A. birds. (*Pl. of* طیر.)

ظ

ظالم (*z̤ālem*) A. oppressor, tyrant.

ظاهر (*z̤āher*) A. apparent; external; outward appearance.

ظاهراً (*z̤āheran*) A. apparently.

ظاهری (*z̤āheri*) *a.* external, seeming.

ظرافت (*z̤arāfat*) A. elegance.

ظرف (*z̤arf*) A. vessel; space, course; capacity.

ظرفیت (*z̤arfiyyat*) A. capacity, tonnage.

ظروف (*z̤oruf*) A. vessels. (*Pl. of* ظرف.)

ظریف (*z̤arif*) A. elegant, fine; witty.

ظریفه (*z̤arifeh*) A. witty saying.

ظفر (*z̤afar*) A. victory.

ظل (*z̤ell*) A. shadow, shade; protection.

ظلم (*z̤olm*) A. oppression, tyranny.

ظلمت (*z̤olmat*) A. darkness.

ظن (*z̤ann*) A. opinion, suspicion.

ظهر (*z̤ahr*) A. back.

ظهر (*z̤ohr*) A. noon. بعد از ظهر (in the) afternoon.

ظهور (*z̤ohur*) A. appearance.

ع

عابد (*'ābed*) A. worshipper.

عابر (*'āber*) A. passer-by, traveller.

عاج (*'āj*) A. ivory.

عاجز (*'ājez*) A. disabled, cripple.

عاجل (*'ājel*) A. hasty; transitory.

عادت (*'ādat*) A. habit, custom.

عادل (*'ādel*) A. just.

عادلانه (*'ādelaneh*) *a.* just(ly), fair(ly).

عادی (*'ādi*) A. customary, habitual, normal.

عار (*'ār*) A. shame, disgrace.

عارض (*'ārez̤*) A. happening; plaintiff; cheek.

عارضه (*'ārez̤eh*) A. accident.

عارضی (*ārez̤i*) A. accidental, adventitious.

عارف (*'āref*) A. knowing; gnostic, mystic.

عاری (*'āri*) A. devoid, destitute.

عاریت (*'āriat*), عاریه (*'ārieh*) A. loan.

عازم (*'āzem*) A. setting out, starting; resolute.

عاشر (*'āsher*) A. tenth.

عاشراً (*'āsheran*) A. tenthly.

عاشق (*'āsheq*) A. lover.

عاصی (*'āṣi*) A. sinful; rebel(lious).

عاطف (*'āṭef*) A. kind, affectionate.

عاطفه (*'āṭefeh*) A. kindness.

عاطل (*'āṭel*) A. idle, futile.

عافیت (*'āfiat*) A. health, welfare.

عاقبت (*'āqebat*) A. end, conclusion,

consequence; in the end, after all.

عاقد (*'āqed*) A. concluder (*of a contract*); signatory (*of a treaty*).

عاقر (*'āqer*) A. barren, sterile.

عاقل (*'āqel*) A. wise, prudent.

عاقلانه (*'āqelāneh*) *a.* wise(ly), prudent(ly).

عالم (*'ālam*) A. world.

عالم (*'ālem*) A. learned; sage, scientist.

عالمانه (*'ālemāneh*) *a.* learned(ly).

عالمتاب (*'ālamtāb*) *a.* world-illuminating.

عالی (*'āli*) A. high, sublime.

عالی رتبه (*'āli rotbeh*) *a.* high-ranking.

عام (*'āmm*) A. common, vulgar; general, universal.

عامل (*'āmel*) A. agent, factor.

عامه (*'āmmeh*) A. common people.

عاید (*'āyed*) A. returning; being earned.

عایدات (*'āyedāt*) A. income(s), revenue.

عائله (*'ā'eleh*) A. family.

عبا (*'abā*) A. cloak.

عبادت (*'ebādat*) A. worship.

عبارت (*'ebārat*) A. phrase, style. عبارت — از بودن to consist of —, to be —.

عبث (*'abaṣ*) A. vain, futile; in vain.

عبد (*'abd*) A. servant, slave (of God).

عبد الله (*'abdo'llāh*) A. *masc. proper name.*

عبرت (*'ebrat*) A. warning, example.

عبری (*'ebri*) A. Hebrew.

عبودیت (*'obudiyyat*) A. servitude, slavery.

عبور (*'obur*) A. passage, crossing, transit. عبور کردن to cross.

عبوس (*'abus*) A. stern, austere.

عبیر (*'abir*) A. ambergris.

عتاب (*'etāb*) A. reproof.

عتبه (*'atabeh*) A. threshold. عتباتِ عالیات the holy shrines at Baghdad, Kerbela, and Najaf.

عتیق (*'atiq*) A. ancient.

عتیقه (*'atiqeh*) A. antiquity.

عثمانی (*'oṣmāni*) A. Ottoman; Turkey.

عجالةً (*'ejālatan*) A. for the time being.

عجائب (*'ajā'eb*) A. wonders.

عجب (*'ajab*) A. wonder, astonishment.

عجز (*'ajz*) A. weakness, inability.

عجله (*'ajaleh*) A. haste.

عجم (*'ajam*) A. non-Arab(s), Persian(s); Persia.

عجمی (*'ajami*) A. Persian.

عجوز (*'ajuz*), عجوزه (*'ajuzeh*) A. old woman.

عجیب (*'ajib*) A. strange, wonderful.

عدالت (*'adālat*) A. justice.

عداوت (*'adāvat*) A. enmity.

عدد (*'adad*) A. number.

عدس (*'adas*) A. lentil.

عدل (*'adl*) A. justice; bale.

عدم (*'adam*) A. non-existence, want, lack. عدمِ موافقت disagreement.

عدن (*'adan*) A. Aden.

عدن (*'adn*) A. Eden.

عدو (*'adovv*) A. enemy.

عدوان (*'odvān*) A. enmity.

عدول (*'odul*) A. deviation.

عده (*'eddeh*) A. number.

عدید (*'adid*) A. numerous.

عدیل (*'adil*) A. equal, equivalent.

عدیم (*'adim*) A. non-existent; destitute.

عذاب (*'azāb*) A. torment, punishment.

عذر (*'ozr*) A. excuse, apology. عذر خواستن to apologize.

عذر خواهی (*'ozr khvāhi*) *a.* apology.

عذوبت (*'ozubat*) A. sweetness.

عرابه (*'arrābeh*) T. cart.

عراده (*'arrādeh*) A. ballista; one piece (*of cannon*); gun carriage.

عراق (*'erāq*) A. Iraq.

عرایض (*'arāyez*) A. petitions, letters. (*Pl. of* عریضه.)

عرب (*'arab*) A. Arab(s).

عربده (*'arbadeh*) A. (drunken) brawl.

عربستان (*'arabestān*) *a.* Arabia.

عربی (*'arabi*) A. Arab(ic).

عرش (*'arsh*) A. throne.

عرصه (*'arṣeh*) A. court, area, space.

عرض (*'arẓ*) A. presentation, exposition; petition; width, latitude. عرض کردن to say, state (*in polite parlance*); to show, represent.

عرض (*'erẓ*) A. reputation.

عرضحال (*'arẓeḥāl*) *a.* petition.

عرعر (*'ar'ar*) A. braying (of an ass).

عرف (*'orf*) A. common law.

عرفاً (*'orfan*) A. according to common law.

عرفان (*'erfān*) A. knowledge; gnosticism.

عرفی (*'orfi*) A. common, civil.

عرق (*'araq*) A. sweat; arrack.

عرق (*'erq*) A. vein; root.

عروس (*'arus*) A. bride.

عروسک (*'arusak*) *a.* doll.

عروسی (*'arusi*) *a.* marriage, wedding.

عروض (*'aruẓ*) A. prosody.

عروق (*'oruq*) A. veins. (*Pl. of* عرق.)

عریان (*'oryān*) A. naked.

عریض (*'ariẓ*) A. wide, broad.

عریضه (*'ariẓeh*) A. petition, letter.

عز (*'ezz*) A. glory, honour.

عزا (*'azā*) A. mourning.

عزادار (*'azādār*) *a.* in mourning; mourner.

عزب (*'azab*) A. bachelor.

عزت (*'ezzat*) A. honour, respect; grandeur.

عزل (*'azl*) A. dismissal.

عزلت (*'ozlat*) A. retirement.

عزم (*'azm*) A. resolution, intention.

عزوبت (*'ozubat*) A. celibacy.

عزیز (*'aziz*) A. great; dear.

عزیمت (*'azimat*) A. (act of) starting. عزیمت کردن to start.

عساکر (*'asāker*) A. armies. (*Pl. of* عسکر.)

عسرت (*'osrat*) A. difficulty, hardship.

عسس (*'asas*) A. night-watch.

عسکر (*'askar*) A. army.

عسل (*'asal*) A. honey.

عشاق (*'oshshāq*) A. lovers. (*Pl. of* عاشق.)

عشائر (*'ashā'er*) A. tribes. (*Pl. of* عشیره.)

عشر (*'ashar*), عشره (*'ashareh*) A. ten.

عشر (*'oshr*) A. tenth; tithe.

عشرات (*'asharāt*) A. tens.

عشرت (*'eshrat*) A. pleasure, enjoyment.

عشق (*'eshq*) A. love.

عشوه (*'eshveh*) A. coquetry.

عشیره (*'ashireh*) A. tribe.

عصا (*'aṣā*) A. staff.

عصار (*'aṣṣār*) A. oil-presser.

عصاره (*'oṣāreh*) A. juice.

عصب (*'aṣab*) A. nerve.

عصبانی (*'aṣabāni*) *a.* nervous; angry.

عصبی (*'aṣabi*) A. nervous.

عصبیت (*'aṣabiyyat*) A. bigotry, prejudice; racial feeling.

عصر (*'aṣr*) A. afternoon, evening; age, epoch.

عصمت (*'eṣmat*) A. chastity; *fem. proper name.*

عصیان (*'eṣyān*) A. sin; rebellion.

عضد (*'aẓod*) A. forearm.

عضله (*'aẓoleh*) A. muscle.

عضو (*'oẓv*) A. limb; member.

عضویت (*'oẓviyyat*) A. membership.

عطا (*'aṭā*) A. gift. عطا فرمودن to bestow.

عطار (*'aṭṭār*) A. druggist; grocer.

عطارد (*'oṭāred*) A. Mercury.

عطر (*'eṭr*) A. perfume.

عطسه (*'aṭseh*) A. sneeze.

عطش (*'aṭash*) A. thirst.

عطف (*'atf*) A. inclination; connection.

عطوفت (*'oṭufat*) A. affection.

عطیه (*'atiyyeh*) A. gift.

عظم (*'aẓm*) A. bone.

عظمت (*'aẓamat*) A. greatness.

عظمی (*'ozmā*) A. greater, greatest. (*Fem. of* اعظم.)

عظیم (*'aẓim*) A. great.

عفت (*'effat*) A. chastity; *fem. proper name.*

عفو (*'afv*) A. pardon, forgiveness. عفو کردن to pardon, forgive.

عفونت (*'ofunat*) A. stench; putrefaction; infection.

عفونی (*'ofuni*) *a.* infected. ضدِ عفونی کردن to disinfect.

عفیف (*'afif*) A. chaste.

عقاب (*'eqāb*) A. punishment.

عقاب (*'oqāb*) A. eagle.

عقائد (*'aqā'ed*) A. beliefs, opinions. (*Pl. of* عقیده)

عقب (*'aqab*) A. heel; rear. عقبِ behind. عقب نشستن to retreat.

عقب نشینی (*'aqab neshini*) *a.* retreat.

عقد (*'aqd*) A. conclusion; marriage contract and ceremony. عقد کردن to marry.

عقد (*'eqd*) A. necklace.

عقده (*'oqdeh*) A. knot; problem.

عقرب (*'aqrab*) A. scorpion; Scorpio.

عقربک (*'aqrabak*) *a.* hand (*of a clock*).

عقل (*'aql*) A. intellect, reason; wisdom.

عقلاً (*'aqlan*) A. reasonably, logically.

عقلی (*'aqli*) A. intellectual ; reasonable, logical ; judicious.

عقوبت (*'oqubat*) A. punishment, torment.

عقیده (*'aqideh*) A. belief, opinion.

عقیق (*'aqiq*) A. cornelian, agate.

عقیم (*'aqim*) A. barren.

عکا (*'akkā*) A. Acre.

عکاس (*'akkās*) A. photographer.

عکاسی (*'akkāsi*) *a.* photography.

عکس (*'aks*) A. reflection ; reverse ; photograph.

عکس العمل (*'akso'l-'amal*) A. reaction.

علاج (*'elāj*) A. remedy, cure.

علاج پذیر (*'elāj pazir*) *a.* remediable, curable.

علاقه (*'alāqeh*) A. attachment, connection ; interest, concern.

علاقه مند (*'alāqeh mand*) *a.* interested, concerned.

علامت (*'alāmat*) A. sign, signal, symptom.

علامه (*'allāmeh*) A. very learned person.

علاوه (*'elāveh*) A. addition. علاوه کردن to add. بعلاوه moreover. علاوه بر in addition to.

علائق (*'alā'eq*) A. connections, interests. (*Pl. of* علاقه.)

علائم (*'alā'em*) A. signs, symptoms. (*Pl. of* علامت.)

علت (*'ellat*) A. cause, reason ; disease. بعلتِ because of.

علف (*'alaf*) A. grass, fodder.

علف زار (*'alaf zār*) *a.* pasture.

علل (*'elal*) A. causes, reasons ; diseases. (*Pl. of* علت.)

علم (*'alam*) A. standard, banner.

علم (*'elm*) A. knowledge, science.

علما (*'olamā*) A. learned men, scientists. (*Pl. of* عالم.)

علم الحیات (*'elmo'l-ḥayāt*) A. biology.

علمی (*'elmi*) *a.* scientific ; theoretical.

علناً (*'alanan*) A. openly.

علنی (*'alani*) A. open, public.

علو (*'olovv*) A. height, elevation.

علوفه (*'olufeh*) A. forage.

علوم (*'olum*) A. sciences. (*Pl. of* عِلم.)

علی (*'ali*) A. *masc. proper name.*

علیا (*'olyā*) A. higher, highest. (*Fem. of* اعلی.)

علیا حضرت (*'olyā ḥaẓrat*) *a.* Her Majesty.

علی الحساب (*'ala'l-ḥesāb*) A. on account.

علی الخصوص (*'ala'l-khoṣuṣ*) A. especially.

علیحده (*'alāḥedeh*) A. separate(ly).

علیل (*'alil*) A. sick, infirm.

علیم (*'alim*) A. learned, wise.

عماد (*'emād*) A. column, pillar.

عمارت (*'emārat*) A. building.

عماری (*'amāri*) *a.* litter.

عمال (*'ommāl*) A. agents, factors. (*Pl. of* عامل.)

عمامه (*'amāmeh*) A. turban.

عمان (*'ammān*) A. Amman.

عمان (*'ommān*) A. Oman.

عمد (*'amd*) A. intention, purpose.

عمداً (*'amdan*) A. intentionally.

عمده (*'omdeh*) A. main, chief.

عمدی (*'amdi*) *a.* intentional, deliberate.

عمر (*'omr*) A. life.

عمر (*'omar*) A. *masc. proper name.*

عمران (*'omrān*) A. prosperity, populousness; reconstruction.

عمق (*'omq*) A. depth.

عمقی (*'omqi*) *a.* deep, profound.

عمل (*'amal*) A. deed, action, operation. بعمل آوردن to carry out. بعمل آمدن to be carried out; to be produced, grown. عمل آوردن to produce, to raise.

عملاً (*'amalan*) A. in practice.

عمله (*'amaleh*) A. labourers, workmen. (*Also used as sing.*)

عملی (*'amali*) A. practical.

عملیات (*'amaliyyāt*) A. activities, operations. (*Used as pl. of* عمل.)

عمو (*'amu*) A. paternal uncle.

عمود (*'amud*) A. column, pillar; perpendicular line.

عمودی (*'amudi*) A. vertical, perpendicular.

عمو زاده (*'amu zādeh*) *a.* cousin.

عموم (*'omum*) A. public.

عموماً (*'omuman*) A. generally; publicly.

عمومی (*'omumi*) *a.* general, public.

عمه (*'ammeh*) A. paternal aunt.

عمیق (*'amiq*) A. deep.

عناب (*'onnāb*) A. jujube.

عناد (*'enād*) A. obstinacy; rebellion.

عناصر (*'anāṣer*) A. elements. (*Pl. of* عنصر.)

عنان (*'enān*) A. rein(s), bridle.

عناوین (*'anāvin*) A. addresses; titles; pretexts. (*Pl. of* عنوان.)

عنایت (*'enāyat*) A. favour.

عنبر (*'anbar*) A. ambergris.

عندلیب (*'andalib*) A. nightingale.

عنصر (*'onṣor*) A. element.

عنف (*'onf*) A. violence.

عنفوان (*'onfovān*) A. flower (of youth).

عنقا (*'anqā*) A. *name of a fabulous bird.*

عنقریب (*'anqarib*) A. presently, shortly.

عنکبوت (*'ankabut*) A. spider.

عنوان (*'onvān*) A. address; title; preface; plea, excuse.

عنود (*'anud*) A. obstinate, rebellious.

عنیف (*'anif*) A. severe, violent; hideous.

عنین (*'ennin*) A. impotent.

عواقب (*'avāqeb*) A. consequences. (*Pl. of* عاقبت).

عوام (*'avāmm*) A. common people. مجلسِ عوام House of Commons.

عوام الناس (*'avāmmo'n-nās*) A. common people, rabble.

عوامل (*'avāmel*) A. agents, factors. (*Pl. of* عامل.)

عوائد (*'avā'ed*) A. incomes, revenue(s).

عوج (*'avaj*) A. crookedness.

عود (*'ud*) A. aloes-wood; lute.

عود (*'oud*) A., عودت (*'oudat*) A. return(ing).

عورت (*'ourat*) A. privy parts; woman.

عوض (*'avaẓ*) A. substitute. عوض کردن to change, exchange. بعوضِ instead of.

عون (*'oun*) A. help.

عهد (*'ahd*) A. promise; covenant, treaty; age. عهد کردن to promise.

عهد نامه (*'ahd nāmeh*) *a.* treaty.

عهده (*'ohdeh*) A. charge, responsibility. از عهدهٔ — بر آمدن to quit oneself of —, to succeed in —. بر عهده گرفتن to undertake.

عهده دار (*'ohdeh dār*) *a.* engaged, charged. عهده دار شدن to undertake.

عیادت (*'iādat*) A. visit (to a sick person).

عیاذاً بالله (*'iāzan bellāh*) A. God forbid!

عیار (*'iār*) A. alloy, assay.

عیار (*'ayyār*) A. cheat, profligate.

عیاش (*'ayyāsh*) A. pleasure-seeker, voluptuary.

عیال (*'ayāl*) A. wife; family.

عیان (*'ayān*) A. evident, manifest.

عیب (*'eib*) A. fault, blemish. عیب ندارد it does not matter.

عیبجوئی (*'eibju'i*) *a.* fault-finding, criticism.

عید (*'eid*) A. festival.

عیدی (*'eidi*) *a.* New Year gift.

عیسوی (*'isavi*) A. Christian.

عیسی (*'isā*) A. Jesus.

عیش (*'eish*) A. pleasure.

عین (*'ein*) A. eye; source, fountain; the thing itself, essence.

عیناً (*'einan*) A. exactly, literally, word for word.

عینک (*'einak*) *a.* spectacles, glasses.

عیوب (*'oyub*) A. faults, defects. (*Pl. of* عیب.)

غ

غار (*ghār*) A. cave.

غارت (*ghārat*) A. plunder. غارت کردن to plunder.

غارتگر (*ghāratgar*) *a.* looter.

غاز (*ghāz*) T. goose.

غازی (*ghāzi*) A. warrior (fighting against the infidel).

غافل (*ghāfel*) A. negligent, unaware.

غالب (*ghāleb*) A. prevailing, conquering; conqueror; most.

غالباً (*ghāleban*) A. mostly, very often.

غالیه (*ghālieh*) A. *name of a perfume composed of musk, ambergris, etc.*

غامض (*ghāmeẓ*) A. obscure, abstruse.

غايب (*ghāyeb*) A. absent.

غايت (*ghāyat*) A. extremity. بغايت extremely.

غائله (*ghā'eleh*) A. anxiety; quarrel.

غبار (*ghobār*) A. dust.

غبغب (*ghabghab*) A. double chin.

غبن (*ghabn*) A. fraud.

غدار (*ghaddār*) A. treacherous, traitor.

غدد (*ghodad*) A. glands. (*Pl. of* غده.)

غدر (*ghadr*) A. treachery.

غده (*ghoddeh*) A. gland.

غدير (*ghadir*) A. pool, pond.

غذا (*gheẕā*) A. food.

غر (*ghor*) murmur. غر زدن to murmur.

غراب (*ghorāb*) A. raven, crow; corvette.

غرابت (*gharābat*) A. strangeness.

غرامت (*gharāmat*) A. indemnification, reparation.

غرائب (*gharā'eb*) A. wonders.

غرب (*gharb*) A. west.

غرباً (*gharban*) A. to the west.

غربال (*gharbāl*) A. sieve.

غربت (*ghorbat*) A. foreign travel, exile.

غربى (*gharbi*) A. western.

غرس (*ghars*) A. (act of) planting.

غرش (*ghorresh*) roar.

غرض (*gharaẓ*) A. motive; self-interest; spite.

غرغره (*ghargharah*) A. gargle, gargling.

غرفه (*ghorfeh*) A. balcony; booth, stall.

غرق (*gharq*) A. (state of) drowning, sinking. غرق شدن to drown (*intr.*).

غرقه (*gharqeh*) *a.* drowned, submerged.

غرم (*ghorm*) mountain sheep.

غروب (*ghorub*) A. sunset; evening.

غرور (*ghorur*) A. pride.

غره (*gharreh*) deluded; proud.

غره (*ghorreh*) A. first day (*of a lunar month*).

غريب (*gharib*) A. strange(r).

غريدن (*ghorridan*) to roar.

غريزه (*gharizeh*) A. instinct.

غريق (*ghariq*) A. drowned, immersed.

غريو (*ghariv*) clamour.

غزال (*ghazāl*) A. gazelle.

غزل (*ghazal*) A. lyrical poem.

غزلاغ (*ghazlāgh*) lark.

غزوه (*ghazveh*) A. war (against the infidel).

غسال (*ghassāl*) A. washer of the dead.

غسل (*ghosl*) A. ceremonial washing.

غش (*ghash*) *a.* faint(ing), fit.

غش (*gheshsh*) A. fraud, guile.

غشا (*gheshā*) A. membrane.

غصب (*ghaṣb*) A. usurpation, extortion. غصب كردن to usurp, to extort.

غصن (*ghoṣn*) A. branch.

غصه (*ghoṣṣeh*) A. grief. غصه خوردن to be grieved.

غضب (*ghaẓab*) A. anger.

غضبناك (*ghaẓabnāk*) *a.* angry.

غضروف (*ghoẓruf*) A. cartilage.

غفار (*ghaffār*) A. (God) the Forgiver.

غفران (*ghafrān*) A. forgiveness.

غفلت (*ghaflat*) A. neglect, negligence.

غفلةً (*ghaflatan*) A. unexpectedly.

غل (*ghel*) roll(ing).

غل (*ghell*) A. fraud, guile.

غلا (*ghalā*) A. dearth.

غلاف (*ghelāf*) A. sheath.

غلام (*gholām*) A. slave, servant.

غلبه (*ghalabeh*) A. predominance; victory.

غلط (*ghalat*) A. mistake, error; false, wrong.

غلطـاندن (*ghalṭāndan*), غلطـانيدن (*ghalṭānidan*) to roll (*tr.*).

غلطيدن (*ghalṭidan*) to roll (*intr.*).

غلغل (*gholghol*) gurgle.

غلغله (*gholgholeh*) *a.* tumult, uproar.

غلو (*gholovv*) A. hyperbole, excess.

غله (*ghalleh*) A. corn, grain.

غليان (*ghalayān*) A. boiling, ebullition; tumult.

غليان (*ghalyān*) hookah.

غليظ (*ghaliẓ*) A. thick; coarse.

غم (*ghamm*) A. grief, anxiety.

غمز (*ghamz*) A. wink(ing); talebearing.

غمزه (*ghamzeh*) A. ogling, coquetry.

غمض (*ghamẓ*) A. connivance.

غمگسار (*ghammgosār*) *a.* sympathetic, sympathizer.

غمگين (*ghammgin*) *a.* sad.

غنا (*ghanā*) A. freedom from want; riches.

غنا (*ghenā*) A. singing; song.

غنائم (*ghanā'em*) A. spoils. (*Pl. of* غنيمت.)

غنچه (*ghoncheh*) bud.

غنودن (*ghonudan*) to sleep, to rest.

غنى (*ghani*) A. rich.

غنيمت (*ghanimat*) A. booty, spoil. غنيمت شمردن to avail oneself of.

غواص (*ghavvāṣ*) A. diver.

غوچ (*ghuch*) T. ram.

غور (*ghour*) A. bottom, depth(s). غور كردن to study profoundly.

غور رسى (*ghour rasi*) *a.* deep research.

غوره (*ghureh*) unripe grape.

غوص (*ghouṣ*) A. (act of) diving.

غوطه (*ghuṭeh*) A. (act of) plunging, diving. غوطه خوردن to plunge, dive.

غوغا (*ghoughā*) A. uproar, riot; quarrel.

غوك (*ghuk*) frog.

غول (*ghul*) A. ogre, ghoul.

غياب (*ghiāb*) A. absence.

غيب (*gheib*) A. the invisible, hidden.

غيبت (*gheibat*) A. backbiting; absence.

غير (*gheir*) A. other, different. غير از except. غيرِ other than, non-.

غيرت (*gheirat*) A. zeal; jealousy.

غيظ (*gheiẓ*) A. anger.

غيور (*ghayur*) A. jealous, zealous.

ف

فاتح (*fāteḥ*) A. victor.

فاتحه (*fāteḥeh*) A. *name of the opening chapter of the Koran.* فاتحه خواندن to read the *fāteḥeh, i.e.* to pray for the dead.

فاجر (*fājer*) A. libertine; adulterer.

فاجع (*fāje'*) A. calamitous, tragic.

فاجعه (*fāje'eh*) A. calamity, catastrophe, tragedy.

فاحش (*fāḥesh*) A. obscene; gross, excessive.

فاحشه (*fāḥesheh*) A. prostitute.

فاخته (*fākhteh*) ringdove.

فاخر (*fākher*) A. fine, rich, sumptuous.

فارس (*fārs*) (province of) Fars.

فارسی (*fārsi*) (native) of Fars; Persian (language)

فارغ (*fāregh*) A. having finished, free, quit.

فارغ التحصيل (*fāregho't-taḥṣil*) A. graduate.

فاسد (*fāsed*) A. corrupt; decayed, rotten.

فاسق (*fāseq*) A. libertine; adulterer.

فاش (*fāsh*) manifest, open.

فاشيست (*fāshist*) F. Fascist.

فاصله (*fāṣeleh*) A. distance, interval, space.

فاضل (*fāẓel*) A. learned (man).

فاطمه (*fāṭemeh*) A. *fem. proper name.*

فاعل (*fā'el*) A. (*in grammar*) agent.

فاقد (*fāqed*) A. lacking.

فاقه (*fāqeh*) A. poverty.

فاكولته (*fākulteh*) F. faculty.

فال (*fāl*) A. omen.

فالگير (*fālgir*) *a.* fortune-teller.

فام (*fām*) colour.

فاميل (*fāmil*) F. family.

فانوس (*fānus*) A. lantern.

فانی (*fāni*) A. transitory, transient.

فايده (*fāyedeh*) A. profit, advantage, use.

فايده مند (*fāyedeh mand*) *a.* profitable, useful.

فائز (*fā'ez*) A. attaining.

فائض (*fā'eẓ*) A. abundant; liberal.

فائق (*fā'eq*) A. excellent, superior.

فبها (*fabehā*) A. well and good.

فتان (*fattān*) A. charming, fascinating.

فتح (*fatḥ*) A. victory.

فتراك (*fetrāk*) saddle-strap.

فترت (*fatrat*) A. interval.

فتق (*fatq*) A. (act of) tearing, rending; hernia, rupture.

فتنه (*fetneh*) A. sedition, riot; plot, intrigue.

فتوت (*fotovvat*) A. generosity, manliness, chivalry.

فتوح (*fotuḥ*) A. victories. (*Pl. of* فتح.)

فتور (*fotur*) A. languor.

فتوی (*fatvā*) A. judicial decree.

فتيله (*fatileh*) A. wick, fuse.

فجأه (*foj'eh*) A. unforeseen accident ; death by apoplexy.

فجر (*fajr*) A. dawn.

فجور (*fojur*) A. debauchery.

فجیعه (*faji'eh*) A. misfortune ; obscene, atrocious act.

فحاش (*faḥḥāsh*) A. scurrilous, obscene.

فحش (*foḥsh*) A. abusive language.

فحشا (*faḥshā*) A. fornication.

فحوی (*faḥvā*) A. tenor, purport.

فخامت (*fakhāmat*) A. greatness, dignity.

فخر (*fakhr*) A. glory, honour, pride.

فخیم (*fakhim*) A. great, dignified.

فدا (*fedā*) A. ransom ; sacrifice.

فدا کار, (*fedā kār*) *a*. self-sacrificing, devoted.

فدا کاری (*fedā kāri*) *a*. self-sacrifice, devotion.

فدائی (*fedā'i*) *a*. devoted, self-sacrificing ; devotee.

فدراسیون (*federāsyun*) F. federation.

فدرال (*federāl*) F. federal.

فدیه (*fedyeh*) A. ransom.

فر (1) (*farr*) splendour, pomp.

فر (2) (*farr*) A. flight.

فرا (*farā*) forward, onwards.

فرات (*forāt*) A. Euphrates.

فراخ (*farākh*) wide, broad ; ample.

فرا خواندن (*farā khvāndan*) to summon, re-call.

فراخور (*farākhor*) fit, worthy.

فرار (*ferār*) A. flight ; desertion. فرار کردن to flee ; to desert.

فراری (*ferāri*) *a*. fugitive. فراری شدن to flee. فراری کردن to put to flight.

فراز (*farāz*) up, above ; top, summit.

فراست (*ferāsat*) A. sagacity ; physiognomy.

فراش (*ferāsh*) A. mattress, bed.

فراش (*farrāsh*) A. footman ; tent-pitcher.

فراغت (*farāghat*) A. leisure, rest, ease.

فراق (*ferāq*) A. separation.

فراکسیون (*frāksion*) F. party (*in the National Assembly*).

فرا گرفتن (*farā gereftan*) to envelop, cover.

فراموش (*farāmush*) forgotten. فراموش کردن to forget.

فراموش کار (*farāmush kār*) forgetful.

فراموشی (*farāmushi*) forgetfulness.

فرانسوی (*farānsavi*) A. French.

فرانسه (*farānseh*) A. France ; French.

فرانک (*frānk*) F. franc.

فراوان (*ferāvān*) abundant, plentiful.

فراوانی (*farāvāni*) plenty, abundance.

فراهم (*farāham*) collected, gathered ; together. فراهم کردن to bring about ; to secure ; to collect.

فرائض (*farā'eẓ*) A. precepts. (*Pl. of* فریضه.)

فربه (*farbeh*) fat. (*The* h *is pronounced.*)

فربهی (*farbehi*) fatness.

فرج (*farj*) A. vulva.

فرجام (*farjām*) end, conclusion.

فرح (*faraḥ*) A. joy, exhilaration.

فرخنده (*farkhondeh*) happy, prosperous ; *fem. proper name.*

فرد (*fard*) A. individual, unit; verse.

فردا (*fardā*) to-morrow.

فردوس (*ferdous*) A. garden, paradise.

فرزان (*farzān*) learning; learned.

فرزانه (*farzāneh*) wise.

فرزند (*farzand*) child, son.

فرزین (*farzin*) queen (*in chess*).

فرس (*fors*) A. Persia(n).

فرستادن (*ferestādan*) to send.

فرستاده (*ferestādeh*) envoy; export.

فرستنده (*ferestandeh*) sender; transmitter.

فرسخ (*farsakh*) A., فرسنگ (*farsang*) parasang.

فرسودن (*farsudan*) to wear, rub, obliterate.

فرش (*farsh*) A. carpet.

فرشته (*fereshteh*) angel.

فرصت (*forṣat*) A. opportunity.

فرض (*farẓ*) A. supposition; duty, obligation.

فرضاً (*farẓan*) A. supposing.

فرط (*farṭ*) A. excess.

فرع (*far'*) A. branch, subdivision, derivative, secondary matter; interest (*on a loan*).

فرعون (*fer'oun*) A. Pharaoh.

فرعی *far'i* A. secondary, subsidiary.

فرفره (*ferfereh*) top (*toy*).

فرق (*farq*) A. difference.

فرقان (*forqān*) A. *name of the Koran.*

فرقه (*ferqeh*) A. sect, party.

فرکندن (*farkandan*) to dig, to tear up.

فرمان (*farmān*) command, order.

فرمان بردار (*farmān bardār*) obedient.

فرمان برداری (*farmān bardāri*) obedience.

فرماندار (*farmāndār*) district governor.

فرمانداری (*farmāndāri*) office of district governor.

فرمانده (*farmāndeh*) commander.

فرماندهی (*farmāndehi*) (high) command.

فرمان روا (*farmān ravā*) ruling, ruler.

فرمان روائی (*farmān ravā'i*) rule.

فرمان روائی کردن to rule.

فرمایش (*farmāyesh*) order, command.

فرمودن (*farmudan*) to command; *polite substitute for* کردن *and* گفتن.

فرنگ (*ferang*) Frank, European.

فرنگستان (*ferangestān*) Europe.

فرنگی (*ferangi*) European.

فرو (*foru*) down.

فرو بردن (*foru bordan*) to swallow; to dip.

فرو تن (*foru tan*) humble.

فرو تنی (*foru tani*) humility.

فروختن (1) (*forukhtan*) to sell.

فروختن (2) (*forukhtan*) to kindle, light.

فرود (*forud*) down, below.

فرودگاه (*forudgāh*) aerodrome, airfield.

فروردین (*farvardin*) *name of the first month of the Persian year.*

فرو رفتن (*foru raftan*) to go down, sink.

فروش (1) (*forush*) sale. بفروش رساندن to sell.

فروش (2) (*forush*) A. carpets. (*Pl. of* فرش.)

فروشنده (*forushandeh*) seller.

فروع (*foru'*) A. branches, divisions. (*Pl. of* فرع.)

فروغ (*forugh*) brightness.

فرو گذار (*foru gozār*) negligent; negligence.

فرو مانده (*foru māndeh*) weary, helpless.

فرو مایه (*foru māyeh*) vile, ignoble.

فروند (*farvand*) *word used in numbering ships.*

فروهر (*foruhar*) essence.

فرهنگ (*farhang*) learning, education, culture; dictionary.

فرهنگستان (*farhangestān*) academy; encyclopædia.

فرهنگی (*farhangi*) educational, cultural.

فریاد (*faryād*) cry, shout; lamentation.

فریب (*ferib*) deceit.

فرید (*farid*) A. single; unique.

فریدون (*faridun*) *name of a mythical king of Persia; masc. proper name.*

فریضه (*farīzeh*) A. religious duty.

فریفتن (*feriftan*) to deceive; to seduce.

فزودن (*fozudan*) to increase.

فزون (*fozun*) more, greater.

فزونی (*fozuni*) surplus, excess.

فساد (*fasād*) A. corruption; putridity; sedition.

فسخ (*faskh*) A. annulment, cancellation.

فسق (*fesq*) A. debauchery, fornication.

فشار (*feshār*) pressure.

فشاردن (*feshārdan*) to press, squeeze.

فشاندن (*feshāndan*) to scatter.

فشردن (*feshordan*) to press, squeeze.

فشنگ (*feshang*) T. cartridge.

فصاحت (*faṣāḥat*) A. eloquence.

فصاد (*faṣṣād*) A. phlebotomist.

فصح (*feṣḥ*) A. Passover; Easter.

فصد (*faṣd*) A. phlebotomy.

فصل (*faṣl*) A. section, chapter; season; settling, deciding.

فصیح (*faṣiḥ*) A. eloquent.

فضا (*faẓā*) A. space.

فضائل (*faẓā'el*) A. virtues. (*Pl. of* فضیلت.)

فضل (*faẓl*) A. grace, favour; excellence; learning.

فضول (*foẓul*) A. busybody.

فضولات (*foẓulāt*) A. refuse; offal; excrement.

فضولی (*foẓuli*) *a.* officiousness.

فضیح (*faẓiḥ*) A. disgraceful, shameful.

فضیحت (*faẓiḥat*) A. shameful act; disgrace.

فضیلت (*faẓilat*) A. excellence, virtue.

فطانت (*faṭānat*) A. intelligence; sagacity.

فطر (*feṭr*) A. (act of) breaking a fast.

فطرت (*feṭrat*) A. nature, temperament.

فطری (*feṭri*) A. natural.

فطیر (*faṭir*) A. unleavened (bread).

فعال (*fa''āl*) A. active.

فعالیت (*fa''āliyyat*) A. activity.

فعل (*fe'l*) A. deed, action; verb.

فعلاً (*fe'lan*) A. at present.

فعله (*fa'aleh*) A. labourer(s). (*Pl. of* فاعل.)

فعلی (*fe'li*) A. present.

فغان (*feghān*) cry, lament.

فغفور (*faghfur*) Chinese Emperor; Chinese porcelain.

فقار (*faqār*) A. vertebræ. (*Pl. of* فقره.)

فقدان (*feqdān*) A. absence, lack, privation, bereavement.

فقر (*faqr*) A. poverty.

فقرا (*foqarā*) A. the poor. (*Pl. of* فقیر.)

فقرالدم (*faqro'd-dam*) A. anæmia.

فقره (*faqareh*) A. vertebra; paragraph; item; penis.

فقط (*faqat*) A. only.

فقه (*feqh*) A. (religious) jurisprudence.

فقید (*faqid*) A. lost, absent.

فقیر (*faqir*) A. poor; fakir, dervish.

فقیه (*faqih*) A. lawyer, jurisconsult.

فک (*fakk*) A. jaw.

فکاهت (*fokāhat*) A. joke.

فکاهی (*fokāhi*) A. humorous.

فکر (*fekr*) A. thought, idea. فکر کردن to think.

فکور (*fakur*) A. deep-thinking.

فلات (*falāt*) A. desert; plateau.

فلاح (*fallāḥ*) A. agriculturalist.

فلاحت (*falāḥat*) A. agriculture.

فلاخن (*falākhon*) sling.

فلاکت (*falākat*) *a.* adversity.

فلان (*folān*) A. such-and-such, so-and-so.

فلج (*falj*) A. paralysis.

فلرانس (*florāns*) F. Florence.

فلز (*felezz*) A. metal.

فلزی (*felezzi*) *a.* metallic.

فلس (*fels*) A. scale (of fish); small coin.

فلسطین (*falasṭin*) A. Palestine.

فلسفه (*falsafeh*) A. philosophy.

فلفل (*felfel*) A. pepper.

فلق (*falaq*) A. dawn.

فلک (1) (*falak*) A. sky, heavens; fortune, destiny.

فلک (2) (*falak*) *name of a wooden instrument with which an offender's feet are held in position for giving him the bastinado;* bastinado.

فلوس (*folus*) A. scales; small coins. (*Pl. of* فلس.)

فم (*fam*) A. mouth.

فن (*fann*) A. art; knack, trick.

فنا (*fanā*) A. destruction, annihilation; nirvana.

فنار (*fanār*) A. lighthouse.

فنجان (*fenjān*) *a.* cup.

فندق (*fondoq*) hazel-nut, filbert.

فندک (*fandak*) tinder-box, lighter.

فنر (*fanar*) (mechanical) spring.

فنلاند (*fanlānd*) F. Finland.

فنی (*fanni*) A. technical.

فواحش (*favāḥesh*) A. prostitutes. (*Pl. of* فاحشه.)

فواره (*favvāreh*) A. jet, spout.

فواصل (*favāṣel*) A. spaces, intervals. (*Pl. of* فاصله.)
فوائد (*favā'ed*) A. advantages, profits. (*Pl. of* فائده.)
فوت (*fout*) A. death.
فوتبال (*futbāl*) F. football.
فوتبالیست (*futbālist*) F. footballer.
فوج (*fouj*) A. regiment.
فور (*four*) A. haste.
فوراً (*fouran*) A. immediately.
فورمول (*formul*) F. formula.
فوری (*fouri*) A. immediate.
فوریت (*fouriyyat*) A. urgency.
فوریه (*fevrieh*) F. February.
فوز (*fouz*) A. victory.
فوفل (*fufel*) A. betel-nut.
فوق (*fouq*) A. upper part. فوقِ above, beyond.
فوق الذکر (*fouqo'z-zekr*) A. above-mentioned.
فوق العاده (*fouqo'l-'ādeh*) A. extra-ordinary.
فوقانی (*fouqāni*) A. upper.
فولاد (*fulād*) steel.
فولادی (*fulādi*) pertaining to steel.
فهرست (*fehrest*) A. list.
فهم (*fahm*) A. understanding.
فهمانیدن (*fahmānidan*) *a.* to give to understand.
فهمیدن (*fahmidan*) *a.* to understand.
فیاض (*fayyāẓ*) A. abundant; generous.
فی الجمله (*fe'l-jomleh*) A. in short.
فی الفور (*fe'l-four*) A. at once.
فیروز (*firuz*) victorious.
فیروزه (*firuzeh*) turquoise.
فیروزی (*firuzi*) victory.
فیزیک (*fizik*) F. physics.
فیش (*fish*) F. indexing card.
فیصل (*feiṣal*) A. arbitration (decision).
فیض (*feiẓ*) A. grace, favour; bounty.
فیل (*fil*) A. elephant; bishop (*in chess*).
فیلبان (*filbān*) *a.* elephant driver.
فیلسوف (*feilasuf*) A. philosopher.
فیلم (*film*) F. film.
فیما بین (*fimā bein*) A. in between. فیما بینِ between.

ق

قاب (1) (*qāb*) T. plate, tray; case; frame.
قاب (2) (*qāb*) ankle-bone, knuckle-bone.
قابل (*qābel*) A. capable, efficient.
قابلمه (*qāblameh*) T. steam-tight stew-pan.
قابله (*qābeleh*) A. midwife.
قابلیت (*qabeliyyat*) A. capability.
قاپو (*qāpu*) T. door; gate.
قاتل (*qātel*) A. murderer.
قاچاق (*qāchāq*) T. contraband, smuggled (goods).
قادر (*qāder*) A. able; powerful.

قادس (*qādes*) A. Cadiz.
قار (*qār*) A. pitch.
قارچ (*qārch*) T. mushroom.
قاره (*qārreh*) A. continent.
قاری (*qāri*) A. reader.
قاز (*qāz*) T. goose.
قاسم (*qāsem*) A. *masc. proper name.*
قاش (*qāsh*) T. slice; splinter.
قاشق (*qāshoq*) T. spoon.
قاصد (*qāṣed*) A. messenger, courier.
قاصر (*qāṣer*) A. falling short, weak.
قاضی (*qāẓi*) A. judge.
قاطبه (*qāṭebeh*) A. the whole, all.
قاطر (*qāṭer*) T. mule.
قاطع (*qāṭe'*) A. cutting, trenchant; decisive, definite.
قاطع الطریق (*qāṭe'o't-ṭariq*) A. highway robber.
قاعده (*qā'edeh*) A. rule; custom; basis; menstruation.
قاعدةً (*qā'edatan*) A. as a rule.
قافله (*qāfeleh*) A. caravan, convoy.
قافیه (*qāfieh*) A. rhyme.
قاقم (*qāqom*) T. ermine.
قالب (*qāleb*) A. mould; model, form.
قالی (*qāli*) T. carpet, rug.
قالیچه (*qālicheh*) rug.
قامت (*qāmat*) A. stature.
قاموس (*qāmus*) A. ocean; dictionary.
قانع (*qāne'*) A. contented, satisfied; persuaded, convinced.
قانع کننده (*qāne' konandeh*) *a.* convincing.
قانون (*qānun*) A. law. قانونِ اساسی constitution.
قانوناً (*qānunan*) A. legally.
قانون گذار (*qānun gozār*) *a.* legislator.
قانون گذاری (*qānun gozāri*) *a.* legislation.
قانونی (*qānuni*) A. legal.
قاهره (*qāhereh*) A. Cairo.
قاه قاه (*qāh qāh*) loud laughter.
قائد (*qā'ed*) A. leader.
قایق (*qāyeq*) T. boat.
قائل (*qā'el*) A. believing.
قائم (*qā'em*) A. erect, upright; perpendicular; firm, secure.
قائم مقام (*qā'em maqām*) A. deputy, successor.
قائن (*qā'en*) A. Cain.
قبا (*qabā*) A. gown, tunic.
قباحت (*qabāḥat*) A. ugliness.
قبال (*qebāl*) A. face, front.
قباله (*qabāleh*) A. deed of sale.
قبائل (*qabā'el*) A. tribes. (*Pl. of* قبیله.)
قبح (*qobḥ*) A. ugliness.
قبر (*qabr*) A. grave, tomb.
قبرس (*qobros*) A. Cyprus.
قبرستان (*qabrestān*) *a.* cemetery.
قبض (*qabẓ*) A. receipt.
قبضه (*qabẓeh*) A. handle, hilt. سه قبضه تفنگ three rifles.
قبل (*qabl*) A. before, ago. قبل از before.
قبلاً (*qablan*) A. beforehand, already.
قبله (*qebleh*) A. point towards which one turns in praying.
قبله نما (*qebleh nomā*) *a.* compass.
قبول (*qabul*) A. acceptance, consent. قبول کردن to accept, consent.
قبه (*qobbeh*) A. cupola, dome.

قبیح (*qabih*) A. ugly, shameful.
قبیل (*qabil*) A. sort, kind.
قبیله (*qabileh*) A. family, tribe.
قپان (*qapān*) T. steelyard.
قتال (*qetāl*) A. battle, war.
قتل (*qaṭl*) A. murder, killing. قتلِ عام massacre.
قحبه (*qaḥbeh*) A. prostitute.
قحط (*qaḥt*) A., قحطی (*qaḥṭi*) *a.* dearth, famine.
قد (*qadd*) A. stature.
قدح (*qadaḥ*) A. bowl, cup.
قدر (*qadr*) A. value; rank; quantity; قدری some, a little.
قدر (*qadar*) A. fate, destiny.
قدرت (*qodrat*) A. power.
قدر دان (*qadr dān*) *a.* appreciative.
قدر دانی (*qadr dāni*) *a.* appreciation.
قدس (*qods*) A. holiness.
قدسی (*qodsi*) *a.* holy; angel.
قدغن (*qadaghan*) T. prohibition; order; forbidden. قدغن کردن to forbid; to order.
قدم (*qadam*) A. step, pace. قدم زدن to walk.
قدما (*qodamā*) A. the ancients. (*Pl. of* قدیم.)
قدمت (*qedmat*) A. antiquity.
قدوم (*qodum*) A. coming, advent.
قدوه (*qodveh*) A. model, pattern.
قدیم (*qadim*) A. old.
قرا (*qorā*) A. villages. (*Pl. of* قریه.)
قرابت (*qarābat*) A. proximity; affinity.
قرار (*qarār*) A. rest, tranquillity; stability; arrangement; decision. قرار بقرارِ, از قرارِ according to. قرار دادن to settle, arrange, fix; to cause to become. قرار گرفتن to settle, alight; to grow calm; to become. قرار شدن to be decided.
قرار داد (*qarār dād*) *a.* appointment; agreement, treaty.
قراض (*qarrāẓ*) A. gnawing; rodent.
قرآن (*qor'ān*) A. Koran.
قران (*qerān*) A. coincidence; conjunction; *name of a monetary unit now replaced by the* rial.
قراول (*qarāvol*) T. sentinel; aim; (gun) sight.
قرائت (*qerā'at*) A. (act of) reading.
قرائت خانه (*qerā'at khāneh*) *a.* reading room.
قرب (*qorb*) A. proximity; affinity.
قربان (*qorbān*) A. sacrifice, victim.
قربانی (*qorbāni*) *a.* sacrificed.
قربت (*qorbat*) A. proximity; affinity.
قرح (*qarḥ*) A. wound, ulcer.
قرص (*qorṣ*) A. disc; loaf.
قرض (*qarẓ*) A. (act of) borrowing; loan; debt.
قرعه (*qor'eh*) A. lot, ballot. قرعه انداختن to cast lots.
قرعه کشی (*qor'eh kashi*) *a.* drawing lots, balloting; lottery.
قرقاول (*qarqāvol*) T. pheasant.
قرقره (*qarqareh*) *a.* (act of) gargling.
قرمز (*qermez*) T. red.
قرمزی (*qermezi*) redness.
قرن (*qarn*) A. century.
قرنطین (*qaranṭin*) F. quarantine.
قرنیه (*qarniyyeh*) A. cornea.

قرون (*qorun*) A. centuries. (*Pl. of* قرن.)

قریب (*qarib*) A. near, close, related.

قریباً (*qariban*) A. shortly, presently.

قریحه (*qariḥeh*) A. talent, genius.

قرین (*qarin*) A. connected, joined; related; companion, mate.

قریه (*qaryeh*) A. village.

قزاق (*qazzāq*) R. Cossack.

قزح (*qozaḥ*) A. *name of an angel presiding over the clouds.* قوسِ قزح rainbow.

قزل آلا (*qezel ālā*) T. trout.

قساوت (*qasāvat*) A. hard-heartedness.

قسط (*qesṭ*) A. instalment.

قسم (*qasam*) A. oath. قسم خوردن to swear.

قسم (*qesm*) A. kind, sort.

قسمت (*qesmat*) A. part, share; fate, destiny.

قشر (*qeshr*) A. peel, rind, crust.

قشلاق (*qeshlāq*) T. winter quarters.

قشنگ (*qashang*) pretty; nice.

قشنگی (*qashangi*) prettiness.

قشون (*qoshun*) M. army.

قصاب (*qaṣṣāb*) A. butcher.

قصاص (*qeṣāṣ*) A. retaliation.

قصائد (*qaṣā'ed*) A. odes (*Pl. of* قصیده.)

قصب (*qaṣab*) A. reed.

قصبه (*qasabeh*) A. town, borough.

قصد (*qaṣd*) A. intention, purpose; attempt.

قصداً (*qaṣdan*) A. intentionally.

قصدی (*qaṣdi*) A. intentional.

قصر (*qaṣr*) A. palace, castle.

قصص (*qeṣaṣ*) A. stories, tales. (*Pl. of* قصه.)

قصور (*qoṣur*) A. failure, shortcoming.

قصه (*qeṣṣeh*) A. story, tale.

قصیده (*qaṣideh*) A. ode.

قصیر (*qaṣir*) A. short.

قضا (*qaẓā*) A. judgment; fate.

قضات (*qoẓāt*) A. judges. (*Pl. of* قاضی.)

قضاوت (*qaẓāvat*) A. judgment. قضاوت کردن to judge.

قضایا (*qaẓāyā*) A. cases, disputes. (*Pl. of* قضیه.)

قضائی (*qaẓā'i*) A. judicial, legal.

قضیه (*qaẓiyyeh*) A. case, law suit.

قطار (*qeṭār*) A. string, file, train.

قطب (*qoṭb*) A. axis, pivot; pole.

قطب نما (*qoṭb nomā*) *a.* compass.

قطبی (*qoṭbi*) A. polar.

قطر (*qoṭr*) A. diameter; calibre; region.

قطران (*qaṭrān*) A. tar.

قطره (*qaṭreh*) A. drop.

قطع (*qaṭ'*) A. (act of) cutting, breaking off, rupture; section, segment; decision. قطع کردن to cut, break off; to settle, decide.

قطعا (*qaṭ'an*) A. certainly, definitely.

قطع نامه (*qaṭ' nāmeh*) *a.* decision, written declaration, resolution.

قطعه (*qeṭ'eh*) A. piece; part.

قطعی (*qaṭ'i*) A. definite, absolute.

قطور (*qoṭur*) A. thick.

قعر (*qa'r*) A. bottom.

قفا (*qafā*) A. nape of the neck.

قفس (*qafas*) A. cage.

قفسه (*qafaseh*) *a.* set of shelves, sideboard, cupboard.

قفقاز (*qafqāz*) Caucasus.

قفل (*qofl*) A. lock.

قلاب (*qollāb*) A. hook.

قلابدوزی (*qollābduzi*) *a.* embroidery.

قلاع (*qelā'*) A. forts, fortresses. (*Pl. of* قلعه.)

قلب (*qalb*) A. heart, centre; counterfeit.

قلبی (*qalbi*) A. hearty, cordial.

قلت (*qellat*) A. scarcity, want.

قلتبان (*qaltabān*) cuckold.

قلع (*qal'*) A. eradication; tin.

قلعه (*qal'eh*) A. fortress, castle.

قلق (*qalaq*) A. anxiety.

قلم (*qalam*) A. pen; item.

قلمتراش (*qalamtarāsh*) *a.* penknife.

قلمداد (*qalamdād*) *a.* enumerated.

قلمدان (*qalamdān*) *a.* pen-case.

قلمرو (*qalamrou*) *a.* realm, jurisdiction.

قلمستان (*qalamestān*) *a.* (tree) nursery.

قلمه (*qalameh*) *a.* slip, cutting (of a tree).

قلندر (*qalandar*) calendar, wandering dervish.

قلوب (*qolub*) A. hearts. (*Pl. of* قلب.)

قله (*qolleh*) A. top, summit.

قليا (*qalyā*) A. alkali.

قليان (*qalyān*) hookah.

قليائی (*qalyā'i*) *a.* alkaline.

قليل (*qalil*) A. little, few.

قمار (*qomār*) A. game of chance, gambling.

قمار باز (*qomār bāz*) *a.* gambler.

قماش (*qomāsh*) A. piece goods, textile fabric.

قمر (*qamar*) A. moon.

قمری (*qamari*) A. lunar.

قمری (*qomri*) A. turtle-dove.

قمع (*qam'*) A. suppression.

قمه (*qameh*) poniard.

قنات (*qanāt*) A. subterranean canal.

قناد (*qannād*) A. confectioner.

قناعت (*qanā'at*) A. contentment. قناعت كردن to be content.

قند (*qand*) A. (lump) sugar.

قند دان (*qand dān*) *a.* sugar-bowl.

قندهار (*qandahār*) Kandahar.

قنوات (*qanavāt*) A. subterranean canals. (*Pl. of* قنات).

قو (*qu*) T. swan.

قوا (*qovā*) A. forces (*Pl. of* قوه.)

قواعد (*qavā'ed*) A. rules, regulations.

قوام (*qavām*) A. consistency; pillar, support.

قوانين (*qavānin*) A. laws, rules, (*Pl. of* قانون.)

قوت (*qut*) A. food, nourishment.

قوت (*qovvat*) A. strength, power.

قوچ (*quch*) T. ram.

قورباغه (*qorbāgheh*) T. frog.

قورخانه (*qurkhāneh*) arsenal.

قوروق (*qoroq*) T. preserve, private hunting ground.

قوروق چی (*qoroq chi*) T. game-keeper.

قوری (*quri*) teapot.

قوز (*quz*) hump.

قوس (*qous*) A. bow; arc; Sagittarius.

قوش (*qūsh*) T. falcon, hawk.

قوطی (*quṭi*) T. (small) box, case.
قول (*qoul*) A. word, promise. قول دادن to promise.
قولنج (*qulenj*) A. colic.
قوم (*qoum*) A. people, tribe.
قومی (*qoumi*) A. national.
قومیت (*qoumiyyat*) A. nationality.
قونسول (*qonsul*) F. consul.
قونسولگری (*qonsulgari*) consulate.
قوه (*qovveh*) A. power, strength, force, energy.
قوی (*qavi*) A. strong.
قویم (*qavim*) A. right, upright.
قهر (*qahr*) A. violence; anger; sulkiness.
قهراً (*qahran*) A. by force.
قهرمان (*qahramān*) hero, champion.
قهقهه (*qahqaheh*) (loud) laughter.
قهوه (*qahveh*) A. coffee.
قی (*qei*) A. (act of) vomiting.
قیاس (*qiās*) A. analogy.
قیافه (*qiafeh*) A. physiognomy.
قیام (*qiām*) A. rising, revolt; starting (*an enterprise*).
قیامت (*qiāmat*) A. resurrection.
قیچی (*qeichi*) T. scissors.
قید (*qeid*) A. tie, bond; restriction; registration. قید کردن to stipulate; to insert.
قیر (*qir*) tar, pitch.
قیراط (*qirāṭ*) A. carat.
قیصر (*qeiṣar*) A. Caesar.
قیل و قال (*qil o qāl*) A. fuss, wrangle.
قیم (*qayyem*) A. guardian.
قیمت (*qeimat*) A. price.
قیمتی (*qeimati*) *a.* precious.
قیمومیت (*qeimumiyyat*) A. guardianship; mandate.
قیود (*qoyud*) A. ties, bonds, restrictions. (*Pl. of* قید)

ک

کابل (*kābl*) F. cable.
کابل (*kābol*) Kabul.
کابوس (*kābus*) A. nightmare.
کابین (*kābin*) marriage portion.
کابینه (*kābineh*) F. cabinet.
کاپیتان (*kāpitān*) F. captain.
کاتب (*kāteb*) A. writer, scribe, secretary.
کاج (*kāj*) pine.
کاخ (*kākh*) palace, mansion.
کاذب (*kāẕeb*) A. lying, false.
کار (*kār*) work; action; affair, thing. کار کردن to work. بکار بردن to use, employ.
کار آزموده (*kār āzmudeh*) experienced.
کار آگاه (*kār āgāh*) detective.
کار آمد (*kār āmad*) skilled; useful.
کار آموز (*kār āmuz*) probationer.
کارت (*kārt*) F. card.
کارت پستال (*kārt postāl*) F. postcard.
کارخانه (*kārkhāneh*) factory.
کارد (*kārd*) knife.

کاردار (*kārdār*) chargé d'affaires.
کارزار (*kārzār*) battle.
کار شکنی (*kār shekani*) obstruction.
کار شناس (*kar shenās*) expert.
کار فرما (*kār farmā*) employer.
کار کن (*kār kon*) labouring; workman. کار کنان personnel.
کارگر (*kārgar*) worker.
کار گزار (*kār gozār*) agent, official.
کار گزاری (*kār gozāri*) agency.
کار گزین (*kār gozin*) personnel officer.
کارمند (*kārmand*) member; employee.
کاروان (*kārvān*) caravan.
کاروانسرای (*kārvānsarāy*) caravanserai.
کاریز (*kāriz*) subterranean canal.
کاز (*kāz*) pruning-scissors.
کاسب (*kāseb*) A. tradesman; hard worker.
کاست (*kāst*) decrease, loss.
کاستن (*kāstan*) to diminish, decrease.
کاسه (*kāseh*) bowl.
کاشانه (*kāshāneh*) cottage; nest.
کاشتن (*kāshtan*) to sow, plant.
کاشف (*kāshef*) A. discovering, revealing; discoverer.
کاشکی (*kāshki*) would that!
کاشی (*kāshi*) glazed tile.
کاظم (*kāẓem*) A. *masc. proper name.*
کاغذ (*kāghaẕ*) paper, letter.
کاغذی (*kāghaẕi*) pertaining to paper.
کافر (*kāfar*) A. unbeliever, infidel.
کافور (*kāfur*) A. camphor.
کافه (*kāffeh*) A. whole, total.
کافه (*kāfeh*) F. café.
کافی (*kāfi*) A. sufficient.
کاکا (*kākā*) negro slave; elder brother.
کاکائو (*kākā'o*) F. cocoa.
کالا (*kālā*) goods.
کالبد (*kālbod*) frame, skeleton; body, corpse.
کالبد شناسی (*kālbod shenāsi*) anatomy.
کالری (*kālori*) F. calorie.
کالسکه (*kāleskeh*) R. carriage.
کام (*kām*) palate; desire, wish.
کامران (*kāmrān*) successful; fortunate.
کامل (*kāmel*) A. perfect, complete.
کاملاً (*kāmelan*) A. perfectly, completely.
کامه (*kāmeh*) desire.
کامیاب (*kāmyāb*) prosperous, successful.
کامیابی (*kāmyābi*) prosperity, success.
کامیون (*kāmion*) F. lorry.
کان (*kān*) mine.
کانال (*kānāl*) F. canal.
کاندید (*kāndid*) F. candidate.
کان شناسی (*kān shenāsi*) mineralogy.
کانون (*kānun*) hearth; brazier; focus; meeting-place.
کانی (*kāni*) mineral.
کاوش (*kāvesh*) digging, excavation; investigation.
کاویدن (*kāvidan*) to dig.
کاه (*kāh*) straw.
کاهش (*kāhesh*) diminution, decrease.
کاهگل (*kāhgel*) cob (*plaster of straw and clay*).
کاهل (*kāhel*) A. indolent.

کاهن (kāhen) A. soothsayer ; priest.

کاهو (kāhu) lettuce.

کاهیدن (kāhidan) to diminish, to be diminished.

کائن (kā'en) A. existing.

کائنات (kā'enāt) A. beings, creatures.

کائوچو (kā'uchu) F. rubber.

کباب (kabāb) A. roast meat.

کبار (kebār) A. Pl. of کبیر.

کبد (kabed) A. liver.

کبر (kebr) A. pride.

کبر (kebar) A. old age.

کبری (kobrā) A. greater, greatest. (Fem. of اکبر.)

کبریت (kebrit) A. sulphur ; match.

کبش (kabsh) A. ram.

کبک (kabk) partridge.

کبوتر (kabutar) pigeon.

کبود (kabud) (dark) blue.

کبی (kabi) ape, monkey.

کبیر (kabir) A. great.

کبیسه (kabiseh) A. intercalary. سالِ کبیسه leap year.

کپیه (kopieh) F. copy.

کت (kot) E. coat.

کتاب (ketāb) A. book.

کتاب (kottāb) A. writers, scribes. (Pl. of کاتب.)

کتابت (ketābat) A. writing, inscription.

کتابچه (ketābcheh) a. small book ; note-book.

کتابخانه (ketābkhāneh) a. library ; bookshop.

کتابدار (ketābdār) a. librarian.

کتابدان (ketābdān) a. book-case.

کتاب فروش (ketāb forush) a. book-seller.

کتان (kattān) A. linen.

کتب (katb) A. writing.

کتب (kotob) A. books. (Pl. of کتاب.)

کتبا (katban) A. in writing.

کتب خانه (kotob khāneh) a. library ; bookshop.

کتری (ketri) H. kettle.

کتف (ketf) A. shoulder(-blade).

کتک (kotak) cudgel ; beating.

کتل (kotal) mountain pass.

کتم (katm) A., کتمان (ketmān) A. (act of hiding, concealing.

کتیبه (katibeh) A. inscription ; battalion.

کتیرا (katirā) gum tragacanth.

کثافت (kaşāfat) A. dirt.

کثرت (kaşrat) A. great number, multitude.

کثیر (kaşir) A. many, much.

کثیف (kaşif) A. dirty.

کج (kaj) crooked, bent.

کجا (kojā) where ? what part ?

کجی (kaji) crookedness.

کحال (kaḥḥāl) A. oculist.

کدام (kodām) which ? هر کدام any one.

کد بانو (kad bānu) mistress of a house, housewife.

کد خدا (kad khodā) mayor, head-man ; head of the household.

کدر (kadar) A. turbidness ; agitation.

کدر (kader) A. turbid ; offended.

کدو (kadu) gourd, squash, pumpkin.

کدورت (*kodurat*) A. turbidness ; displeasure, resentment.

کذاب (*kazzāb*) A. liar.

کذلك (*kazāleka*) A. thus ; likewise.

کر (*kar*) deaf.

کراچي (*karāchi*) Karachi.

کراراً (*kerāran*) A. repeatedly.

کرامت (*karāmat*) A. generosity, magnanimity ; miracle.

کران (*karān*), کرانه (*karāneh*) border ; coast.

کراهت (*karāhat*) A. aversion, disgust.

کرایه (*kerāyeh*) A. rent, hire, freight.

کرباس (*karbās*) canvas.

کرجی (*karaji*) boat.

کرچك (*karchak*) castor-oil plant.

کرد (*kord*) Kurd.

کردار (*kerdār*) deed, action ; way, manner.

کردگار (*kerdegār*) Creator.

کردن (*kardan*) to do, to make.

کرست (*korset*) F. corset.

کرسی (*korsi*) A. throne, chair ; stool (*covered with rugs under which a brazier is placed and round which the family sit with their legs tucked under the rugs*).

کرشمه (*kereshmeh*) ogle, wink.

کرك (*kork*) T. down, fluff.

کرگدان (*kargedān*) rhinoceros.

کرگس (*kargas*) vulture.

کرم (*karam*) A. generosity, nobility.

کرم (*kerm*) worm.

کرم (*krem*) F. (face) cream.

کرنا (*karnā*) trumpet.

کروی (*koravi*) A. round, spherical.

کرویت (*koraviyyat*) A. roundness.

کره (*kareh*) butter.

کره (*karreh*) A. time, turn. بکرات repeatedly.

کره (1) (*koreh*) A. globe, sphere.

کره (2) (*koreh*) F. Korea.

کره (*korreh*) colt, foal.

کریم (*karim*) A. generous, liberal, noble.

کریمه (*krimeh*) F. Crimea.

کژ (*kazh*) crooked.

کس (*kas*) person. کسان relatives. کسانیکه those who.

کس (*kos*) vulva.

کساد (*kasād*) A. dullness (*of market*) ; dull.

کسادی (*kasādi*) *a.* dullness (*of market*).

کسالت (*kasālat*) A. indisposition.

کسب (*kasb*) A. business ; acquisition, earning. کسب کردن to acquire.

کسبه (*kasabeh*) A. tradesmen. (*Pl. of* کاسب).

کسده (*kosdeh*) prostitute. (*The final* h *is pronounced.*)

کسر (*kasr*) A. fraction ; deduction ; shortage. کسر کردن to deduct ; to depreciate.

کسری (*kesrā*) A. Chosroes.

کسکش (*koskash*) pimp.

کسل (*kasel*) A. indisposed, weary.

کسوت (*kesvat*) A. clothing.

کسوف (*kosuf*) A. eclipse of the sun.

کش (*kesh*) indiarubber ; elastic.

کشاف (*kashshāf*) A. discoverer.

کشاکش (*kashākash*) struggle.

کشانیدن (*kashānidan*) to (cause to) draw, pull.

کشاورز (*keshāvarz*) farmer, cultivator.

کشاورزی (*keshāvarzi*) agriculture.

کشت (*kesht*) sown field, sowing.

کشتار (*koshtār*) slaughter, carnage. کشتار کردن to slaughter.

کشتزار (*keshtzār*) cultivated land.

کشتن (*keshtan*) to sow, plant.

کشتن (*koshtan*) to kill.

کشتی (*kashti*) ship.

کشتی (*koshti*) wrestling. کشتی گرفتن to wrestle.

کشتی رانی (*kashti rāni*) navigation.

کشش (*kashesh*) drawing, haulage; attraction, allurement.

کشف (*kashf*) A. discovery. کشف کردن to discover.

کشف (*kashaf*) tortoise; Cancer.

کشک (*kashk*) dried whey.

کشمش (*keshmesh*) raisins.

کشمکش (*kashmakash*) conflict, struggle.

کشمیر (*kashmir*) Kashmir.

کشو (*keshou*) drawer.

کشور (*keshvar*) country. وزارت کشور the Ministry of the Interior.

کشور گشا (*keshvar goshā*) conqueror.

کشور گشائی (*keshvar goshā'i*) conquest.

کشوری (*keshvari*) civil.

کشیده (*kashideh*) drawn, pulled; slap.

کشیدن (*kashidan*) to draw, pull.

کشیش (*kashish*) priest.

کشیک (*keshik*) T. guard, sentry.

کعب (*ka'b*) A. ankle; dice; cube root.

کعبه (*ka'beh*) A. Kaaba.

کف (*kaf*) froth, foam, scum, lather.

کف (*kaff*) A. (palm of the) hand.

کفاش (*kaffāsh*) *a.* shoemaker.

کفاف (*kafāf*) A. sufficiency; daily bread.

کفالت (*kafālat*) A. bail, surety.

کفایت (*kefāyat*) A. sufficiency; efficiency.

کفتار (*kaftār*) hyena.

کفتر (*kaftar*) pigeon.

کفر (*kofr*) A. impiety.

کفش (*kafsh*) shoe.

کفش دوز (*kafsh duz*) shoemaker.

کفگیر (*kafgir*) skimmer.

کفل (*kafal*) A. buttocks.

کفن (*kafan*) A. winding-sheet.

کفور (*kafur*) A. ungrateful, impious.

کفیل (*kafil*) A. surety, bail; acting (*minister, etc.*).

کل (*kal*) bald.

کل (*koll*) A. whole, general, chief.

کلاس (*klās*) F. class.

کلاغ (*kalāgh*) crow.

کلاف (*kalāf*) skein.

کلام (*kalām*) A. speech.

کلان (*kalān*) great, big.

کلانتر (*kalāntar*) elder; mayor; commissioner.

کلاه (*kolāh*) hat.

کلب (*kalb*) A. dog.

کلبتین (*kalbatein*) A. forceps.

کلبه (*kolbeh*) cottage, hut.

کلبی (*kalbi*) A. canine; cynic.

کلده (*kaldeh*) F. Chaldea.
کلفت (*kolfat*) A. maid-servant.
کلفت (*koloft*) thick, rough; hoarse.
کلک (*kelk*) reed; pen.
کلم (*kalam*) cabbage.
کلمه (*kalemeh*) A. word.
کلنگ (*kolang*) pick; crane (*bird*).
کلوب (*klub*) F. club.
کلوخ (*kolukh*) clod.
کله (*kalleh*) head.
کلی (*kolli*) A. general, universal. بکلی entirely.
کلید (*kelid*) key.
کلیسا (*kelisā*) church.
کلیشه (*klisheh*) F. cliché, stereotype plate.
کلیمی (*kalimi*) *a.* Jew, Jewish.
کلیه (*kolliyyeh*) A. totality, all.
کم (*kam*) little, few. کم کم little by little. دستِ کم at least.
کماج (*komāj*) thick, flat, round unleavened bread.
کما فی الصابق (*kamā fe'ṣ-ṣābeq*), کماکان (*kamākān*) A. as before.
کما ینبغی (*kamā yanbaghi*) A. as is fitting, duly.
کمال (*kamāl*) A. perfection. با کمالِ آزادی with the utmost freedom.
کمان (*kamān*) bow; Sagittarius.
کمبود (*kambud*) deficiency, deficit.
کمپانی (*kompāni*) F. company.
کمتر (*kamtar*) less.
کمترین (*kamtarin*) least.
کمدی (*komedi*) F. comedy.
کمر (*kamar*) loins, waist; girdle.
کمر بند (*kamar band*) girdle, belt, cummerbund.
کمر شکن (*kamar shekan*) onerous, insupportable.
کم رنگ (*kam rang*) pale; weak (*tea*).
کمک (*komak*) T. help, assistance.
کمند (*kamand*) lasso, noose, trap, snare.
کمونیست (*komunist*) F. Communist.
کمی (*kami*) fewness, shortage.
کمیاب (*kamyāb*) scarce, rare.
کمیابی (*kamyābi*) scarcity.
کمیت (*komeit*) A. dark bay horse.
کمیت (*kammiyyat*) A. quantity.
کمیته (*komiteh*) F. committee.
کمیساریا (*komisāriā*) F. commissariat.
کمیسر (*komiser*) F. commissar, commissioner.
کمیسیون (*komisyun*) F. commission, committee.
کمین (*kamin*) A. ambush.
کمین (*kamin*), کمینه (*kamineh*) least.
کنار (*kanār*) side; bank, shore.
کناره (*kanāreh*) side, edge. کناره گرفتن to retire.
کناره کیری (*kanāreh giri*) resignation, retirement, abdication.
کناس (*kannās*) A. scavenger.
کنام (*konām*) thicket; lair, nest.
کنایه (*kenāyeh*) A. allusion; metaphor.
کنتال (*kantāl*) F. quintal.
کنترات (*kontrāt*) F. contract.
کنترل (*kontrol*) F. control.
کنج (*konj*) corner.
کنجد (*konjed*) sesame.

کند (*kond*) blunt, dull; slow.

کندن (*kandan*) to dig; to pull out.

کندو (*kandu*) beehive.

کنده (*kandeh*) dug; ditch, moat.

کنده (*kondeh*) log, block, stump; stocks.

کندی (*kondi*) bluntness; slowness.

کنسرت (*konsert*) F. concert.

کنسرو (*konserv*) F. preserves, tinned goods.

کنسول (*konsul*) F. consul.

کنسول خانه (*konsul khāneh*) consulate (building).

کنسولگری (*konsulgari*) consulate.

کنش (*konesh*) action.

کنشت (*konesht*) synagogue, church.

کنعان (*kan'ān*) A. Canaan.

کنف (1) (*kanaf*) jute.

کنف (2) (*kanaf*) A. wing; side.

کنفرانس (*konferāns*) F. conference; lecture.

کنگ (*kang*) wing; arm.

کنگاش (*kangāsh*) M. counsel, deliberation.

کنگره (*kongereh*) cog; turret, battlement.

کنگره (*kongreh*) F. congress.

کنون (*konun*) now.

کنونی (*konuni*) present.

کنه (*konh*) A. bottom, depth; essence, substance.

کنیه (*konyeh*) A. patronymic.

کنیز (*kaniz*) slave-girl, maidservant.

کنیزک (*kanizak*) female slave, maidservant; kept mistress.

کنیسه (*kaniseh*) A. synagogue.

کنین (*kenin*) F. quinine.

کو (*ku*) where is, are ?

کواکب (*kavākeb*) stars. (*Pl. of* کوکب.)

کوبیدن (*kubidan*) to beat, to pound, to crush.

کوپال (*kupāl*) mace, club.

کوتاه (*kutāh*) short.

کوتاهی (*kutāhi*) shortness.

کوچ (*kuch*) T. decampment.

کوچك (*kuchek*) little, small.

کوچکی (*kucheki*) littleness, smallness.

کوچولو (*kuchulu*) little, tiny.

کوچه (*kucheh*) lane; street.

کود (*kud*) manure, dung.

کودتا (*kudetā*) F. coup d'état.

کودك (*kudak*) child.

کودکستان (*kudakestān*) kindergarten.

کودن (*koudan*) stupid.

کور (*kur*) blind.

کوران (*kurān*) F. draught (of air).

کور کورانه (*kur kurāneh*) blind(ly).

کوره (*kureh*) furnace, kiln.

کوری (*kuri*) blindness.

کوز (*kuz*) hump; crooked.

کوزه (*kuzeh*) pot, jar.

کوزه گر (*kuzeh gar*) potter.

کوزه گری (*kuzeh gari*) pottery.

کوس (*kus*) (kettle-)drum.

کوسه (*kuseh*) thin-bearded. کوسه ماهی swordfish.

کوش (*kush*) F. hotbed.

کوشش (*kushesh*) endeavour.

کوشك (*kushk*) palace.

کوشیدن (*kushidan*) to endeavour, to strive.

کوفتن (*kuftan*) to beat, thresh, pound.

کوفته (*kufteh*) rissole.

کوک (*kuk*) (act of) tuning; winding up. کوک کردن to tune; wind up.

کوکب (*koukab*) A. star.

کوکو (*kuku*) cuckoo.

کون (*koun*) A. existence, world.

کون (*kun*) anus.

کونی (*kuni*) catamite.

کوه (*kuh*) mountain.

کوهان (*kouhān*) hump (of camel).

کوهسار (*kuhsār*), کوهستان (*kuhestān*) hilly country.

کوهستانی (*kuhestāni*) hilly.

کوه نورد (*kuh navard*) mountaineer.

کوهی (*kuhi*) mountainous; wild.

کوی (*kuy*) lane.

کویت (*koveit*) A. Koweit.

کویر (*kavir*) salt desert.

که (1) (*keh*) small, young. (*The* h *is pronounced.*)

که (2) (*keh*) that, who, which.

کهتر (*kehtar*) smaller, younger, junior.

کهربا (*kahrobā*) amber.

کهف (*kahf*) A. cave.

کهکشان (*kahkashān*) Milky Way.

کهن (*kohan*) old.

کهنه (*kohneh*) old, worn; rag, clout.

کی (*kei*) when?

کیاست (*kiāsat*) A. ingenuity.

کیخسرو (*keikhosrou*) *name of a legendary king of Persia*; *masc. proper name.*

کید (*keid*) A. deceit, fraud, stratagem.

کیر (*kir*) penis.

کیسه (*kiseh*) bag, sack.

کیسه بر (*kiseh bor*) *a.* cutpurse.

کیش (1) (*kish*) religion, faith.

کیش (2) (*kish*) quiver.

کیف (*kif*) purse, bag.

کیف (*keif*) A. exhilaration (*produced by intoxicant*).

کیفر (*keifar*) reward, retribution, punishment.

کیفیت (*keifiyyat*) A. quality; circumstance.

کیک (*keik*) flea.

کیکاوس (*keikāus*) *name of a legendary king of Persia.*

کیلو (*kilo*) F. kilo.

کیلوات (*kilovāt*) F. kilowatt.

کیلومتر (*kilometer*) F. kilometre.

کیلومتری (*kilometri*) distance of — kilometres. در ٤ کیلومتریِ شهر at a distance of 4 kilometres from the town.

کیمیا (*kimiā*) elixir, alchemy.

کیمیاگر (*kimiāgar*) alchemist.

کین (*kin*) spite; revenge.

کینه (*kineh*) spite, hatred.

کیوان (*keivān*) Saturn.

کیومرث (*kayumarṣ*) *name of a legendary king of Persia; the Persian Adam.*

کیهان (*keihān*) world.

گ

گار (*gār*) F. railway station.

گاراژ (*gārāzh*) F. garage.

گارد (*gārd*) F. guard.

گاری (*gāri*) H. cart.

گاز (1) (*gāz*) bite. گاز گرفتن to bite.

گاز (2) *gāz*) F. gas.

گاله (*gāleh*) wide-mouthed sack.

گام (*gām*) step, pace.

گاو (*gāv*) cow; ox. گاوِ ماده cow. گاوِ نر bull, ox.

گاو آهن (*gāv āhan*) ploughshare.

گاودار (*gāvdār*) dairyman.

گاو صندوق (*gāv ṣanduq*) *a.* strong box, safe.

گاو میش (*gāv mish*) buffalo.

گاه (*gāh*) time; place. گاهی sometimes.

گاهگاهی (*gāhgāhi*) from time to time.

گائیدن (*gā'idan*) to copulate.

گبر (*gabr*) Guebre, Zoroastrian.

گچ (*gach*) plaster. سنگِ گچ gypsum.

گدا (*gadā*) beggar.

گداختن (*godākhtan*) to melt, to smelt.

گدار (*godār*) ford.

گذاردن (*goẕārdan*), گذاشتن (*goẕāshtan*) to put, lay; to let, allow.

گذر (*goẕar*) passage.

گذرانیدن (*goẕarānidan*) to pass, spend.

گذر نامه (*goẕar nāmeh*) passport.

گذشتن (*goẕashtan*) to pass, cross. از — گذشتن to overlook, spare, forgive —; to forbear from —.

گذشته (*goẕashteh*) past. گذشته از apart from.

گر (*gar*) *contracted form of* اگر.

گراز (*gorāz*) boar.

گرازیدن (*gorāzidan*) to strut.

گرام (*gerām*), dear; revered, respected.

گرام (*grām*) F. gramme.

گرامافون (*grāmāfon*) F. gramophone.

گرامی (*gerāmi*) dear; respected, honourable.

گران (*gerān*) dear, expensive; heavy.

گرانبها (*gerānbahā*) valuable.

گرانفروش (*gerānforush*) profiteer.

گرانی (*gerāni*) dearness; scarceness; heaviness.

گراور (*grāvur*) F. engraving.

گرائیدن (*gera'idan*) to be inclined, tend.

گربز (*gorboz*) sly (person).

گربه (*gorbeh*) cat.

گرجستان (*gorjestān*) Georgia.

گرچه (*garcheh*) although.

گرد (*gard*) dust.

گرد (*gerd*) round. گردِ around. گرد آوردن to accumulate.

گرد (*gord*) hero; brave.

گرداب (*gerdāb*) whirlpool.

گرداگردِ (*gerdāgerde*) round about.

گردان (*gardān*) turning, revolving.

گردان (*gordān*) battalion.

گردانیدن (*gardānidan*) to turn, change.

گردباد (*gerdbād*) whirlwind.

گرد بر (*gerd bor*) gimlet.

گردش (*gardesh*) turn, revolution, circulation; walk. گردش کردن to turn, revolve; to take a walk.

گردن (*gardan*) neck.

گردن فراز (*gardan ferāz*) haughty.

گردنه (*gardaneh*) pass, defile.

گردو (*gerdu*) walnut.

گرده (*gordeh*) kidney.

گردیدن (*gardidan*) to become.

گرز (*gorz*) club, mace.

گرسنگی (*gorosnegi*) hunger.

گرسنه (*gorosneh*) hungry.

گرفتار (*gereftār*) seized, prisoner; embarrassed; busy.

گرفتاری (*gereftāri*) captivity; embarrassment, preoccupation.

گرفتن (*gereftan*) to take, receive; to seize; to cover; to be stopped; to be eclipsed.

گرگ (*gorg*) wolf.

گرم (*garm*) warm; hot; enthusiastic, zealous.

گرم (*gram*) F. gramme.

گرما (*garmā*) heat.

گرمابه (*garmābeh*) bath.

گرمسیر (*garmsir*) warm region; tropical country.

گرمی (*garmi*) warmth, heat.

گرنه (*garnah*) otherwise. (*The* h *is not pronounced.*)

گرو (*gerou*) pledge, wager.

گروه (*goruh*) multitude, company, troop; squad.

گروهبان (*goruhbān*) corporal.

گرویدن (*geravidan*) to adhere to, follow.

گره (*gereh*) knot; *measure of length* $= 2\frac{1}{2}$ *in. approx.*

گریبان (*geribān*) collar.

گریپ (*grip*) F. influenza.

گریختن (*gorikhtan*) to flee.

گریز (*goriz*) flight.

گریستن (*geristan*) to weep.

گریه (*geryeh*) (act of) weeping. گریه کردن to weep.

گز (*gaz*) ell.

گزارش (*gozāresh*) explanation, interpretation; report.

گزاف (*gezāf*) extravagant, enormous.

گزند (*gazand*) injury, harm.

گزیدن (*gazidan*) to bite, to sting.

گزیدن (*gozidan*) to choose, select.

گزیده (*gozideh*) chosen; choice, excellent.

گزین (*gozin*) choice.

گساردن (*gosārdan*) to drink.

گستاخ (*gostākh*) bold; rude, impudent.

گستاخانه (*gostākhāneh*) rude(ly).

گستاخی (*gostākhi*) rudeness, impudence.

گستردن (*gostardan*) to spread.

گسترش (*gostaresh*) deployment.

گسستن (*gosestan*) to break off.

گسیختن (*gosikhtan*) to break off.

گسیل (*gosil*) (act of) sending off, dispatch.

گشاد (*goshād*) wide, loose.

گشادن (*goshādan*) to open; to conquer.

گشایش (*goshāyesh*) (act of) opening; relief.

گشت (*gasht*) walk, excursion.

گشتی (*gashti*) patrol.

گشن (*goshn*) male; rut, heat.

گفتار (*goftār*) speech, saying.

گفتگو (*goftogu*) conversation. گفتگو کردن to converse.

گفتن (*goftan*) to say, to call.

گل (*gel*) mud, clay.

گل (*gol*) flower, rose.

گلاب (*golāb*) rose-water.

گلابی (*golābi*) pear.

گلچینی (*golchini*) (act of) gathering flowers; selection.

گلخانه (*golkhāneh*) greenhouse.

گلدان (*goldān*) vase, flower-pot.

گلدسته (*goldasteh*) nosegay; minaret.

گلستان (*golestān*) rose-garden.

گلگیر (*gelgir*) dashboard.

گلو (*galu*) throat.

گلو بند (*galu band*) necklace.

گلوله (*goluleh*) bullet.

گله (*geleh*) complaint.

گله (*galleh*) flock, herd.

گلی (*geli*) earthern.

گلیم (*gelim*) coarse carpet; blanket.

گم (*gom*) lost. گم کردن to lose.

گماشتن (*gomāshtan*) to appoint; to entrust.

گماشته (*gomāshteh*) appointed; deputy.

گمان (*gamān*) opinion. گمان کردن to think, suppose.

گمراه (*gomrāh*) astray, misled.

گمرک (*gomrok*) T. customs.

گمنام (*gomnām*) obscure, nameless.

گناه (*gonāh*) sin, crime; fault.

گناهکار (*gonāhkār*) sinful, sinner.

گنبد (*gonbad*) dome, cupola.

گنج (*ganj*) treasure.

گنجایش (*gonjāyesh*) capacity.

گنجشک (*gonjeshk*) sparrow.

گنجفه (*ganjefeh*) playing-cards.

گنجیدن (*gonjidan*) to be contained; to contain.

گنجینه (*ganjineh*) treasure; store.

گند (*gand*) stench.

گندم (*gandom*) wheat.

گندم گون (*gandom gun*) swarthy.

گنده (*gandeh*) fetid.

گنده (*gondeh*) big, huge; fat.

گندیدن (*gandidan*) to putrefy, to stink.

گنگ (*gong*) dumb, mute.

گنه گنه (*geneh geneh*) quinine.

گو (*gou*) hero; brave.

گو (*gu*), گوی (*guy*) ball.

گوارا (*govārā*) digestible, palatable.

گوارش (*govāresh*) digestion.

گواریدن (*gavāridan*) to be digested; to digest.

گواه (*govāh*) witness.

گواهی (*govāhi*) testimony.

گواهی نامه (*govāhi nāmeh*) certificate.

گوجه (*goujeh*) *name of a small green plum.* گوجهٔ فرنگی tomato.

گود (*goud*) deep, low; pit.

گودال (*goudāl*) ditch, trench.

گور (1) (*gur*) grave.

گور (2) (*gur*) wild ass, onager.

گورستان (*gurestān*) cemetery.

گوز (*guz*) *crepitus ventris.*

گوزن (*gavazn*) deer, stag.

گوزیدن (*guzidan*) to break wind.

گوساله (*gusāleh*) calf.

گوسفند (*gusfand*) sheep.

گوش (*gush*) ear.

گوشت (*gusht*) flesh, meat.

گوشت آلود (*gusht ālud*) plump, corpulent.

گوشتخوار (*gushtkhvār*) carnivorous.

گوشزد (*gushzad*) heard; report. گوشزد کردن to report, notify.

گوشواره (*gushvāreh*) ear-ring.

گوشه (*gusheh*) corner, angle.

گوشه نشین (*gusheh neshin*) retired, secluded; recluse, hermit.

گوشی (*gushi*) (telephone) receiver.

گوگرد (*gugerd*) sulphur.

گول (*gul*) deceit. گولِ — خوردن to be deceived by —.

گون (*gun*) colour; kind, sort.

گوناگون (*gunāgun*) variegated, various.

گونه (1) (*guneh*) colour; kind, sort.

گونه (2) (*guneh*) cheek.

گونی (*guni*) gunny-bag.

گوهر (*gouhar*) jewel; essence; origin, stock.

گویا (*guyā*) speaking; seemingly, perhaps.

گوینده (*guyandeh*) speaker, orator.

گه (*goh*) excrement.

گهواره (*gahvāreh*) cradle.

گیاه (*giāh*) grass; plant, herb.

گیاه شناس (*giāh shenās*) botanist.

گیاه شناسی (*giāh shenāsi*) botany.

گیتی (*giti*) world.

گیج (*gij*) giddy, bewildered.

گیر (*gir*) hold, grasp. گیر کردن to get caught.

گیراندن (*girāndan*) to ignite.

گیرنده (*girandeh*) (wireless) receiver.

گیر و دار (*gir o dār*) conflict, brawl.

گیره (*gireh*) vice; pincers.

گیس (*gis*) (woman's) hair; curl, ringlet.

گیسو (*gisu*) tress, ringlet.

گیلاس (1) (*gilās*) cherry.

گیلاس (2) (*gilās*) glass, tumbler.

گیوه (*giveh*) cotton shoe.

گیهان (*gihān*) world.

ل

لا ابالی (*lā obāli*) A. nonchalant, reckless.

لا اقل (*lā aqall*) A. at least.

لا بد (*lā bodd*) A. necessarily.

لابوراتوار (*lāborātvār*) F. laboratory.

لابه (*lābeh*) supplication.

لات (*lāt*) destitute ; street Arab.

لا جرم (*lā jaram*) A. necessarily ; certainly ; therefore.

لاجورد (*lājvard*) lapis lazuli, azure.

لاحق (*lāḥeq*) A. attached, following.

لاحقه (*lāḥeqeh*) A. annexe.

لازم (*lāzem*) A. necessary. لازم داشتن to need.

لازمه (*lāzemeh*) A. requisite ; inference.

لاستیک (*lāstik*) F. rubber ; tyre.

لاش (*lāsh*) corpse, carcass.

لاشخور (*lāshkhor*) kite ; vulture.

لاشه (*lāsheh*) corpse.

لاطاری (*lāṭāri*) E. lottery.

لاغر (*lāghar*) thin, lean.

لاف (*lāf*) (act of) boasting. لاف زدن to boast.

لاقید (*lā qeid*) A. careless, unconcerned.

لاک (1) (*lāk*) lac, wax.

لاک (2) (*lāk*) wooden cup ; shell (of the tortoise).

لاک پشت (*lāk posht*) tortoise.

لال (*lāl*) dumb.

لاله (*lāleh*) tulip.

لامپ (*lāmp*) F. lamp ; electric light bulb ; wireless valve.

لامسه (*lāmeseh*) A. (sense of) touch.

لانه (*lāneh*) nest.

لاوک (*lāvak*) wooden pan.

لاهه (*lāheh*) F. the Hague.

لا یتجزا (*lā yatajazzā*) A. indivisible.

لا یتناهی (*lā yatanāhi*) A. infinite.

لایحه (*lāyeḥeh*) A. bill (*project of a law*).

لایق (*lāyeq*) A. worthy.

لا ینقطع (*lā yanqaṭe'*) A. incessant(ly).

لائیدن (*lā'idan*) to bark.

لب (*lab*) lip ; edge.

لب (*lobb*) A. pith, marrow ; gist, essence.

لباس (*lebās*) A. clothing, clothes.

لبخند (*labkhand*) smile.

لبریز (*labriz*) overflowing.

لبنان (*lobnān*) A. Lebanon.

لت (*lat*) blow ; deficit ; piece.

لثه (*leṣeh*) A. gum (of the teeth).

لج (*lajj*) A. grudge, spite.

لجاجت (*lajājat*) A. obstinacy ; spite.

لجن (*lajan*) black mud.

لجوج (*lajuj*) A. obstinate.

لجه (*lojjeh*) A. the deep.

لحاظ (*leḥāẓ*) A. respect, point of view.

لحاف (*leḥāf*) A. quilt.

لحد (*laḥd*) A. niche (*in the side of a tomb*).

لحظه (*laḥzeh*) A. moment.

لحن (*laḥn*) A. tune, melody ; tone.

لحیم (*laḥim*) A. solder.

لحیه (*leḥyeh*) A. beard.

لخت (*lokht*) naked, bare. لخت کردن to strip ; to rob.

لختی (*lakhti*) some; a little while; somewhat.

لذا (*lezā*) A. therefore.

لذت (*lazzat*) A. pleasure.

لذیذ (*laziz*) A. pleasant, delicious.

لر (*lor*) Lur.

لرزه (*larzeh*) tremor.

لرزیدن (*larzidan*) to tremble.

لزج (*lazej*) A. viscous, slimy.

لزوم (*lozum*) A. necessity.

لژ (*lozh*) F. box (*in the theatre*).

لسان (*lesān*) A. tongue, language.

لشکر (*lashgar*) army; division.

لشکر کشی (*lashgar kashi*) (military) expedition.

لشکری (*lashgari*) military.

لطافت (*laṭāfat*) A. kindness; elegance; wit; tenderness, thinness.

لطف (*loṭf*) A. kindness.

لطمه (*laṭmeh*) A. blow, injury.

لطیف (*laṭif*) A. kind; elegant; witty; delicate, tender, thin.

لطیفه (*laṭifeh*) A. jest, witticism.

لعاب (*lo'āb*) A. saliva; mucus, slime.

لعب (*la'b*) A. play, sport.

لعبت (*lo'bat*) A. toy, plaything; game.

لعل (*la'l*) *a.* ruby.

لعنت (*la'nat*) A. curse.

لغت (*loghat*) A. word; dictionary; language, dialect.

لغزش (*laghzesh*) slip, error; offence.

لغزیدن (*laghzidan*) to slip, stumble.

لغو (*laghv*) A. cancellation; nonsense. لغو کردن to cancel.

لفاف (*lefāf*) A. packing paper.

لفظ (*lafẓ*) A. word.

لفظی (*lafẓi*) A. literal.

لق (*laq*) loose.

لقا (*leqā*) A. countenance; encounter.

لقب (*laqab*) A. title.

لقلق (*laqlaq*) stork.

لقمه (*loqmeh*) A. mouthful, morsel.

لکنت (*loknat*) A. (act of) stammering.

لکه (*lakkeh*) spot, blemish.

لگام (*legām*) bridle, reins.

لگد (*lagad*) kick. لگد زدن to kick.

لگن (*lagan*) basin.

لله (*laleh*) T. tutor.

لم (*lam*) lolling.

لمس (*lams*) A. (act of) touching, feeling. لمس کردن to touch, feel.

لمعه (*lam'eh*) A. flash.

لم یزرع (*lam yazra'*) A. uncultivated.

لم یزل (*lam yazal*) A. eternal, everlasting.

لند لند (*lond lond*) grumbling.

لندن (*landan*) E. London.

لنگ (*lang*) lame.

لنگر (*langar*) anchor.

لنگیدن (*langidan*) to limp.

لو (*lou*) A. if. (*Occurs only in the phrase* ولو آنکه, even if.)

لوا (*levā*) A. standard, banner.

لوازم (*lavāzem*) A. necessaries; accessories; outfit. (*Pl. of* لازمه.)

لواش (*lavāsh*) thin, flat bread.

لوایح (*lavāyeḥ*) A. bills. (*Pl. of* لایحه.)

لوبیا (*lubiā*) kidney bean.

لوچ (*luch*) squint-eyed.

لوح (*louḥ*) A. tablet, slate.

لوحه (*louḥeh*) A. tablet.

لوط (*luṭ*) A. Lot.

لوطی (*luṭi*) *a*. pederast ; rogue.

لوکس (*luks*) F. luxury.

لوکوموتیو (*lokomotiv*) F. locomotive.

لولا (*loulā*) hinge.

لولو (*lulu*) bugbear.

لؤلؤ (*lo'lo'*) A. pearl.

لوله (*luleh*) tube, pipe.

لوله کشی (*luleh kashi*) (laying of) pipeline.

لون (*loun*) A. colour.

لوند (*lavand*) prostitute.

له (*lah*) R. Pole.

له (*leh*) squeezed, crushed, trampled. (*The* h *is pronounced.*)

لهذا (*lehāẕā*) A. therefore.

لهجه (*lahjeh*) A. dialect ; accent, tone.

لهستان (*lahestān*) Poland.

لهو (*lahv*) A. play.

لیاقت (*liāqat*) A. merit, worthiness.

لیبی (*libi*) F. Libya.

لیتر (*litr*) F. litre.

لیدر (*lider*) F. (political) leader.

لیز (*liz*) slippery.

لیسیدن (*lisidan*) to lick.

لیف (*lif*) A. fibre.

لیل (*leil*), لیله (*leileh*) A. night.

لیکن (*likan*) *a*. but.

لیمو (*limu*) lemon.

لیموناد (*limonād*) F. lemonade.

لینت (*linat*) A. softness.

لئیم (*la'im*) A. mean, base.

م

ما (*mā*) we.

ماء (*mā'*) A. water.

مآب (*ma'āb*) A. resort, refuge ; style, mode. فرنگی مآب fond of European ways.

مابعد (*māba'd*) A. following, subsequent.

مابقی (*mābaqi*) A. rest, remainder.

ما بین (*mā bein*) A. middle. ما بینِ between.

مات (*māt*) A. checkmate(d) ; astonished.

مآت (*me'āt*) A. hundreds.

ماتم (*mātam*) A. mourning.

ماتیک (*mātik*) F. cosmetic.

مآثر (*ma'āṯer*) A. memorable deeds.

ماجرا (*mājarā*) A. event, occurrence ; adventure.

ماجرا جو (*mājarā ju*) *a*. adventurer.

ماچ (*māch*) kiss. ماچ کردن to kiss.

ما حضر (*mā ḥazar*) A. food prepared in haste.

مأخذ (*ma'khaẕ*) A. source, origin ; basis.

مأخوذ (*ma'khuẕ*) A. taken, received.

مادام (1) (*mādām*) A. duration. مادامیکه while; as long as.
مادام (2) (*mādām*) F. madame.
مادر (*mādar*) mother. مادرِ بزرگ grandmother.
مادر زاد (*mādar zād*) innate, congenital.
مادر زن (*mādar zan*) mother-in-law (*wife's mother*).
مادر شوهر (*mādar shouhar*) mother-in-law (*husband's mother*).
مادری (*mādari*) maternal.
ماده (*mādeh*) female.
ماده (*māddeh*) A. matter, material; article.
مادی (*māddi*) A. material.
مادیان (*mādiān*) mare.
مار (*mār*) snake.
مار پیچ (*mār pich*) spiral.
مار چوبه (*mār chubeh*) asparagus.
مارس (*mārs*) F. March.
مارسی (*mārsei*) F. Marseilles.
مارش (*mārsh*) F. march.
مارشال (*mārshāl*) F. marshal.
مارک (*mārk*) F. mark.
مار ماهی (*mār māhi*) eel.
مارملاد (*mārmelād*) F. marmelade, jam.
مازاد (*māzād*) A. surplus, excess.
مازو (*māzu*) gallnut, oak-apple.
ماساژ (*māsāzh*) F. massage.
ماسبق (*māsabaq*) A. the foregoing.
ماست (*māst*) curds.
ماسک (*māsk*) F. mask.
ماسوره (*māsureh*) fuse.
ماسه (*māseh*) (fine) sand.
ماش (*māsh*) vetch.
ماشأ الله (*māshā' allāh*) A. well done!
ماشین (*māshin*) F. machine; engine, train.
ماشین آلات (*māshin ālāt*) *a.* machinery.
ماضی (*māẓi*) A. past, preterite.
ما فوقِ (*mā fouqe*) *a.* beyond.
ماقبل (*māqabl*) A. antecedent.
ماکو (*māku*) weaver's shuttle.
ماکول (*ma'kul*) A. victual.
ماکیان (*mākiān*) hen.
مال (*māl*) A. property, wealth.
مآل (*ma'āl*) A. return; end, conclusion.
مالاً (*mālan*) A. financially.
مآلاً (*ma'ālan*) A. consequently, ultimately.
مالاریا (*mālāriā*) F. malaria.
مال الاجاره (*mālo'l-ejāreh*) A. rent.
مال التجاره (*mālo't-tejāreh*) A. merchandise.
مالت (*mālt*) F. Malta.
مالخولیا (*mālkhuliā*) A. melancholy.
مالک (*mālek*) A. proprietor, landlord.
مالکیت (*mālekiyyat*) A. ownership.
مألوف (*ma'luf*) A. usual, customary; familiar.
ماله (*māleh*) towel.
مالی (*māli*) A. financial.
مالیات (*māliāt*) A. tax(es), revenue.
مالیدن (*mālidan*) to rub.
مالیه (*māliyyeh*) A. finance(s).
ماما (*māmā*) midwife; mamma.
مأمن (*ma'man*) A. place of refuge.

مأمور (*ma'mur*) A. official, functionary; charged, commissioned.

مأموريت (*ma'muriyyat*) A. commission.

مانچوری (*mānchuri*) F. Manchuria.

ماندن (*māndan*) to remain.

مانستن (*mānestan*) to resemble.

مانع (*māne'*) A. hindering; obstacle.

مانع للغير (*māne'on lel-gheir*) A. exclusive.

مانند (*mānand*) resembling. مانندِ like.

مانور (*mānovr*) F. manœuvre.

مأنوش (*ma'nus*) A. familiar, intimate.

مانیکور (*mānikur*) F. manicure.

مأوی (*ma'vā*) A. dwelling, abode.

ما ورا اردن (*mā varā ordonn*) A. Transjordan.

ماه (*māh*) moon; month.

ماهتاب (*māhtāb*) moonlight.

ماهر (*māher*) A. skilful.

ماهه (*māheh*) space of — months.

ماهوت (*māhut*) broadcloth.

ماهی (*māhi*) fish. ماهي ريشدار barbel. ماهي سيم bream.

ماهیانه (*māhiāneh*) monthly (wages).

ماهیت (*māhiyyat*) A. quiddity, nature, essence.

ماهی تابه (*māhi tābeh*) frying-pan.

ماهی خوار (*māhi khvār*) heron.

ماهی گیر (*māhi gir*) fisherman.

مایچه (*māycheh*) muscle.

ما یحتاج (*mā yaḥtāj*) A. necessaries.

مائده (*mā'edeh*) A. table.

مایع (*māye'*) A. liquid.

مایل (*māyel*) A. inclined, willing, fond.

مأیوس (*ma'yus*) A. disappointed, despairing.

مایه (*māyeh*) leaven, yeast; capital, funds; source; essence, matter; vaccine.

مائی (*mā'i*) A. watery, aqueous.

مباح (*mobāḥ*) A. lawful.

مباحثه (*mobāḥeṣeh*) A. discussion, dispute, controversy.

مبادا (*mabādā*) God forbid! lest.

مبادرت (*mobāderat*) A. (act of) hurrying, setting about (*a task*). مبادرت کردن to hurry, set about (*a task*).

مبادله (*mobādeleh*) A. exchange. مبادله کردن to exchange.

مبادی (*mabādi*) A. beginnings, elements. (*Pl. of* مبدأ.)

مبادی (*mobādi*) A. beginning, beginner.

مبارز (*mobārez*) A. fighter, duellist.

مبارزه (*mobārezeh*) A. combat, duel, fight. مبارزه کردن to combat, to fight.

مبارك (*mobārak*) A. blessed.

مباشر (*mobāsher*) A. supervisor, superintendent.

مباشرت (*mobāsherat*) A. supervision.

مبال (*mabāl*) A. lavatory.

مبالغه (*mobālegheh*) A. exaggeration.

مبالغه آمیز (*mobālegheh āmiz*) *a.* exaggerated.

مباهات (*mobāhāt*) A. glory.

مباین (*mobāyen*) A. separate, discordant.

مباینت (*mobāyenat*) A. separation, discordance.

مبتدا (*mobtadā*) A. subject (*in grammar*).

مبتدی (*mobtadi*) A. beginner.

مبتذل (*mobtazal*) A. hackneyed, commonplace.

مبتلا (*mobtalā*) A. afflicted.

مبتنی (*mobtani*) A. based, founded.

مبحث (*mabhaṣ*) A. (subject for) debate.

مبدا (*mabdā*) A. origin, beginning.

مبدل (*mobaddal*) A. changed.

مبذول (*mabzul*) A. bestowed. مبذول داشتن to bestow.

مبرا (*mobarrā*) A. free, exempt; innocent.

مبرم (*mobrem*) A. pressing, urgent.

مبرهن (*mobarhan*) A. proved.

مبسوط (*mabsuṭ*) A. extended; detailed.

مبشر (*mobashsher*) A. bearer of good tidings, evangelist.

مبعوث (*mab'uṣ*) A. sent; delegate, envoy, apostle.

مبل (*mobl*) F. furniture.

مبلغ (*mablagh*) A. amount, sum.

مبلغ (*moballegh*) A. missionary.

مبنی (*mabni*) A. based, founded.

مبنی (*mabnā*) A. foundation, basis.

مبهم (*mobham*) A. vague, obscure, ambiguous.

مبهوت (*mabhut*) A. dumb-struck.

مبهی (*mobahhi*) A. aphrodisiac.

مبین (*mobayyen*) A. explaining.

متابعت (*motābe'at*) A. (act of) following; obedience.

متأثر (*mota'aṣṣer*) A. touched, moved.

متأخر (*mota'akhkher*) A. modern.

متارکه (*motārekeh*) A. truce, armistice.

متأسف (*mota'assef*) A. regretful, sorry.

متأسفانه (*mota'assefāneh*) *a.* unfortunately.

متأسی (*mota'assi*) A. following, follower.

متاع (*matā'*) A. goods, merchandise.

متألم (*mota'allem*) A. grieved.

متانت (*matānat*) A. firmness, constancy.

متأنی (*mota'anni*) A. lingering, slow.

متأهل (*mota'ahhel*) A. married.

متبادل (*motabādel*) A. alternate, alternative; reciprocal.

متبحر (*motabaḥḥer*) A. erudite.

متبرک (*motabarrek*) A. sacred, holy.

متبسم (*motabassem*) A. smiling.

متبلور (*motabalver*) A. crystallized.

متبوع (*matbu'*) A. followed, obeyed. دولتِ متبوعه the state to which one belongs.

متتبع (*motatabbe'*) A. one who carries out research.

متجاسر (*motajāser*) A. daring; insurgent.

متجانس (*motajānes*) A. homogeneous.

متجاوز (*motajāvez*) A. exceeding; aggressor. متجاوز از more than.

متجدد (*motajadded*) A. modern.

متجمل (*motajammel*) A. luxurious.

متحارب (*motaḥāreb*) A. belligerent.

متحد (*mottaḥed*) A. united, allied. متحدین allies.

متحرک (*motaḥarrek*) A. movable, mobile.

متحصن (*motaḥaṣṣen*) A. taking refuge.

متحمل (*motaḥammel*) A. suffering. متحمل شدن to suffer.

متحیر (*motaḥayyer*) A. astonished, amazed.

متخاصم (*motakhāṣem*) A. (mutually) hostile.

متخذ (*mottakhaẕ*) A. taken, adopted.

متخصص (*motakhaṣṣeṣ*) A. specialist.

متداول (*motadāvel*) A. current, popular, fashionable.

متدرجاً (*motadarrejan*) A. gradually.

متدین (*motadayyen*) A. religious, pious.

متذکر (*motaẕakker*) A. remembering, reminding متذکر شدن to remember, remind.

متر (*metr*) F. metre.

مترادف (*motarādef*) A. successive; synonym(ous).

متراکم (*motarākem*) A. piled up, accumulated.

مترجم (*motarjem*) A. translator; interpreter.

متردد (*motaradded*) A. irresolute, hesitant.

مترشح (*motarashsheḥ*) A. exuding.

مترصد (*motaraṣṣed*) A. watching for, expecting.

مترقب (*motaraqqab*) A. expected.

مترقی (*motaraqqi*) A. progressive.

متروک (*matruk*) A. abandoned; obsolete.

متزاید (*motazāyed*) A. increasing.

متزلزل (*motazalzel*) A. shaking, trembling; unstable.

متساوی (*motasāvi*) A. equal.

متشابه (*motashābeh*) A. resembling, similar. (*The* h *is pronounced.*)

متشکر (*motashakker*) A. thankful.

متشکل (*motashakkel*) A. formed.

متشکی (*motashakki*) A. complaining; plaintiff.

متشنج (*motashannej*) A. convulsive.

متشیع (*motashayye'*) A. Shiite.

متصاعد (*motaṣā'ed*) A. rising, ascending.

متصدی (*motaṣaddi*) A. person in charge.

متصرف (*motaṣarref*) A. possessing. متصرف شدن to take possession of, to occupy.

متصرفی (*motaṣarrefi*) *a.* occupied.

متصل (*mottaṣel*) A. connected; adjoining; continual.

متصلاً (*mottaṣelan*) A. continually.

متصور (*motaṣavvar*) A. imagined.

متصوف (*motaṣavvef*) A. Sufi.

متضاد (*motaẓādd*) A. opposed; antonym.

متضمن (*motaẓammen*) A. containing, comprising.

متظلم (*motaẓallem*) A. complaining of injustice; petitioner.

متعارف (*mota'āref*) A. paying compliments.

متعارفی (*mota'ārefi*) *a.* usual, ordinary.

متعاقب (*mota'āqeb*) A. following, subsequent.

متعال (*mota'āl*) A. high, lofty.

متعاهد (*mota'āhed*) A. contracting (party).

متعجب (*mota'ajjeb*) A. surprised.

متعدد (*mota'added*) A. numerous.

متعدی (*mota'addi*) A. aggressive, aggressor; transitive.

متعذر (*mota'azzer*) A. apologizing; impossible.

متعرض (*mota'arrez*) A. aggressive, molesting.

متعصب (*mota'asseb*) A. bigot(ted), fanatic(al).

متعفن (*mota'affen*) A. putrefied; infected.

متعلق (*mota'alleq*) A. belonging.

متعلم (*mota'allem*) A. student.

متعهد (*mota'ahhed*) A. undertaking.

متغیر (*motaghayyer*) A. changed, changeable; angry, offended.

متفاوت (*motafāvet*) A. different, distinct.

متفرع (*motafarre'*) A. branching.

متفرعات (*motafarre'āt*) A. by-products.

متفرق (*motafarreq*) A. dispersed; miscellaneous.

متفق (*mottafeq*) A. united, allied. متفقین allies.

متفکر (*motafakker*) A. thoughtful, reflective.

متقابل (*motaqābel*) A. opposite, reciprocal.

متقارب (*motaqāreb*) A. convergent; *name of a poetical metre.*

متقاطع (*motaqāte'*) A. intersecting.

متقاعد (*motaqā'ed*) A. retired.

متقدم (*motaqaddem*) A. anterior, ancient.

متقلب (*motaqalleb*) A. cheat, adulterator.

متکا (*mottakā, motakkā*) A. bolster, pillow.

متکبر (*motakabber*) A. proud.

متکفل (*motakaffel*) A. guaranteeing, undertaking.

متکلم (*motakallem*) A. speaking, speaker; first person (*in grammar*).

متکی (*mottaki*) A. based, founded.

متلاشی (*motalāshi*) A. decomposed, broken up.

متلون (*motalavven*) A. many-coloured; fickle.

متمادی (*motamādi*) A. prolonged.

متمایز (*motamāyez*) A. distinct, distinguished.

متمایل (*motamāyel*) A. inclined.

متمتع (*motamatte'*) A. enjoying.

متمدن (*motamadden*) A. civilized.

متمرد (*motamarred*) A. disobedient, rebellious.

متمرکز (*motamarkez*) A. concentrated.

متمکن (*motamakken*) A. well-established.

متملق (*motamalleq*) A. flattering, flatterer.

متمنی (*motamanni*) A. requesting, asking.

متموج (*motamavvej*) A. undulating.

متمول (*motamavvel*) A. wealthy.

متن (*matn*) A. text.

متنازع فيه (*motanāza'on fih*) A. disputed about, litigious.

متناسب (*motanāseb*) A. proportionate, symmetrical.

متناقض (*motanāqez̤*) A. contradictory.

متناوب (*motanāveb*) A. alternate, recurring.

متناهى (*motanāhi*) A. finished.

متنبه (*motanabbeh*) A. wakened, vigilant; admonished. (*The* h *is pronounced.*)

متنفذ (*motanaffez̤*) A. influential.

متنفر (*motanaffer*) A. abhorring.

متنكر (*motanakker*) A. disguised.

متنوع (*motanavve'*) A. various, variable.

متواتر (*motavāter*) A. successive.

متوارى (*motavāri*) A. hidden.

متوارى شدن to hide.

متوازى (*motavāzi*) A. parallel.

متواضع (*motavāz̤e'*) A. humble.

متوالى (*motavāli*) A. successive.

متوجه (*motavajjeh*) A. facing, turning; attentive.

متوحش (*motavaḥḥesh*) A. frightened.

متوسط (*motavasseṭ*) A. middle, medium, average.

متورم (*motavarrem*) A. swollen, inflated.

متوسل (*motavassel*) A. resorting.

متوطن (*motavaṭṭen*) A. making one's home, settling down.

متوفى (*motavaffā*) A. deceased.

متوقع (*motavaqqe'*) A. expecting.

متوقف (*motavaqqef*) A. halting, stopped.

متوكل (*motavakkel*) A. trusting.

متولد (*motavalled*) A. born.

متولى (*motavalli*) A. administrator, custodian.

مته (*matteh*) gimlet.

متهاجم (*motahājem*) A. attacking.

متهم (*mottaham*) A. accused (person).

متهم (*mottahem*) A. accusing, accuser.

متين (*matin*) A. strong, firm.

متينگ (*meting*) F. (political) meeting.

مثابه (*maṣābeh*) A. position, rank.

مثال (*maṣāl*) A. example; likeness.

مثانه (*maṣāneh*) A. bladder.

مثبت (*moṣbat*) A. proved; positive, affirmative.

مثقال (*meṣqāl*) A. *name of a Persian weight, the sixteenth part of a* سير.

مثل (*maṣal*) A. proverb, example.

مثل (*mesl*) A. likeness. مثلِ like.

مثلاً (*maṣalan*) A. for example, e.g.

مثلث (*moṣallaṣ*) A. triangular, triangle.

مثمر (*moṣmer*) A. fruitful.

مثنوى (*maṣnavi*) A. poetry in rhymed couplets.

مثنى (*moṣannā*) A. doubled; dual.

مجادله (*mojādeleh*) A. dispute.

مجار (*majār*) Magyar, Hungarian.

مجارستان (*majārestān*) Hungary.

مجارى (*majāri*) A. channels. (*Pl. of* مجرى.)

مجاز (*majāz*) A. metaphor.

مجاز (*mojāz*) A. permitted, authorized.

مجازات (*mojāzāt*) A. punishment. مجازات کردن to punish.

مجال (*majāl*) A. leisure, opportunity.

مجال کردن to find an opportunity.

مجالس (*majāles*) A. assemblies, meetings. (*Pl. of* مجلس).

مجامعت (*mojāme'at*) A. copulation.

مجاناً (*majjānan*) A. gratis.

مجانی (*majjāni*) A. gratuitous.

مجاور (*mojāver*) A. neighbouring.

مجاورت (*mojāverat*) A. neighbourhood, proximity.

مجاهد (*mojāhed*) A. warrior of the Faith; fighter for freedom.

مجاهدت (*mojāhedat*) A. endeavour; engagement in a Holy War; fighting for freedom.

مجبور (*majbur*) A. compelled, forced.

مجتمع (*mojtame'*) A. assembled.

مجتهد (*mojtahed*) A. Shia divine.

مجد (*majd*) A. glory.

مجدد (*mojaddad*) A. renewed.

مجدداً (*mojaddadan*) A. again.

مجذوب (*majẕub*) A. attracted.

مجرب (*mojarrab*) A. experienced.

مجرد (*mojarrad*) A. bare, naked; single, unmarried; incorporeal. بمجردِ immediately upon.

مجرم (*mojrem*) A. guilty, criminal.

مجروح (*majruḥ*) A. wounded.

مجری (*majrā*) A. channel.

مجری (*mojrā*) A. executed, carried out.

مجری (*mojri*) A. executive.

مجزی (*mojazzā*) A. separate, distinct.

مجسم (*mojassam*) A. incarnate, corporeal.

مجسمه (*mojassameh*) A. statue.

مجعد (*moja''ad*) A. curly.

مجلد (*mojallad*) A. bound; volume.

مجلس (*majles*) A. assembly, meeting; party. مجلسِ شوراي ملی National Consultative Assembly.

مجلل (*mojallal*) A. splendid, magnificent.

مجله (*majalleh*) A. magazine.

مجمع (*majma'*) A. assembly.

مجمع الجزایر (*majma'o'l-jazāyer*) A. archipelago.

مجمل (*mojmal*) A. brief, concise.

مجملا (*mojmalan*) A. briefly.

مجموع (*majmu'*) A. total (sum); tranquil.

مجموعه (*majmu'eh*) A. collection; miscellany; magazine; tray.

مجنون (*majnun*) A. insane, madman.

مجوز (*mojavvaz*) A. permitted.

مجوس (*majus*) A. Magian, Magi.

مجوف (*mojavvaf*) A. hollow.

مجهز (*mojahhaz*) A. equipped.

مجهول (*majhul*) A. unknown.

مجید (*majid*) A. glorious.

مچ (*moch*) wrist.

محاذی (*moḥāẕi*) A. opposite.

محارب (*moḥāreb*) A. belligerent.

محاربه (*moḥārebeh*) A. war, battle.

محاسب (*moḥāseb*) A. accountant.

محاسبه (*moḥāsebeh*) A. calculation, account.

محاسن (*mahāsen*) A. good deeds; beauties; beard.

محاصر (*mohāser*) A. besieging, besieger.

محاصره (*mohāṣereh*) A. siege.

محاصره کردن to besiege.

محاضره (*mohāẓereh*) A. conversation.

محافظ (*mohāfeẓ*) A. guardian, keeper.

محافظت (*mohāfezat*) A. guardianship, custody, protection.

محافظه کار (*mohāfeẓeh kār*) *a.* Conservative.

محافل (*mahāfel*) A. circles. (*Pl. of* محفل.)

محاکمه (*mohākemeh*) A. trial.

محال (*mohāl*) A. impossible.

محال (*mahāll*) A. districts, suburbs. (*Pl. of* محل.)

محاوره (*mohāvereh*) A. conversation.

محب (*mohebb*) A. loving; lover, friend.

محبت (*mahabbat*) A. love.

محبس (*mahbas*) A. prison.

محبوب (*mahbub*) A. beloved, popular.

محبوبیت (*mahbubiyyat*) A. popularity.

محبوس (*mahbus*) A. imprisoned.

محتاج (*mohtāj*) A. needing, needy.

محترق (*mohtareq*) A. inflammable, combustible, explosive.

محترم (*mohtaram*) A. honourable, respectable.

محتسب (*mohtaseb*) A. municipal officer.

محتشم (*mohtasham*) A. magnificent; respectable.

محتکر (*mohtaker*) A. speculator, monopolizer.

محتمل (*mohtamel*) A. probable.

محتوی (*mohtavi*) A. containing.

محجر (*mahjar*) A. railing, fence.

محجوب (*mahjub*) A. modest.

محدب (*mohaddab*) A. convex.

محدود (*mahdud*) A. limited, bounded.

محذور (*mahẕur*) A. obstacle.

محراب (*mehrāb*) A. niche in the side of a mosque.

محرر (*moharrer*) A. writer.

محرف (*moharraf*) A. corrupted, altered.

محرک (*moharrek*) A. motor; motive; stimulant; agitator.

محرم (*mahram*) A. confidant.

محرم (*moharram*) A. forbidden; *name of the first month of the Arabic lunar year.*

محرمانه (*mahramāneh*) *a.* secret.

محروم (*mahrum*) A. deprived.

محزون (*mahzun*) A. sad.

محسن (*mohsen*) A. beneficent, benefactor; *masc. proper name.*

محسنات (*mohassanāt*) A. virtues, advantages.

محسوب (*mahsub*) A. reckoned.

محسود (*mahsud*) A. envied.

محسوس (*mahsus*) A. perceptible, tangible.

محشر (*mahshar*) A. (gathering-place on) the Day of Judgment.

محصل (*mohaṣṣel*) A. collector; student.

محصن (*mohṣen*) A. chaste.

محصور (*mahṣur*) A. besieged.

محصول (*mahṣul*) A. crop; produce, product.

محض (*maḥẓ*) A. mere, pure. محضِ only for.

محضر (*maḥẓar*) A. presence; nature; protocol.

محظور (*maḥẓur*) A. obstacle.

محظوظ (*maḥẓuẓ*) A. pleased, delighted.

محفظه (*maḥfaẓeh*) A. case, chest.

محفل (*maḥfel*) A. assembly, circle.

محفوظ (*maḥfuẓ*) A. protected.

محقر (*moḥaqqar*) A. despised, contemptible.

محقق (*moḥaqqaq*) A. ascertained, verified; certain.

محقق (*moḥaqqeq*) A. investigator, critic.

محققاً (*moḥaqqaqan*) A. certainly.

محک (*meḥakk*) A. touchstone. محکِ تجربه criterion, test case.

محکم (*moḥkam*) A. firm, strong.

محکمه (*maḥkameh*) A. law court; clinic.

محکوم (*maḥkum*) A. condemned.

محل (*maḥall*) A. place.

محلل (*moḥallel*) A. solvent.

محلول (*maḥlul*) A. dissolved; solution.

محله (*maḥalleh*) A. quarter, district.

محلی (*maḥalli*) A. local.

محمد (*moḥammad*) A. Mohammed.

محمدی (*moḥammadi*) A. pertaining to Mohammed, Mohammedan. گلِ محمدی Damascus rose.

محمل (*maḥmel*) A. camel-litter.

محمود (*maḥmud*) A. praiseworthy; *masc. proper name.*

محمول (*maḥmul*) A. loaded, shipped.

محمولات (*maḥmulāt*) A. cargo.

محمی (*maḥmi*) A. protected.

محنت (*meḥnat*) A. toil, suffering.

محو (*maḥv*) A. obliteration, erasure. محو کردن to obliterate, erase. محو — بودن to be fascinated by—.

محور (*meḥvar*) A. pivot, axis.

محول (*moḥavval*) A. changed; delivered.

محیر العقول (*moḥayyero'l-'oqul*) A. stupendous.

محیط (*moḥiṭ*) A. surrounding; circumference; environment, atmosphere.

محیل (*moḥil*) A. cunning.

محیی (*moḥyi*) A. reviving.

مخابره (*mokhābereh*) A. correspondence; message. مخابره کردن to communicate; to wire, telegraph.

مخارج (*makhārej*) A. expenses.

مخاصم (*mokhāṣem*) A. antagonist(ic).

مخاصمت (*mokhāṣemat*) A. antagonism.

مخاطب (*mokhāṭab*) A. (person) addressed; second person (*in grammar*).

مخاطب (*mokhāṭeb*) A. speaker.

مخاطبت (*mokhāṭebat*) A. speech, address.

مخاطره (*mokhāṭereh*) A. risk, danger.

مخالطه (*mokhāleṭeh*) A. intercourse.

مخالف (*mokhālef*) A. contrary, opposed; opponent.

مخالفت (*mokhālefat*) A. opposition.

مخبر (*mokhber*) A. correspondent.

مخبط (*mokhabbaṭ*) A. insane.

مختار (*mokhtār*) A. free, independent, authorized. وزیرِ مختار minister plenipotentiary.

مخترع (*mokhtare'*) A. inventor.

مختص (*mokhtaṣṣ*) A. peculiar, special.

مختصر (*mokhtaṣar*) A. brief ; slight.

مختل (*mokhtall*) A. confused, disordered.

مختلس (*mokhtales*) A. embezzler.

مختلط (*mokhtaleṭ*) A. mixed.

مختلف (*mokhtalef*) A. different, various.

مختوم (*makhtum*) A. sealed ; concluded.

مخدر (*mokhadder*) A. narcotic.

مخدوم (*makhdum*) A. served ; master.

مخرب (*mokhreb*) A. destructive, destroyer.

مخرج (*makhraj*) A. outlet, way out ; denominator ; pronunciation.

مخروب (*makhrub*) A. destroyed, ruined.

مخروط (*makhruṭ*) A. cone.

مخروطی (*makhruṭi*) *a.* conical ; cone.

مخزن (*makhzan*) A. storehouse, treasury.

مخصوص (*makhṣuṣ*) A. special ; specific ; private.

مخصوصاً (*makhsusan*) A. especially.

مخطط (*mokhaṭṭaṭ*) A. striped.

مخفی (*makhfi*) A. hidden, secret.

مخل (*mokhell*) A. disturbing, disturber.

مخلد (*mokhallad*) A. eternal, permanent.

مخلص (*mokhleṣ*) A. sincere, devoted (friend).

مخلوط (*makhluṭ*) A. mixed ; mixture.

مخلوق (*makhluq*) A. created, produced.

مخمل (*makhmal*) A. velvet.

مخملک (*makhmalak*) *a.* scarlet fever.

مخمور (*makhmur*) A. intoxicated.

مخنث (*mokhannaṣ*) A. effeminate, hermaphrodite.

مخوف (*makhuf*) A. terrible, dreadful.

مد (*madd*) A. extension ; ebb, flow.

مد (*mod*) F. fashion(able).

مداح (*maddāḥ*) A. panegyrist.

مداخل (*madākhel*) A. indirect earnings, income.

مداخله (*modākheleh*) A. intervention, interference. مداخله کردن to intervene, to interfere.

مداد (*medād*) A. pencil.

مدار (*madār*) A. orbit, pivot ; circle, tropic.

مدارا (*modārā*) A. caution, dissimulation, courtesy.

مدارج (*madārej*) A. degrees.

مدارس (*madāres*) A. schools. (*Pl. of* مدرسه).

مدارک (*madārek*) A. documents. (*Pl. of* مدرک.)

مدافع (*modāfe'*) A. defending, defender ; barrister.

مدافعه (*modāfe'eh*) A. defence.

مدال (*medāl*) F. medal.

مدام (*modām*) A. continual(ly), always.

مداوا (*modāvā*) A. medical treatment.

مداوم (*modāvem*) A. continual; persevering.

مداومت (*modāvemat*) A. continuance; perseverance.

مدبر (*modabber*) A. prudent, skilful; manager.

مدبر (*modber*) A. unfortunate (person).

مدت (*moddat*) A. space of time.

مدح (*madḥ*) A. praise.

مدحت (*medḥat*) A. praise.

مدخل (*madkhal*) A. entrance.

مدد (*madad*) A. help, assistance.

مدرس (*modarres*) A. teacher.

مدرسه (*madraseh*) A. school.

مدرك (*madrak*) A. evidence, document.

مدعو (*mad'ovv*) A. invited; guest.

مدعی (*modda'i*) A. pretender, claimant, plaintiff.

مدعی العموم (*modda'io 'l-'omum*) A. attorney-general.

مدعی علیه (*modda'ā 'aleyh*) A. defendant.

مدفن (*madfan*) A. tomb.

مدفوع (*madfu'*) A. repulsed; excrement.

مدفون (*madfun*) A. buried.

مدل (*model*) F. model.

مدلل (*modallal*) A. proved, demonstrated.

مدلول (*madlul*) A. purport, tenour.

مدنی (*madani*) A. civil, civic.

مدنیت (*madaniyyat*) A. civilization.

مدور (*modavvar*) A. round, spherical.

مدون (*modavvan*) A. collected in a *divan*; codified.

مدهوش (*madhush*) A. dumbfounded; unconscious.

مدیترانه (*mediterāneh*) F. Mediterranean.

مدید (*madid*) A. long.

مدیر (*modir*) A. director, administrator, manager.

مدینه (*madineh*) A. city; Medina.

مدیون (*madyun*) A. debtor, indebted. مدیون بودن to owe.

مذاق (*maẕāq*) A. taste, palate.

مذاکره (*moẕākereh*) A. conversation, negotiation, discussion.

مذاهب (*maẕāheb*) A. religions. (*Pl. of* مذهب.)

مذبح (*maẕbaḥ*) A. altar.

مذبوح (*maẕbuḥ*) A. slaughtered.

مذکر (*moẕakkar*) A. masculine.

مذکور (*maẕkur*) A. (above) mentioned.

مذلت (*maẕallat*) A. abjectness, baseness.

مذمت (*maẕammat*) A. blame, reproach.

مذموم (*maẕmum*) A. reprehensible.

مذهب (*maẕhab*) A. religion.

مذهبی (*maẕhabi*) A. religious.

مرآت (*mer'āt*) A. mirror.

مراتب (*marāteb*) A. degrees; storeys; facts, particulars. (*Pl. of* مرتبه.)

مراتع (*marāte'*) A. pastures. (*Pl. of* مرتع.)

مراجعت (*morāje'at*) A. return.
 مراجعت کردن to return.

مراجعه (*morāje'eh*) A. reference, resort, application.

مراحم (*marāḥem*) A. kindnesses, favours. (*Pl. of* مرحمت.)

مراد (*morād*) A. desire; intention, meaning.

مرارت (*marārat*) A. suffering, hardship.

مراسله (*morāseleh*) A. letter.
 مراسلات correspondence.

مراسم (*marāsem*) A. customs; ceremonies.

مراعات (*morā'āt*) A. observance, regard.

مرافعه (*morāfe'eh*) A. litigation, lawsuit.

مراقب (*morāqeb*) A. watchful, observant.

مراقبت (*morāqebat*) A. watchfulness, observation.

مراکز (*marākez*) A. centres. (*Pl. of* مرکز.)

مراکش (*marākash*) A. Morocco.

مرال (*marāl*) T. ibex.

مرام (*marām*) A. desire, wish; aim, purpose; (political) platform, ideology.

مراوده (*morāvedeh*) A. intercourse.

مربا (*morabbā*) A. jam.

مربع (*marabba'*) A. square.

مربوط (*marbuṭ*) A. connected, related, relevant; dependent.

مربی (*morabbi*) A. tutor.

مرتب (*morattab*) A. arranged, orderly, regular.

مرتباً (*morattaban*) A. regularly.

مرتبه (*martabeh*) A. Step, degree; storey; time. یکمرتبه once.

مرتجع (*mortaje'*) A. reactionary.

مرتد (*mortadd*) A. apostate.

مرتع (*marta'*) A. pasture.

مرتعش (*morta'esh*) A. trembling.

مرتفع (*mortafe'*) A. high, lofty.
 مرتفع کردن to remove; to meet (*requirements*).

مرتکب (*mortakeb*) A. perpetrator; guilty.

مرثیه (*marṣieh*) A. elegy.

مرجان (*marjān*) A. coral.

مرجع (*marja'*) A. place of reference, destination.

مرحبا (*marḥabā*) A. welcome! bravo!

مرحله (*marḥaleh*) A. stage.

مرحمت (*marḥamat*) A. pity; kindness, favour.

مرحوم (*marḥum*) A. deceased.
 — مرحومِ the late —.

مرخص (*morakhkhaṣ*) A. dismissed, permitted to leave.

مرخصی (*morakhkhaṣi*) *a.* leave, furlough.

مرد (*mard*) man.

مرداب (*mordāb*) lagoon; marsh.

مرداد (*mordād*) *name of the fifth month of the Persian year.*

مردار (*mordār*) carrion.

مردانگی (*mardānegi*) manliness.

مردانه (*mardāneh*) manly; belonging to men, men's.

مردد (*moraddad*) A. hesitating, wavering.

مردم (*mardom*) people; mankind.

مردم خوار (*mardom khvār*) cannibal.

مردم شناسی (*mardom shenāsi*) anthropology.

مردن (*mordan*) to die.

مردود (*mardud*) A. rejected.

مرده (*mordeh*) dead.

مردی (*mardi*) manhood, manliness.

مرز (*marz*) frontier, boundary; region, country.

مرز دار (*marz dār*) frontier guard.

مرسل (*morsal*) A. sent.

مرسوم (*marsum*) A. custom(ary).

مرشد (*morshed*) A. spiritual guide.

مرصد (*marṣad*) A. observatory.

مرصع (*moraṣṣa'*) A. studded with jewels.

مرض (*maraẓ*) A. disease.

مرضی (*marẓā*) A. patients. (*Pl. of* مریض.)

مرضی (*marẓi*) A. admirable, laudable.

مرطوب (*marṭub*) A. moist, damp.

مرعوب (*mar'ub*) A. terrified.

مرعی (*mar'i*) A. observed, regarded.

مرغ (*margh*) meadow.

مرغ (*morgh*) bird; domestic fowl.

مرغابی (*morghābi*) duck.

مرغزار (*marghzār*) meadow.

مرغوب (*marghub*) A. desired, desirable; in demand.

مرفق (*merfaq*) A. elbow.

مرقد (*marqad*) A. tomb.

مرقع (*moraqqa'*) A. patched, ragged.

مرقوم (*marqum*) A. written; aforesaid.

مرقومه (*marqumeh*) A. letter.

مرکب (*markab*) A. mount (*horse, camel, etc.*); ship.

مرکب (*morakkab*) A. composed, compound; ink.

مرکبات (*morakkabāt*) A. compounds; citrous fruits.

مرکز (*markaz*) A. centre; headquarters.

مرکزی (*markazi*) *a.* central.

مرگ (*marg*) death.

مرمت (*marammat*) A. reparation, repair. مرمت کردن to repair.

مرمر (*marmar*) marble.

مرموز (*marmuz*) A. cryptic, occult.

مروارید (*marvārid*) pearl.

مروت (*morovvat*) A. manliness, humanity.

مرور (*morur*) A. passing, lapse.

مرهم (*marham*) A. ointment, poultice, plaster.

مریخ (*merrikh*) A. Mars.

مرید (*morid*) A. disciple, novice.

مریض (*mariẓ*) A. sick, ill.

مریضخانه (*mariẓkhāneh*) *a.* hospital.

مریم (*maryam*) A. Mary.

مرئی (*mar'i*) A. visible.

مزاج (*mezāj*) A. temperament, constitution.

مزاحم (*mozāḥem*) A. molesting, inconvenient.

مزاحمت (*mozāḥemat*) A. molestation; inconvenience.

مزار (*mazār*) A. tomb.

مزارع (*mazāre'*) A. fields. (*Pl. of* مزرعه.)

مزاوجت (*mozāvejat*) A. marriage.

مزایا (*mazāyā*) A. advantages, virtues. (*Pl. of* مزیت.)

مزایده (*mozāyedeh*) A. auction.

مزبور (*mazbur*) A. aforesaid.

مزد (*mozd*) wages, hire.

مزدور (*mozdur*) hired (labourer).

مزرعه (*mazra'eh*) A. field.

مزروع (*mazru'*) A. cultivated; crop, harvest.

مزمن (*mozmen*) A. chronic.

مزور (*mozavver*) A. deceitful; impostor.

مزه (*mazeh*) taste, flavour.

مزیت (*maziyyat*) A. advantage, excellence, virtue.

مزید (*mazid*) A. increase.

مزین (*mozayyan*) A. adorned.

مژده (*mozhdeh*) glad tidings.

مژه (*mozheh*) eyelash.

مس (*mes*) copper.

مسابقه (*mosābeqeh*) A. competition.

مساجد (*masājed*) A. mosques. (*Pl. of* مسجد.)

مساح (*massāḥ*) A. surveyor.

مساحت (*mesaḥat*) A. land-measurement, surveying; area.

مساعد (*mosā'ed*) A. assisting, favourable.

مساعدت (*mosā'edat*) A. assistance.

مساعده (*mosā'edeh*) A. advance (money).

مساعی (*masā'i*) A. efforts.

مسافت (*masāfat*) A. distance.

مسافر (*mosāfer*) A. traveller; passenger.

مسافرت (*mosāferat*) A. journey.

مسالمت (*mosālemat*) A. peacefulness, tranquillity.

مسامحه (*mosāmeḥeh*) A. negligence.

مساوات (*mosāvāt*) A. equality.

مساوی (*mosāvi*) A. equal.

مسائل (*masā'el*) A. questions, problems. (*Pl. of* مسئله.)

مسبب (*mosabbeb*) A. causing, one who causes.

مسبوق (*masbuq*) A. informed, aware.

مست (*mast*) drunk; in rut.

مستأصل (*mosta'ṣal*) A. eradicated; helpless.

مستأجر (*mosta'jer*) A. tenant, lessee.

مستبد (*mostabedd*) A. despot(ic).

مستتر (*mostatar*) A. veiled, hidden.

مستثنی (*mostaṣnā*) A. excepted, exceptional.

مستجاب (*mostajāb*) A. (favourably) answered, granted.

مستحاث (*mostaḥāṣ*) A. fossil.

مستحضر (*mostaḥẓar*) A. informed.

مستحق (*mostaḥaqq*) A. deserving; needy.

مستحکم (*mostaḥkam*) A. firm, solid.

مستحیل (*mostaḥil*) A. transmuted.

مستخدم (*mostakhdem*) A. employee.

مستخلص (*mostakhlaṣ*) A. released, liberated.

مستدعی (*mostad'i*) A. requesting.

مستدیر (*mostadir*) A. round, circular, spherical.

مستراح (*mostarāḥ*) A. lavatory.

مسترد (*mostaradd*) A. returned, restored, withdrawn.

مستسقی (*mostaqsi*) A. dropsical (person).

مستشار (*mostashār*) A. adviser, counsellor.

مستشرق (*mostashreq*) A. orientalist.

مستطاب (*moṣtaṭāb*) A. excellent.

مستطیل (*mostaṭil*) A. oblong, rectangular.

مستظرف (*mostaẓraf*) A. fine, elegant.

مستعجل (*mosta'jel*) A. hasty.

مستعد (*mosta'edd*) A. prepared, ready; able, apt.

مستعفی (*mosta'fi*) A. resigned, resigning.

مستعمره (*mosta'mareh*) A. colony.

مستعمل (*mosta'mal*) A. used, second-hand; current.

مستغرق (*mostaghraq*) A. drowned; absorbed.

مستغل (*mostaghall*) A. landed property, real estate.

مستفاد (*mostafād*) A. made use of; understood.

مستفیض (*mostafiẓ*) A. deriving benefit, profiting.

مستقبل (*mostaqbal*) A. future (tense).

مستقبل (*mostaqbel*) A. one that goes to meet, welcomer.

مستقر (*mostaqerr*) A. fixed, established.

مستقل (*mostaqell*) A. independent.

مستقیم (*mostaqim*) A. direct.

مستقیماً (*mostaqiman*) A. directly.

مستلزم (*mostalzem*) A. necessitating.

مستمر (*mostamerr*) A. constant.

مستمری (*mostamerri*) *a.* pension.

مستمسک (*mostamsak*) A. basis; pretext.

مستمع (*mostame'*) A. listener.

مستملک (*mostamlak*) A. possessed.

مستملکات (*mostamlakāt*) A. colonies.

مستمند (*mostamand*) unhappy; poor.

مستند (*mostanad*) A. supported, based; support, base.

مستنطق (*mostanṭeq*) A. examining magistrate.

مستوجب (*mostoujeb*) A. deserving, worthy.

مستور (*mastur*) A. veiled, covered; chaste.

مستوفی (*mostoufi*) A. state accountant.

مستولی (*mostouli*) A. seizing, occupying; predominant, prevalent.

مستوی (*mostavi*) A. plane, level; straight; equal.

مستهجن (*mostahjan*) A. obscene.

مستهلک (*mostahlak*) A. ruined; amortized.

مستی (*masti*) drunkenness.

مسجد (*masjed*) A. mosque.

مسح (*masḥ*) A. annointment.

مسخ (*maskh*) A. metamorphosis.

مسخر (*mosakhkhar*) A. conquered.

مسخرگی (*maskharegi*) *a.* buffoonery.

مسخره (*maskhareh*) A. buffoon; laughing-stock.

مسدود (*masdud*) A. closed, stopped.

مسرت (*masarrat*) A. joy.

مسرف (*mosref*) A. prodigal, extravagant; spendthrift.

مسرور (*masrur*) A. glad, happy.

مسروق (*masruq*) A. stolen.

مسری (*mosri*) A. contagious.

مسطح (*mosaṭṭaḥ*) A. flat, level, plane.

مسطر (*mesṭar*) A. ruler.

مسطور (*masṭur*) A. written; aforesaid.

مسعود (*mas'ud*) A. auspicious; *masc. proper name.*

مسقط (*mosqeṭ*) A. abortive.

مسقط الرأس (*masqaṭo'r-ra's*) A. birthplace.

مسقف (*mosaqqaf*) A. roofed.

مسکر (*mosker*) A. intoxicating.

مسکرات (*moskerāt*) A. intoxicants.

مسکن (*maskan*) A. dwelling.

مسکن (*mosakken*) A. alleviating; anodyne.

مسکو (*maskou*) Moscow.

مسکوت عنه (*maskuton 'anh*) A. passed over in silence; left in abeyance.

مسکوک (*maskuk*) A. coin(ed).

مسکین (*meskin*) A. poor, wretched.

مسگر (*mesgar*) coppersmith.

مسلح (*mosallaḥ*) A. armed.

مسلسل (*mosalsal*) A. concatenated, linked; consecutive, continuous; machine-gun.

مسلط (*mosallaṭ*) A. predominant.

مسلک (*maslak*) A. way, path; method, policy, principle.

مسلم (*mosallam*) A. certain, confirmed, established.

مسلم (*moslem*) A. Moslem.

مسلماً (*mosallaman*) A. certainly.

مسلمان (*mosalmān*) *a.* Mohammedan.

مسلمانی (*mosalmāni*) *a.* Mohammedanism.

مسلوب (*maslub*) A. deprived, divested.

مسلول (*maslul*) A. consumptive.

مسمار (*mesmār*) A. nail, peg.

مسموع (*masmu'*) A. heard; valid, plausible.

مسموعات (*masmu'āt*) A. rumours.

مسموم (*masmum*) A. poisoned.

مسمی (*mosammā*) A. called, named.

مسن (*mosenn*) A. aged.

مسند (*masnad*) A. seat; cushion; throne.

مسواک (*mesvāk*) A. toothbrush.

مسوده (*mosavvadeh*) A. rough draft.

مسهل (*mos-hel*) A. purgative.

مسیح (*masiḥ*) A. Messiah.

مسیحی (*masiḥi*) A. Christian.

مسیر (*masir*) A. line, path, course.

مسئله (*mas'aleh*) A. question, problem.

مسیو (*mosyu*) F. monsieur.

مسئول (*mas'ul*) A. responsible.

مسئولیت (*mas'uliyyat*) A. responsibility.

مشابه (*moshābeh*) A. resembling, similar. (*The* h *is pronounced*).

مشابهت (*moshābehat*) A. likeness, similarity.

مشاجره (*moshājereh*) A. quarrel, dispute.

مشار اليه (*moshāron eleih*) A. the aforesaid.

مشار بالبنان (*moshāron be'l-banān*) A. famous, illustrious.

مشارکت (*moshārekat*) A. partnership, association.

مشاطه (*mashāṭṭeh*) A. bride-dresser; lady's maid.

مشاع (*moshā'*) A. joint, undivided.

مشاعره (*moshā'ereh*) A. poetical contest.

مشاق (*mashshāq*) A. instructor.

مشام (*mashāmm*) A. sense of smell.

مشاور (*moshāver*) A. counsellor. وزيرِ مشاور minister without portfolio.

مشاوره (*moshāvereh*) A. consultation.

مشاهره (*moshāhedeh*) A. observation. مشاهده کردن to observe.

مشاهير (*mashāhir*) A. famous people. (*Pl. of* مشهور.)

مشايخ (*mashāyekh*) A. elders, learned men, sheikhs. (*Pl. of* شيخ.)

مشايعت (*moshāye'at*) A. (act of) escorting.

مشت (*mosht*) fist, handful.

مشتاق (*moshtāq*) A. eager, desirous.

مشتبه (*moshtabeh*) A. doubtful, ambiguous. (*The* h *is pronounced.*)

مشترک (*moshtarek*) A. joint, common; partner; subscriber.

مشتری (*moshtari*) A. customer; the planet Jupiter.

مشتعل (*moshta'el*) A. aflame, kindled.

مشتق (*moshtaqq*) A. derived.

مشتقات (*moshtaqqāt*) A. derivatives, by-products.

مشتمال (*moshtmāl*) massage.

مشجر (*moshajjar*) A. planted with trees.

مشحون (*mashḥun*) A. crammed full.

مشخص (*moshakhkhaṣ*) A. specified.

مشدد (*moshaddad*) A. strengthened; pronounced double.

مشرف (*mosharraf*) A. honoured.

مشرف (*moshref*) A. imminent; overlooking; on the verge.

مشرق (*mashreq*) A. East.

مشرقی (*mashreqi*) *a.* eastern.

مشرک (*moshrek*) A. polytheist.

مشروب (*mashrub*) A. drinkable; drink; irrigated.

مشروح (*mashruḥ*) A. detailed; explained.

مشروط (*mashruṭ*) A. conditional.

مشروطه (*mashruṭeh*) A. constitution(al).

مشروطيت (*mashruṭiyyat*) A. constitution.

مشروع (*mashru'*) A. legal, legitimate.

مشعر (*mosh'er*) A. indicating.

مشعشع (*mosha'sha'*) A. brilliant.

مشعل (*maɛh'al*) A. torch.

مشعوف (*mash'uf*) A. delighted.

مشغله (*mashghaleh*) A. business, occupation.

مشغول (*mashghul*) A. occupied, busy.
مشفق (*moshfeq*) A. kind, sympathetic.
مشق (*mashq*) A. drill, exercise.
مشقت (*mashaqqat*) A. toil, hardship.
مشك (*mashk*) water-skin.
مشك (*meshk*) musk.
مشكل (*moshkel*) A. difficult.
مشكلات (*moshkelāt*) A. difficulties.
مشكوك (*mashkuk*) A. doubtful.
مشكی (*meshki*) black.
مشكين (*meshkin*) musky.
مشمع (*moshamma'*) A. covered with wax; oilcloth.
مشمعی (*moshamma'i*) *a.* made of oilcloth.
مشمول (*mashmul*) A. included, incorporated; conscript.
مشوب (*mashub*) A. poisoned, tainted.
مشورت (*mashvarat*) A. consultation, counsel.
مشورتی (*mashvarati*) *a.* consultative.
مشوش (*moshavvash*) A. disturbed, confused.
مشوق (*moshavveq*) A. encourager, patron.
مشهود (*mashhud*) A. witnessed.
مشهور (*mashhur*) A. famous.
مشهی (*moshhi*) A. voluptuous; aphrodisiac.
مشی (*mashy*) A. gait; course, policy.
مشير (*moshir*) A. counsellor.
مصاحبت (*moṣāḥebat*) A. society.
مصاحبه (*moṣāḥebeh*) A. interview.
مصادر (*maṣāder*) A. sources. (*Pl. of* مصدر.) مصادرِ امور the authorities.
مصادره (*moṣādereh*) A. confiscation.
مصادف (*moṣādef*) A. coinciding.
مصادم (*moṣādem*) A. colliding.
مصارف (*maṣāref*) A. expenses. (*Pl. of* مصرف.)
مصاف (*maṣāff*) A. battle fields; battle.
مصافحه (*moṣāfeḥeh*) A. (act of) shaking hands.
مصالح (*maṣāleḥ*) A. interests; materials. (*Pl. of* مصلحت.)
مصالحه (*moṣāleḥeh*) A. reconciliation; compromise.
مصائب (*maṣā'eb*) A. calamities, misfortunes. (*Pl. of* مصيبت.)
مصب (*maṣabb*) A. river mouth.
مصباح (*meṣbāḥ*) A. light, candle.
مصحح (*moṣaḥḥeḥ*) A. corrector, editor.
مصحف (*moṣḥaf*) A. book.
مصدر (*maṣdar*) A. source, origin; infinitive.
مصدع (*moṣadde'*) A. importunate.
مصدق (*moṣaddaq*) A. certified.
مصر (*meṣr*) A. Egypt.
مصر (*moṣerr*) A. insistent.
مصرع (*meṣra'*) A. hemistich.
مصرف (*maṣraf*) A. use, consumption, expenditure. مصرف كردن to consume.
مصرف كننده (*maṣraf konandeh*) *a.* consumer.
مصروف (*maṣruf*) A. used, spent.
مصطلح (*moṣṭaleḥ*) A. idiomatic.
مصفی (*moṣaffā*) A. purified, strained.
مصلا (*moṣallā*) A. meeting place for prayer (*outside a town*).

مصلح (*moṣleḥ*) A. pacifier, peace-maker; corrector, reformer.

مصلحت (*maṣlaḥat*) A. welfare, benefit; the best thing to do; affair.

مصلوب (*maṣlub*) A. crucified.

مصمم (*moṣammam*) A. determined.

مصنف (*moṣannef*) A. author.

مصنوع (*maṣnu'*) A. made, created.

مصنوعات (*maṣnu'āt*) A. manufactures.

مصنوعی (*masnu'i*) *a.* artificial.

مصوب (*moṣavvab*) A. approved.

مصور (*moṣavvar*) A. illustrated.

مصون (*maṣun*) A. immune.

مصیبت (*maṣibat*) A. misfortune, calamity.

مضارع (*moẓāre'*) A. aorist.

مضاعف (*moẓā'af*) A. redoubled.

مضاف (*moẓāf*) A. added, joined; noun followed by the *eẓāfat*.

مضاف الیه (*moẓāfon eleih*) A. noun preceded by the *eẓāfat*.

مضایقه (*moẓāyeqeh*) A. (act of) refraining, withholding. مضایقه داشتن to refrain.

مضبوط (*maẓbut*) A. seized, confiscated; recorded; managed.

مضحک (*moẓḥek*) A. ridiculous.

مضر (*moẓerr*) A. harmful, injurious.

مضرب (*maẓrab*) A. multiple.

مضرت (*maẓarrat*) A. injury, harm.

مضروب (*maẓrub*) A. struck; multiplicand.

مضطرب (*moẓṭareb*) A. disturbed, anxious.

مضغ (*maẓgh*) A. mastication.

مضمحل (*moẓmaḥel*) A. destroyed, annihilated. مضمحل کردن to destroy.

مضمون (*maẓmun*) A. contents.

مضیقه (*maẓiqeh*) A. strait, difficulty.

مطابق (*moṭābeq*) A. conforming, conformable.

مطابقت (*moṭābeqat*) A. conformity, concord.

مطاع (*moṭā'*) A. (that must be) obeyed.

مطالب (*maṭāleb*) A. subjects, questions. (*Pl. of* مطلب.)

مطالبه (*moṭālebeh*) A. claim, demand.

مطالعه (*moṭāle'eh*) A. study, consideration.

مطب (*maṭabb*) A. clinic.

مطبخ (*maṭbakh*) A. kitchen.

مطبعه (*maṭba'eh*) A. printing office.

مطبوخ (*maṭbukh*) A. cooked (food).

مطبوع (*maṭbu'*) A. printed; pleasant.

مطبوعات (*maṭbu'āt*) A. press.

مطر (*meṭr*) F. metre.

مطران (*maṭrān*) A. metropolitan, archbishop.

مطرب (*moṭreb*) A. minstrel.

مطربی (*moṭrebi*) *a.* minstrelsy.

مطرح (*maṭraḥ*) A. open to discussion. مطرح کردن to debate.

مطفی (*moṭfi*) A. fireman.

مطلا (*moṭallā*) *a.* gilt.

مطلب (*maṭlab*) A. object of desire; subject, question.

مطلع (*maṭla'*) A. opening distich (*of a poem*).

مطلع (*moṭṭale'*) A. (well) informed.

مطلق (*moṭlaq*) A. absolute.

مطلقاً (*moṭlaqan*) A. absolutely, altogether.

مطلوب (*maṭlub*) A. desired, desirable; desire, wish.

مطمح (*maṭmaḥ*) A. place looked at. مطمح نظر object of desire.

مطمئن (*moṭma'en*) A. sure, safe.

مطیع (*moṭi'*) A. obedient.

مظالم (*maẓālem*) A. cruelties, tyrannies. (*Pl. of* مظلمت.)

مظاهر (*maẓāher*) A. manifestations. (*Pl. of* مظهر.)

مظفر (*moẓaffar*) A. victorious.

مظلم (*moẓlem*) A. dark, gloomy.

مظلمت (*maẓlamat*) A. cruelty, tyranny.

مظلوم (*maẓlum*) A. oppressed; submissive.

مظنون (*maẓnun*) A. suspect(ed).

مظنه (*maẓanneh*) A. opinion, suspicion; current rate; probably.

مظهر (*maẓhar*) A. manifestation.

معا (*ma'ā*) A. intestine.

معابد (*ma'ābed*) A. temples. (*Pl. of* معبد.)

معاد (*ma'ād*) A. resurrection.

معادل (*mo'ādel*) A. equivalent.

معادن (*ma'āden*) A. mines. (*Pl. of* معدن.)

معارض (*mo'āreẓ*) A. opposing, hindering; opponent.

معارضه (*mo'āreẓeh*) A. opposition; dispute.

معارف (*ma'āref*) A. sciences; education. (*Pl. of* معرفت.)

معاش (*ma'āsh*) A. livelihood.

معاشر (*mo'āsher*) A. companion, associate.

معاشرت (*mo'āsherat*) A. association.

معاصر (*mo'āṣer*) A. contemporary.

معاضد (*mo'āẓed*) A. assistant.

معاضدت (*mo'āẓedat*) A. assistance.

معاف (*mo'āf*) A. exempt(ed); excused.

معافیت (*mo'āfiyyat*) A. exemption.

معالج (*mo'ālej*) A. treating, healing.

معالجه (*mo'ālejeh*) A. (medical) treatment; healing, curing.

معامله (*mo'āmeleh*) A. negotiation, dealing, transaction.

معاند (*mo'āned*) A. obstinate.

معانقه (*mo'āneqeh*) A. (act of) embracing.

معانی (*ma'āni*) A. meanings. (*Pl. of* معنی.)

معاودت (*mo'āvedat*) A. return(ing).

معاوضه (*mo'āveẓeh*) A. exchange, compensation.

معاون (*mo'āven*) A. assistant; under-secretary.

معاونت (*mo'āvenat*) A. assistance; office of under-secretary.

معاهده (*mo'āhedeh*) A. treaty, alliance; contract.

معایب (*ma'āyeb*) A. faults.

معاینه (*mo'āyeneh*) A. examination, inspection.

معبد (*ma'bad*) A. place of worship, temple.

معبر (*ma'bar*) A. passage, ford.

معبود (*ma'bud*) A. worshipped; object of worship.

معتاد (*mo'tād*) A. accustomed; usual.

معتبر (*mo'taber*) A. reputable; considerable, large.

معتدل (*mo'tadel*) A. moderate, temperate.

معترض (*mo'tareẓ*) A. objecting, protesting, hindering.

معترف (*mo'taref*) A. confessing, acknowledging.

معتزل (*mo'tazel*) A. schismatic(al).

معتصب (*mo'taṣeb*) A. striker.

معتقد (*mo'taqed*) A. believing. معتقد بودن to believe.

معتكف (*mo'takef*) A. retiring for prayer.

معتمد (*mo'tamad*) A. trustworthy.

معتنا به (*mo'tanā beh*) A. considerable. (*The* h *is pronounced*).

معجزه (*mo'jezeh*) A. miracle.

معدلت (*ma'dalat*) A. justice.

معدن (*ma'dan*) A. mine.

معدنچی (*ma'danchi*) *a.* miner.

معدنیات (*ma'daniyyāt*) A. minerals.

معدود (*ma'dud*) A. numbered; limited.

معدوم (*ma'dum*) A. annihilated.

معده (*me'deh*) A. stomach.

معذرت (*ma'ẕarat*) A. excuse.

معذلك (*ma'aẕālek*) A. nevertheless.

معذور (*ma'ẕur*) A. excused.

معراج (*me'rāj*) A. ascension.

معرض (*ma'raẓ*) A. place of exposure.

معرف (*mo'arref*) A. introducing, introducer.

معرفت (*ma'refat*) A. knowledge, learning, education.

معرفة الارض (*ma'refato'l-arẓ*) A. geology.

معرفة الارضی (*ma'refato'l-arẓi*) *a.* geological.

معرفی (*mo'arrefi*) *a.* introduction. معرفی کردن to introduce.

معرق (*mo'arreq*) A. diaphoretic.

معرکه (*ma'rekeh*) A. battlefield.

معروض (*ma'ruẓ*) A. presented, offered; submitted, reported.

معروف (*ma'ruf*) A. famous, well-known.

معزول (*ma'zul*) A. deposed, dismissed.

معزی الیه (*mo'azzā eleih*) A. (the person) referred to.

معشر (*ma'shar*) A. assembly.

معشوق (*ma'shuq*) A. beloved.

معشوقه (*ma'shuqeh*) A. beloved, sweetheart. (*Fem. of* معشوق*.*)

معصوم (*ma'ṣum*) A. innocent.

معصیت (*ma'ṣiat*) A. sin; rebellion.

معضل (*mo'ẓel*) A. difficult.

معضلات (*mo'ẓelāt*) A. difficulties.

معطر (*mo'aṭṭar*) A. perfumed, fragrant.

معطل (*mo'aṭṭal*) A. delayed, detained.

معطلی (*mo'aṭṭali*) *a.* delay, detention.

معطوف (*ma'ṭuf*) A. inclined, turned.

معظم (*mo'zam*) A. great.

معظّم (*mo'azzam*) A. honourable.

معفو (*ma'fovv*) A. pardoned.

معقول (*ma'qul*) A. rational, reasonable; polite.

معکوس (*ma'kus*) A. inverted, reversed.

معلق (*mo'allaq*) A. hanging, suspended. معلق زدن to turn a somersault.

معلم (*mo'allem*) A. teacher.

معلول (*ma'lul*) A. caused, effected; effect; weak, infirm.

معلوم (*ma'lum*) A. known; evident, obvious.

معلومات (*ma'lumāt*) A. qualifications.

معمار (*me'mār*) A. architect.

معماری (*me'māri*) *a.* architecture.

معمور (*ma'mur*) A. cultivated, inhabited; flourishing.

معمول (*ma'mul*) A. usual, customary. معمول داشتن to practise.

معمولاً (*ma'mulan*) A. usually.

معمى (*mo'ammā*) A. riddle, enigma.

معنوی (*ma'navi*) A. spiritual.

معنى (*ma'nā*) A. meaning.

معوق (*mo'avvaq*) A. delayed.

معهذا (*ma'ahāzā*) A. nevertheless.

معهود (*ma'hud*) A. promised; customary.

معیار (*me'yār*) A. standard.

معیت (*ma'iyyat*) A. company.

معیشت (*ma'ishat*) A. livelihood.

معین (*mo'ayyan*) A. fixed, specified.

معین (*mo'in*) A. assistant.

معیوب (*ma'yub*) A. defective, damaged.

مغ (*mogh*) Magian, fire-worshipper.

مغاره (*maghāreh*) A. cave.

مغازه (*maghāzeh*) store.

مغاک (*maghāk*) pit.

مغایر (*moghāyer*) A. contrary, contradictory.

مغایرت (*moghāyerat*) A. contradiction, disagreement.

مغبون (*maghbun*) A. cheated.

مغتنم (*moghtanam*) A. regarded as booty.

مغذی (*moghazzi*) A. nutritive.

مغرب (*maghreb*) A. west.

مغربی (*maghrebi*) A. western.

مغرض (*moghrez*) A. self-interested.

مغرور (*maghrur*) A. proud; deluded.

مغروق (*maghruq*) A. drowned.

مغز (*maghz*) pith, marrow; kernel; brain.

مغشوش (*maghshush*) A. confused, disordered.

مغضوب (*maghzub*) A. exposed to anger.

مغفر (*meghfar*) A. helmet.

مغفرت (*maghferat*) A. forgiveness.

مغفور (*maghfur*) A. forgiven; deceased.

مغلطه (*maghlateh*) A. misleading question.

مغلق (*moghlaq*) A. abstruse.

مغلوب (*maghlub*) A. defeated.

مغلوبیت (*maghlubiyyat*) A. defeat.

مغلوط (*maghlut*) A. faulty, corrupt.

مغموم (*maghmum*) A. grieved.

مغناطیس (*maghnāṭis*) A. magnet.
مغنی (*moghanni*) A. singer.
مغنیه (*moghannieh*) A. female singer.
مغول (*moghol*) Mongol.
مغولستان (*mogholestān*) Mongolia.
مفاجات (*mofājāt*) A. unexpected attack.
مفاخر (*mafākher*) A. glories. (*Pl. of* مفخرت.)
مفاخرت (*mofākherat*) A. (act of) priding oneself, boasting.
مفاد (*mafād*) A. purport, tenour.
مفارقت (*mofāreqat*) A. separation.
مفاصل (*mafāṣel*) A. joints. (*Pl. of* مفصل.)
مفت (*moft*) gratis; idle, nonsensical.
مفتاح (*meftāḥ*) A. key.
مفتخر (*moftakher*) A. honoured.
مفت خور (*moft khor*) parasite.
مفتش (*mofattesh*) A. inspector.
مفتضح (*moftaẓaḥ*) A. disgraced.
مفتوح (*maftuḥ*) A. opened; conquered.
مفتول (*maftul*) A. twisted; wire.
مفتون (*maftun*) A. fascinated, charmed.
مفتی (*mofti*) A. mufti.
مفخرت (*mafkharat*) A. glory.
مفرح (*mofarreḥ*) A. exhilarating.
مفرد (*mofrad*) A. single; singular (*in grammar*).
مفرط (*mofreṭ*) A. excessive.
مفرغ (*mafragh*) gun metal, bronze.
مفروز (*mafruz*) A. separated.
مفروش (*mafrush*) A. carpeted.
مفروق (*mafruq*) A. subtracted; subtrahend.
مفروق منه (*mafruqon menh*) A. minuend.
مفسد (*mofsed*) A. seditious (person), mischief-maker.
مفسده (*mafsadeh*) A. wickedness, evil.
مفسر (*mofasser*) A. commentator.
مفصل (*mafṣel*) A. joint, articulation.
مفصل (*mofaṣṣal*) A. detailed, lengthy.
مفصلاً (*mofaṣṣalan*) A. in detail, at length.
مفعول (*maf'ul*) A. object (*of a verb.*)
مفقود (*mafqud*) A. lost, missing.
مفکر (*mofakker*) A. thinking deeply, deep thinker.
مفلس (*mofles*) A. poor, bankrupt.
مفوض (*mofavvaẓ*) A. entrusted, ceded.
مفهوم (*mafhum*) A. understood; purport, sense.
مفید (*mofid*) A. useful, profitable.
مقابل (*moqābel*) A. opposite; corresponding; equal. (در) مقابلِ opposite. دو مقابل twice as much.
مقابله (*moqābeleh*) A. comparison, collation; confronting; reciprocity.
مقاتله (*moqāteleh*) A. battle, combat.
مقادیر (*maqādir*) A. quantities. (*Pl. of* مقدار.)
مقاربت (*moqārebat*) A. sexual intercourse.
مقاربتی (*moqārebati*) *a.* venereal.

مقارن (*moqāren*) A. close, connected; simultaneous.

مقارنت (*moqārenat*) A. connection; simultaneity.

مقاصد (*maqāṣed*) A. destinations; intentions. (*Pl. of* مقصد.)

مقاطعه (*moqāṭe'eh*) A. contract.

مقاطعه کار (*moqāṭe'eh kār*) *a.* contractor.

مقال (*maqāl*) A. speech, discourse.

مقاله (*maqāleh*) A. treatise, article.

مقام (*maqām*) A. position, rank, office.

مقامات (*maqāmāt*) A. positions, ranks; authorities.

مقاوله (*moqāveleh*) A. agreement, convention.

مقاومت (*moqāvemat*) A. resistance.

مقایسه (*moqāyeseh*) A. comparison. مقایسه کردن to compare.

مقبره (*maqbareh*) A. graveyard, cemetery; tomb.

مقبل (*moqbel*) A. fortunate.

مقبوض (*maqbuẓ*) A. received.

مقبول (*maqbul*) A. accepted; agreeable, pretty.

مقتبس (*moqtabas*) A. borrowed, extracted.

مقتدا (*moqtadā*) A. imitated; leader.

مقتدر (*moqtader*) A. powerful.

مقتصد (*moqtaṣed*) A. economic(al); economist.

مقتضا (*moqtaẓā*) A. necessity, exigency.

مقتضی (*moqtaẓi*) A. expedient; necessary.

مقتول (*maqtul*) A. killed.

مقدار (*meqdār*) A. quantity.

مقدر (*moqaddar*) A. destined, fated.

مقدرات (*moqaddarāt*) A. destinies.

مقدس (*moqaddas*) A. holy.

مقدم (*moqaddam*) A. prior; preferred.

مقدم (*maqdam*) A. arrival.

مقدمات (*moqaddamāt*) A. preliminaries.

مقدماتی (*moqaddamāti*) *a.* preliminary.

مقدمه (*moqaddameh*) A. introduction, preamble.

مقدور (*maqdur*) A. predestined; practicable, possible.

مقدونیه (*maqduniyyeh*) A. Macedonia.

مقر (*maqarr*) A. residence, abode. مقرِ سلطنت capital.

مقر (*moqerr*) A. confessing.

مقراض (*meqrāẓ*) A. scissors.

مقرر (*moqarrar*) A. established, fixed, stipulated.

مقررات (*moqarrarāt*) A. provisions, regulations.

مقرری (*moqarrari*) *a.* salary, pension.

مقروض (*maqruẓ*) A. indebted.

مقرون (*maqrun*) A. connected, joined.

مقسوم (*maqsum*) A. divided; dividend.

مقسوم علیه (*maqsumon 'aleih*) A. divisor.

مقصد (*maqṣad*) A. destination; intention.

مقصر (*moqaṣṣer*) A. guilty (person), criminal.

مقصود (*maqṣud*) A. purpose.

مقصور (*maqṣur*) A. shortened; defective.

مقطر (*moqaṭṭar*) A. distilled.

مقطع (*moqaṭṭa'*) A. cut; interrupted; abbreviated.

مقطع (*maqṭa'*) A. section.

مقطوع (*maqṭu'*) A. cut (off), severed.

مقعر (*moqa''ar*) A. concave.

مقفی (*moqaffā*) A. rhymed.

مقلد (*moqalled*) A. imitator, buffoon.

مقلوب (*maqlub*) A. inverted.

مقمر (*moqammar*) A. moonlit.

مقنع (*moqne'*) A. satisfying, convincing.

مقنن (*moqannan*) A. legal.

مقنن (*moqannen*) A. legislative; legislator.

مقوا (*moqavvā*) A. cardboard.

مقوس (*moqavvas*) A. arched.

مقوله (*maquleh*) A. topic; category.

مقوم (*moqavvem*) A. appraiser.

مقوی (*moqavvi*) A. strengthening, fortifying; tonic.

مقهور (*maqhur*) A. subdued, conquered.

مقیاس (*meqyās*) A. measure; scale.

مقید (*moqayyad*) A. bound; recorded.

مقیم (*moqim*) A. dwelling, resident.

مقیی (*moqayyi*) A. emetic.

مکابره (*mokābereh*) A. haughtiness; contention.

مکاتب (*makāteb*) A. schools. (*Pl. of* مکتب.)

مکاتبه (*mokātebeh*) A. correspondence.

مکاره (*makāreh*) R. fair.

مکارم (*makārem*) A. noble actions. (*Pl. of* مکرمت.)

مکاشفه (*mokāshefeh*) A. revelation.

مکافات (*mokāfāt*) A. retribution.

مکافی (*mokāfi*) A. equal; parabolic.

مکالمه (*mokālemeh*) A. conversation.

مکان (*makān*) A. place; dwelling.

مکانیزه (*mekānizeh*) F. mechanized.

مکانیک (*mekānik*) F. mechanics.

مکتب (*maktab*) A. school.

مکتسب (*moktaseb*) A. acquiring, earning.

مکتوب (*maktub*) A. written; letter.

مکتوم (*maktum*) A. hidden; secret.

مکث (*makṣ*) A. halt, pause.

مکدر (*mokaddar*) A. turbid; offended.

مکر (*makr*) A. craft, wile, trick.

مکرر (*mokarrar*) A. repeated.

مکرراً (*mokarraran*) A. repeatedly.

مکرم (*mokarram*) A. honoured.

مکرمت (*makramat*) A. generosity; noble action.

مکروه (*makruh*) A. hated, abominable.

مکزیک (*mekzik*). F. Mexico.

مکشوف (*makshuf*) A. discovered.

مکعب (*moka''ab*) A. cubic.

مکفی (*mokfi*) A. sufficient.

مکلف (*mokallaf*) A. bound, charged; of age, liable to taxation.

مکمل (*mokammal*) A. complete(d).

مکمل (*mokammel*) A. complement(ary).

مکنت (*meknat*) A. power; wealth.

مکون (*mokavvan*) A. created.

مکون (*mokavven*) A. creating, creator.

مکه (*makkeh*) A. Mecca.

مکیدن (*makidan*) to suck.

مکیف (*mokayyef*) A. intoxicating, intoxicant.

مکین (*makin*) A. established, dwelling; dweller.

مگر (*magar*) except; *an interrogative particle.*

مگس (*magas*) fly.

مل (*mol*) wine.

ملا (*malā*) A. fulness; crowd, public.

ملا (*mollā*) *a.* theologian, preacher.

ملاح (*mallāḥ*) A. sailor.

ملاحت (*malāḥat*) A. beauty, elegance.

ملاحظه (*molāḥeẓeh*) A. observation. ملاحظه کردن to observe.

ملاذ (*malāẕ*) A. asylum.

ملازم (*molāzem*) A. attending, attendant.

ملازمت (*molāzemat*) A. assiduity; attendance.

ملاطفت (*molāṭefat*) A. kindness.

ملاعین (*malā'in*) A. accursed ones. (*Pl. of* ملعون.)

ملافه (*malāfeh*) *a.* sheet.

ملاقات (*molāqāt*) A. (act of) meeting, interview. ملاقات کردن to meet.

ملاقی (*molāqi*) A. meeting.

ملاک (*mallāk*) A. landowner.

ملال (*malāl*), ملالت (*malālat*) A. weariness; sadness; vexation.

ملامت (*malāmat*) A. blame, reproach.

ملائکه (*malā'ekeh*) A. angels. (*Pl. of* ملک.)

ملایم (*molāyem*) A. mild, temperate.

ملایمت (*molāyemat*) A. mildness, moderation.

ملبس (*molabbas*) A. clothed, dressed.

ملبوس (*malbus*) A. clothing, clothes.

ملت (*mellat*) A. nation.

ملتجی (*moltaji*) A. taking refuge.

ملتحمه (*moltaḥemeh*) A. conjunctiva.

ملتزم (*moltazem*) A. bound, obliged; attendant.

ملتفت (*moltafet*) A. aware; attentive. ملتفت شدن to understand.

ملتقی (*moltaqā*) A. confluence.

ملتمس (*moltamas*) A. requested; request.

ملتهب (*moltaheb*) A. inflamed.

ملجا (*maljā*) A. refuge, asylum.

ملح (*melḥ*) A. salt.

ملحد (*molḥed*) A. atheist.

ملحفه (*melḥafeh*) A. sheet, cover.

ملحق (*molḥaq*) A. joined, annexed.

ملحوظ (*malḥuẓ*) A. viewed, considered.

ملخ (*malakh*) locust; propeller.

ملزم (*molzam*) A. bound, obliged.

ملزوم (*malzum*) A. necessitated, needed; inseparable.

ملزومات (*malzumāt*) A. supplies, munitions.

ملصق (*molṣaq*) A. fastened, stuck.

ملعون (*mal'un*) A. cursed.

ملغی (*molghā*) A. cancelled, annulled.

ملفوظ (*malfuẓ*) A. pronounced.

ملفوف (*malfuf*) A. wrapped, enclosed.

ملفه (*malaffeh*) A. sheet, bed clothes.

ملقب (*molaqqab*) A. endowed with a title, entitled.

ملک (*malak*) A. angel.

ملک (*malek*) A. king.

ملک (*molk*) A. kingdom.

ملک (*melk*) A. landed property.

ملکوت (*malakut*) A. Kingdom of Heaven.

ملکه (*malekeh*) A. queen.

ملکیت (*molkiyyat*) A. ownership.

ملل (*melal*) A. nations (*Pl. of* ملت.)

ملمع (*molamma'*) A. many-coloured, variegated; piebald.

ملموس (*malmus*) A. touched, tangible.

ملوان (*malavān*) sailor.

ملوث (*molavvaṣ*) A. polluted, defiled.

ملوک (*moluk*) A. kings. (*Pl. of* ملک.)

ملوکانه (*molukāneh*) *a.* royal.

ملول (*malul*) A. weary, bored; sad.

ملون (*molavvan*) A. coloured.

ملهم (*molham*) A. inspired.

ملی (*melli*) A. national.

ملیار (*melyār*) F. billion.

ملیت (*melliyyat*) A. nationality.

ملیح (*maliḥ*) A. graceful; melodious.

ملین (*molayyen*) A. laxative.

ملیون (*melyun*) F. million.

ملیون (*melliyyun*) A. nationalists.

ممات (*mamāt*) A. death.

ممارست (*momāresat*) A. assiduity, practice.

ممالک (*mamālek*) A. countries. (*Pl. of* مملکت.)

ممانعت (*momāne'at*) A. prevention, prohibition.

ممتاز (*momtāz*) A. distinguished, excellent.

ممتحن (*momtaḥan*) A. examined, examinee.

ممتحن (*momtaḥen*) A. examiner.

ممتد (*momtadd*) A. protracted, drawn out.

ممتنع (*momtane'*) A. impossible.

ممد (*momedd*) A. extending, helping.

ممدوح (*mamduḥ*) A. praised, laudable; object of praise, patron.

ممدود (*mamdud*) A. extended.

ممر (*mamarr*) A. pass, passage.

ممرز (*mamraz*) hornbeam.

ممزوج (*mamzuj*) A. mixed.

ممسک (*momsek*) A. parsimonious, miser(ly.)

ممکن (*momken*) A. possible.

مملکت (*mamlakat*) A. country.

مملکتی (*mamlakati*) *a.* belonging to the state.

مملو (*mamlovv*) A. full.

مملوک (*mamluk*) A. possessed, owned; slave.

ممنوع (*mamnu'*) A. forbidden, prohibited.

ممنون (*mamnun*) A. obliged, grateful.

ممه (*mameh*) breast.

ممهور (*mamhur*) A. sealed.

مميز (*momayyez*) A. discerning, discriminating; auditor; decimal point.

من (1) (*man*) I.

من (2) (*man*) maund.

منابر (*manāber*) A. pulpits. (*Pl. of* منبر.)

منابع (*manābe'*) A. sources. (*Pl. of* منبع.)

منات (*manāt*) R. rouble.

مناجات (*monājāt*) A. prayer, litany.

منادات (*monādāt*) A. proclamation.

منادی (*monādi*) A. herald.

مناره (*manāreh*) A. minaret; lighthouse.

منازع (*monāze'*) A. litigious, litigant.

منازعت (*monāze'at*) A. litigation.

منازل (*manāzel*) A. dwellings, stages. (*Pl. of* منزل.)

مناسب (*monāseb*) A. suitable, fit, proper.

مناسبت (*monāsebat*) A. relation, connection; proportion; comparison; suitability; occasion, ground.

مناسک (*manāsek*) A. ceremonies, rites.

مناص (*manāṣ*) A. refuge, asylum.

مناط (*manāṭ*) A. basis, example, distance.

مناطق (*manāṭeq*) A. zones. (*Pl. of* منطقه.)

مناظر (*manāẓer*) A. views, landscapes. (*Pl. of* منظره.)

مناظره (*monāẓereh*) A. dispute, debate.

مناعت (*manā'at*) A. inaccessibility; magnanimity.

منافات (*monāfāt*) A. inconsistency, incompatibility.

منافع (*manāfe'*) A. profits, advantages. (*Pl. of* منفعت.)

منافی (*monāfi*) A. inconsistent, incompatible.

مناقشه (*monāqesheh*) A. dispute, quarrel.

مناقصه (*monāqeṣeh*) A. purchase from the lowest bidder; calling for tenders.

مناقض (*monāqeẓ*) A. contrary, repugnant.

مناکحت (*monākeḥat*) A. marriage.

منبت (*monbet*) A. fertile.

منبت (*monabbat*) A. inlaid, embossed.

منبر (*menbar*) A. pulpit.

منبسط (*monbaseṭ*) A. expanded.

منبع (*manba'*) A. source.

منبعد (*menba'd*) A. henceforth.

منبه (*monabbeh*) A. awakening. (*The* h *is pronounced.*)

منت (*mennat*) A. grace, favour; obligation; thanks, praise.

منتبه (*montabeh*) A. awake, alert. (*The* h *is pronounced.*)

منتج (*montáj*) A. resulting; deduced.

منتخب (*montakhab*) A. chosen.

منتخب (*montakheb*) A. elector; elective.

منتزع (*montaze'*) A. wrested.

منتشر (*montasher*) A. published. منتشر کردن to publish.

منتظر (*montaẓar*) A. expected.

منتظر (*montaẓer*) A. expecting, awaiting.

منتظم (*montaẓam*) A. arranged, regular.

منتفع (*montafe'*) A. profiting, gaining.

منتقد (*montaqed*) A. criticizing; critic.

منتقل (*montaqel*) A. transferred.

منتهی (*montahā*) A. extremity, maximum, utmost.

منتهی (*montahi*) A. terminating, resulting.

منتهی الیه (*montahā eleih*) A. end, extremity.

منجر (*monjarr*) A. drawn; terminating, resulting.

منجلاب (*manjelāb*) *a.* dirty water; cesspool, sewer.

منجلی (*monjali*) A. clear, evident.

منجم (*monajjem*) A. astrologer, astronomer.

منجمد (*monjamed*) A. frozen, congealed.

منجمله (*menjomleh*) A. among others; such as.

منجنیق (*manjeniq*) A. ballista, mangonel.

منجی (*monji*) A. saviour.

منحرف (*monḥaref*) A. deviated.

منثور (*manṣur*) A. (written in) prose.

منحصر (*monḥaṣer*) A. limited, restricted; monopolized; exclusive.

منحصراً (*monḥaṣeran*) A. exclusively.

منحل (*monḥall*) A. dissolved.

منحنی (*monḥani*) A. curved.

منحوس (*manḥus*) A. sinister, wretched.

من حیث المجموع (*men heiṣa'l-majmu'*) A. on the whole.

منخسف (*monkhasef*) A. eclipsed (*said of the moon*).

مندرج (*mondarej*) A. inserted.

مندرجات (*mondarejāt*) A. contents.

مندرس (*mondares*) A. obliterated; worn out.

مندفع (*mondafe'*) A. repulsed.

مندیل (*mandil*) A. handkerchief; turban.

منزجر (*monzajer*) A. disgusted; averse.

منزل (*manzel*) A. lodging, house, dwelling; stage.

منزل (*monzal*) A. sent down (*from heaven*).

منزله (*manzaleh*) A. rank. بمنزلهٔ in the rank of, as.

منزوی (*monzavi*) A. retired, secluded; hermit.

منزه (*monazzah*) A. pure, guiltless.

منسوب (*mansub*) A. related, connected; attributed, charged.

منسوج (*mansuj*) A. woven, textile.

منسوخ (*mansukh*) A. abolished, annulled.

منش (*manesh*) nature, disposition.

منشاء (*mansha'*) A. source, origin.

منشعب (*monsha'eb*) A. branching, ramified.

منشور (*manshur*) A. prism; patent, diploma. منشورِ اطلس Atlantic Charter.

منشی (*monshi*) A. secretary.

منصب (*manṣab*) A. office, post.

منصرف (*monṣaref*) A. desisting, dispensing (*with*).

منصف (*monṣef*) A. just, equitable.

منصوب (*manṣub*) A. appointed; set up, erected.

منصور (*manṣur*) A. victorious; *masc. proper name.*

منضم (*monẓamm*) A. annexed, joined.

منطق (*manṭeq*) A. logic.

منطقه (*menṭaqeh*) A. zone.

منطقی (*manṭeqi*) A. logical.

منظر (*manẓar*) A. appearance, phase.

منظره (*manẓareh*) A. view, landscape.

منظم (*monaẓẓam*) A. regular, arranged.

منظور (*manẓur*) A. seen, considered, provided for; object, goal.

منظوم (*manẓum*) A. versified, in verse.

منع (*man'*) A. prohibition, prevention. منع کردن to prohibit, to prevent.

منعدم (*mon'adem*) A. destroyed, annihilated.

منعزل (*mon'azel*) A. dismissed.

منعقد (*mon'aqed*) A. concluded (*as a treaty*); held (*as a meeting*). منعقد کردن to conclude; to hold.

منعکس (*mon'akes*) A. reflected.

منعم (*mon'em*) A. beneficent; rich.

منفجر (*monfajer*) A. exploding. منفجر شدن to explode.

منفذ (*manfaẕ*) A. hole.

منفرد (*monfared*) A. single, isolated.

منفصل (*monfaṣel*) A. detached, separate; dismissed.

منفعت (*manfa'at*) A. profit, advantage.

منفعل (*monfa'el*) A. ashamed, put to shame.

منفک (*monfakk*) A. separated.

منفور (*manfur*) A. abhorred, detested.

منفی (*manfi*) A. negative.

منقاد (*monqād*) A. obedient.

منقار (*menqār*) A. beak.

منقاش (*menqāsh*) A. tweezers.

منقبض (*monqabeẓ*) A. contracted.

منقرض (*monqareẓ*) A. overthrown, extinct.

منقسم (*monqasem*) A. divided.

منقصت (*manqaṣat*) A. deficiency.

منقضی (*monqaẓi*) A. elapsed, expired.

منقطع (*monqaṭe'*) A. cut off, interrupted.

منقلب (*monqaleb*) A. turned, converted, overturned, upset.

منقوش (*manqush*) A. engraved, carved.

منقول (*manqul*) A. transported; movable; narrated.

منکر (*monkar*) A. denied; unlawful, wicked; sin.

منکر (*monker*) A. denying.

منکر شدن to deny.

منکسر (*monkaser*) A. broken.

منکسف (*monkasef*) A. eclipsed (*said of the sun*).

منکوب (*mankub*) A. afflicted (with a calamity).

منکوحه (*mankuḥeh*) A. married (woman).

منگنه (*manganeh*) press, vice.

منوال (*menvāl*) A. manner, method.

منوچهر (*manuchehr*) *name of a legendary king of Persia; masc. proper name.*

منور (*monavvar*) A. illuminated.

منوط (*manuṭ*) A. dependent.

منوم (*monavvem*) A. soporific.

منها (*menhā*) A. minus.

منهدم (*monhadem*) A. destroyed.

منهزم (*monhazem*) A. routed, put to flight.

منهی (*manhi*) A. forbidden; sin.

منی (1) (*mani*) A. semen.

منی (2) (*mani*) egotism.

منیر (*munir*) A. shining, bright.

منیع (*mani'*) A. inaccessible.

مو (*mu*) hair.

مو (*mou*) vine.

مواج (*mavvāj*) A. stormy (*sea*).

مواجب (*mavājeb*) A. salary.

مواجه (*movājeh*) A. facing, confronting. (*The* h *is pronounced.*)

مواجهه (*movājeheh*) A. (act of) confronting, meeting face to face.

مؤاخذه (*mo'ākheẕeh*) A. remonstration; chastisement.

مواد (*mavādd*) A. materials, stuffs; articles. (*Pl. of* ماده.)

موارد (*mavāred*) A. cases, instances. (*Pl. of* مورد.)

موازات (*movāzāt*) A. parallelism.

موازن (*movāzen*) A. equal in weight.

موازنه (*movāzeneh*) A. equilibrium, balance.

موازی (*movāzi*) A. parallel; equal, equivalent.

مواشی (*mavāshi*) A. quadrupeds, cattle.

مواصلت (*movāṣelat*) A. conjunction, union; communication.

مواضع (*mavāẓe'*) A. places, situations. (*Pl. of* موضع.)

مواضیع (*mavāẓi'*) A. subjects, topics. (*Pl. of* موضوع.)

مواظب (*movāẓeb*) A. careful, attentive.

مواظبت (*movāẓebat*) A. assiduity, attention. مواظبت کردن to take care of; to apply oneself to.

مواعید (*mavā'id*) A. promises. (*Pl. of* موعود.)

موافق (*movāfeq*) A. agreeing, conformable.

موافقت (*movāfeqat*) A. agreement.
مواقع (*mavāqe'*) A. occasions, times. (*Pl. of* موقع.)
مواقعه (*movāqe'eh*) A. attack, fight; sexual intercourse.
موانع (*mavāne'*) A. obstacles. (*Pl. of* مانع.)
موبد (*moubad*) Zoroastrian priest.
موت (*mout*) A. death.
مؤتمن (*mo'taman*) A. trusted, trustworthy.
موتور (*motor*) F. motor, engine.
موتورسیکلت (*motor siklet*) F. motor cycle.
موتوریزه (*motorizeh*) F. motorized.
مؤثر (*mo'aṣṣer*) A. effective.
موثق (*movaṣṣaq*) A. reliable, trustworthy.
موج (*mouj*) A. wave.
موجب (*mujab*) A. rendered necessary; consequence, result. بموجبِ in accordance with.
موجب (*mujeb*) A. causing; cause.
موجز (*mujaz*) A. brief, laconic.
موجود (*moujud*) A. existing, available.
موجودی (*moujudi*) *a.* stock, cash on hand.
موجه (*movajjah*) A. plausible.
موحد (*movaḥḥed*) A. monotheist.
موحش (*muḥesh*) A. frightful.
مؤاخر (*mo'akhkhar*) A. hinder, latter; postponed, delayed.
مؤدب (*mo'addab*) A. polite.
مودت (*mavaddat*) A. friendship, affection.
مودت آمیز (*mavaddat āmiz*) *a.* friendly.
مؤدی (*mo'addi*) A. paying, payer.
مؤذن (*mo'azzen*) A. muezzin.
موذی (*muẕi*) A. harmful, noxious.
مور (*mur*) ant.
مورب (*movarrab*) A. oblique.
مورج (*movarrej*) A. propagator.
مورچه (*murcheh*) ant.
مورخ (*movarrakh*) A. dated.
مورخ (*movarrekh*) A. historian.
مورد (*murd*) myrtle.
مورد (*moured*) A. case, instance.
موردِ subject to, exposed to.
موروث (*moruṣ*) A., موروثی (*moruṣi*) *a.* hereditary, inherited.
موریانه (*muriāneh*) termite; rust.
موز (*mouz*) A. banana.
موزع (*movazze'*) A. distributor.
موزون (*mouzun*) A. rhythmical, symmetrical.
موزه (1) (*muzeh*) boot.
موزه (2) (*muzeh*) F. museum.
موزیك (*muzik*) F. music, band.
مؤسس (*mo'asses*) A. founder, organizer.
مؤسسه (*mo'assaseh*) A. establishment, institution.
موسم (*mousem*) A. season.
موسوم (*mousum*) A. named.
موسوی (*musavi*) A. Mosaic; Jew(ish).
موسی (*musā*) A. Moses.
موسیقی (*musiqi*) A. music(al).
موسیو (*mosyu*) F. monsieur.
موش (*mush*) mouse. موشِ کور mole.
موش خرما (*mush khormā*) mongoose.

موشک (*mushak*) little mouse; rocket.

موشگیر (*mushgir*) sparrowhawk.

موصل (*mouṣel*) A. Mosul.

موصوف (*mouṣuf*) A. qualified, characterized.

موضع (*mouẓe'*) A. place, locality; situation.

موضعی (*mouẓe'i*) *a.* local.

موضوع (*mouzu'*) A. subject, matter.

موطن (*mouṭan*) A. mother country, birth-place.

موظف (*movaẓẓaf*) A. charged, bound.

موعد (*mou'ed*) A. (fixed) time, term.

موعظه (*mou'eẓeh*) A. preaching, sermon.

موعود (*mou'ud*) A. promised; invited.

موفق (*movaffaq*) A. successful. موفق شدن to succeed.

موفقیت (*movaffaqiyyat*) A. success.

موفور (*moufur*) A. abundant, copious.

موقتاً (*movaqqatan*) A. temporarily, provisionally.

موقتی (*movaqqati*) *a.* temporary, provisional.

موقر (*movaqqar*) A. grave, dignified.

موقع (*mouqe'*) A. occasion, time. بموقع خود in due course. موقعیکه when.

موقعیت (*mouqe'iyyat*) A. situation.

موقف (*mouqef*) A. station, place.

موقوف (*mouquf*) A. suspended, stopped; dependent; endowed for a pious foundation.

موقوفه (*mouqufeh*) A. pious bequest, foundation.

موکب (*moukeb*) A. retinue.

مؤکد (*mo'akkad*) A. emphatic, strict.

موکل (*movakkal*) A. appointed, delegated; agent.

موکل (*movakkel*) A. client, principal (*in a lawsuit*).

موکول (*moukul*) A. dependent; trusted. موکول کردن to trust, confide; to postpone.

مولی (*moulā*) A. lord, master.

مولد (*mouled*) A. birth-place.

مولد (*movalled*) A. generating; generator.

مؤلف (*mo'allaf*) A. compiled.

مؤلف (*mo'allef*) A. compiler, author.

مولفات (*mo'allafāt*) A. compositions, writings.

مؤلم (*mo'allem*) A. sad.

مولود (*moulud*) A. born; birth; birthday.

موم (*mum*) wax.

مؤمن (*mo'men*) A. believer.

مومیا (*mumiā*) mineral asphalt; preservative for making mummies.

مومیائی (*mumiā'i*) mummified; mummy.

مؤنث (*mo'annaṣ*) A. feminine.

مونس (*munes*) A. intimate, familiar; companion.

مؤول (*mo'avval*) A. paraphrased, allegorized.

موهبت (*mouhebat*) A. gift, present.

موهن (*muhen*) A. humiliating, offensive.

موهوم (*mouhum*) A. imaginary; imagination; superstition.

مؤید (*mo'ayyad*) A. assisted (*by God*); confirmed.

مؤید (*mo'ayyed*) A. confirmatory.

مویز (*maviz*) currants.

مه (1) (*meh*) fog, mist. (*The* h *is pronounced.*)

مه (2) (*meh*) great. (*The* h *is pronounced.*)

مه (3) (*meh*) F. May.

مهاجر (*mohājer*) A. emigrant, émigré.

مهاجرت (*mohājerat*) A. emigration. مهاجرت کردن to emigrate.

مهاجم (*mohājem*) A. attacker, assailant.

مهاجمه (*mohājemeh*) A. attack.

مهار (*mahār*) halter; mooring, painter.

مهارت (*mahārat*) A. skill.

مهتاب (*mahtāb*) moonlight.

مهتر (1) (*mehtar*) greater.

مهتر (2) (*mehtar*) groom.

مهجور (*mahjur*) A. separated; abandoned.

مهد (*mahd*) A. cradle.

مهدی (*mahdi*) A. *title of the twelfth Imam; masc. proper name.*

مهذب (*mohazzab*) A. polished, refined.

مهر (*mahr*) A. marriage-portion.

مهر (1) (*mehr*) sun.

مهر (2) (*mehr*) love, kindness.

مهر (3) (*mehr*) *name of the seventh month of the Persian year.*

مهر (*mohr*) seal.

مهربان (*mehrebān*) kind.

مهربانی (*mehrebāni*) kindness.

مهره (*mohreh*) shell; bead; marble; piece in chess; glaze; vertebra.

مهره دار (*mohreh dār*) glazed; vertebrate.

مهلت (*mohlat*) A. respite.

مهلك (*mohlek*) A. deadly, fatal.

مهلکه (*mahlakeh*) A. dangerous place, situation; danger.

مهم (*mohemm*) A. important; great.

مهمات (*mohemmāt*) A. munitions, ammunition.

مهمان (*mehmān*) guest.

مهمان خانه (*mehmān khāneh*) hotel.

مهمان نواز (*mehmān navāz*) hospitable.

مهمان نوازی (*mehmān navāzi*) hospitality.

مهمانی (*mehmāni*) feast, banquet.

مهمل (*mohmal*) A. neglected, obsolete; nonsensical.

مهملات (*mohmalāt*) A. nonsense.

مهمیز (*mehmiz*) *a.* spur.

مهندس (*mohandes*) A. engineer.

مهی (*mehi*) greatness.

مهیا (*mohayyā*) A. prepared, ready.

مهیب (*mohib*) A. dreadful.

مهیج (*mohayyej*) A. exciting, stimulating; stimulant.

می (*mei*) wine.

می (*mi*) *a particle used in forming the present and imperfect tenses.*

میادین (*mayādin*) A. squares; arenas. (*Pl. of* میدان.)

میان (*miān*) middle, centre; loins. میانِ in the middle of, between, among. از میان بر داشتن to eliminate.

میان تهی (*miān tohi*) hollow.

میانجی (*miānji*) mediator.

میانجیگری (*miānjigari*) mediation.

میانه (*miāneh*) middle; middling, mediocre, average; connection, relations.

میثاق (*miṣāq*) A. agreement, alliance.

میخ (*mikh*) nail, peg.

میخانه (*meikhāneh*) tavern.

میخی (*mikhi*) nail-shaped; cuneiform.

میدان (*meidān*) A. square; arena.

میراث (*mirāṣ*) A. inheritance.

میز (*miz*) table.

میزان (*mizān*) A. pair of scales; Libra; amount; metre; balance.

میزان الحراره (*mizāno 'l-ḥarāreh*) A. thermometer.

میزان الهوا (*mizāno'l-havā*) A. barometer.

میزبان (*mizbān*) host.

میسر (*moyassar*) A. possible; procurable.

میسره (*meisareh*) A. left wing.

میش (*mish*) ewe.

میشن (*mishan*) sheep leather.

میعاد (*mi'ād*) A. rendezvous.

میعان (*maya'ān*) A. liquidity.

میغ (*migh*) cloud; fog, mist.

میکرب (*mikrob*) F. microbe.

میکروسکپ (*mikroskop*) F. microscope.

میکروفون (*mikrofon*) F. microphone.

میگسار (*meigosār*) winedrinker.

میل (*meil*) A. inclination; wish. میل داشتن to wish, to like.

میل (1) (*mil*) A. bodkin; bar, rod, axle; obelisk.

میل (2) (*mil*) A. mile.

میلاد (*milād*) A. birth (of Christ).

میلادی (*milādi*) *a.* of the Christian era.

میلان (*mayalān*) A. inclination.

میلان (*milān*) F. Milan.

میله (*mileh*) *a.* rod, bar.

میلیار (*milyār*) F. billion.

میلیون (*milyon*) F. million.

میمنه (*meimaneh*) A. right wing.

میمون (1) (*meimun*) A. auspicious, fortunate.

میمون (2) (*meimun*) monkey.

مین (*min*) F. (*explosive*) mine.

مینا (*minā*) enamel.

مینو (*minu*) paradise.

مینوت (*minut*) F. minute, draft.

مینیاتور (*miniatur*) F. miniature.

میوه (*miveh*) fruit.

میهمان (*mihmān*) guest.

میهمانخانه (*mihmānkhāneh*) hotel, inn.

میهمانی (*mihmāni*) feast, banquet.

میهن (*mihan*) native land.

میهن پرست (*mihan parast*) patriot.

ن

نا (*nā*) *a prefix corresponding to E.* un-, in-.

نا امن (*nā amn*) *a.* insecure; disorderly.

نا امید (*nā omid*) hopeless, desperate.

نا امیدی (*nā omidi*) hopelessness, despair.

نا اهل (*nā ahl*) *a.* unworthy.

ناب (*nāb*) pure, clear.

نا باب (*nā bāb*) unsuitable.

نابغه (*nābegheh*) A. genius.

نابود (*nābud*) non-existent. نابود کردن to annihilate.

نا بکار (*nā bekār*) good-for-nothing, wicked (person).

نا بینا (*nā binā*) blind.

نا پاک (*nā pāk*) unclean, impure, dirty.

نا پدید (*nā padid*) invisible, disappearing.

نا پسند (*nā pasand*) displeasing, disagreeable.

ناپل (*nāpl*) F. Naples.

نا تمام (*nā tamām*) *a.* incomplete, imperfect.

نا توان (*nā tavān*) powerless, weak, feeble.

نا چار (*nā chār*) helpless; compelled.

نا چیز (*nā chiz*) worthless.

ناحیه (*nāḥieh*) A. region.

ناخدا (1) (*nākhodā*) (naval) captain.

ناخدا (2) (*nākhodā*) godless.

نا خلف (*nā khalaf*) *a.* degenerate, undutiful.

ناخن (*nākhon*) nail.

ناخوش (*nākhosh*) ill.

ناخوشی (*nākhoshi*) illness.

نادان (*nādān*) ignorant.

نادانی (*nādāni*) ignorance.

نادر (*nāder*) A. rare.

نادم (*nādem*) A. penitent.

نار (1) (*nār*) pomegranate.

نار (2) (*nār*) A. (hell)fire.

نا راست (*nā rāst*) false; dishonest.

نا راستی (*nā rāsti*) falsehood; dishonesty.

نا راحت (*nā rāḥat*) *a.* uneasy, uncomfortable.

نا راضی (*nā rāẓi*) *a.* dissatisfied.

ناردان (*nārdān*) pomegranate seed.

نارس (*nāras*) unripe.

نا رسیده (*nā rasideh*) unripe, immature.

نارگیل (*nārgil*) coconut.

نارنج (*nāranj*) (sour) orange.

نارنجک (*nāranjak*) grenade, shell, bomb.

نارنگی (*nārangi*) tangerine.

ناروان (*nārvān*) elm-tree.

ناز (*nāz*) coquetry, blandishment.

نازک (*nāzok*) thin; delicate.

نازل (*nāzel*) A. descending; low.

نازنین (*nāzanin*) delicate, tender.

نازی (*nāzi*) F. Nazi.

نا سازگار (*nā sāzgār*) unsuitable, unwholesome.

ناسخ (*nāsekh*) A. abrogating, annulling.

ناسره (*nāsareh*) bad, base (*said of money*).

ناسزا (*nāsazā*) indecent; abusive language.

ناسک (*nāsek*) A. ascetic.

نا شایسته (*nā shāyesteh*) indecent; unworthy.

ناشتا (*nāshtā*) fast(ing); breakfast.

ناشر (*nāsher*) A. publisher. ناشرِ افکار organ (*of a party*).

ناشی (1) (*nāshi*) A. arising, springing.

ناشی (2) (*nāshi*) unskilful.

ناشیگری (*nāshigari*) unskilfulness.

ناصح (*nāṣeḥ*) A. adviser.

ناصر (*nāṣer*) A. assister, defender; *masc. proper name.*

ناصیه (*nāṣieh*) A. forehead.

ناطق (*nāṭeq*) A. speaking, speaker; rational.

ناظر (*nāẓer*) A. seeing; spectator, observer; overseer, supervisor.

ناظم (*nāẓem*) A. regulator, superintendent.

ناف (*nāf*) navel.

نافذ (*nāfez̲*) A. penetrating; everywhere obeyed.

نا فرمان (*nā farmān*) disobedient.

نا فرمانی (*nā farmāni*) disobedience.

نافع (*nāfe'*) A. useful, advantageous.

نا فهم (*nā fahm*) *a.* dull, stupid.

نا قابل (*nā qābel*) *a.* incapable; insignificant.

ناقص (*nāqeṣ*) A. defective.

ناقض (*nāqeẓ*) A. violating, cancelling.

ناقل (*nāqel*) A. narrator; transmitter, conductor.

نا کس (*nā kas*) base, vile.

نا گاه (*nāgāh*) suddenly.

نا گزیر (*nā gozir*) helpless; inevitable.

نا گوار (*nāgovār*) indigestible, unpalatable, unpleasant.

نا گه (*nāgah*), نا گهان (*nāgahān*) suddenly.

نا لایق (*nā lāyeq*) *a.* unworthy; incapable.

ناله (*nāleh*) complaint.

نالیدن (*nālidan*) to complain, lament.

نام (*nām*) name. حسن نام called Hasan.

نام آور (*nām āvar*) illustrious, famous.

نامبرده (*nāmbordeh*) aforesaid.

نا متناهی (*nā motanāhi*) *a.* infinite.

نامجو (*nāmju*) seeking fame.

نا محدود (*nā maḥdud*) *a.* infinite, boundless.

نا محرم (*nā maḥram*) *a.* not intimate; stranger.

نامدار (*nāmdār*) celebrated, famous.

نا مربوط (*nā marbuṭ*) *a.* unconnected, incoherent; abusive (language.)

نا مرد (*nā mard*) coward(ly).

نا مردم (*nā mardom*) inhumane.

نا مردی (*nā mardi*) cowardice.

نا مرئی (*nā mar'i*) *a.* invisible.

نامزد (*nāmzad*) nominated; candidate; betrothed, fiancée.

نا مطلوب (*nā maṭlub*) *a.* undesirable.

نا معلوم (*nā ma'lum*) *a.* unknown.

نا مناسب (*nā monāseb*) *a.* unsuitable.

نامور (*nāmvar*) celebrated, famous.

ناموس (*nāmus*) principle, law; chastity; reputation.

نامه (*nāmeh*) book; letter.

نامی (*nāmi*) famous, celebrated.

نامیدن (*nāmidan*) to name, call.

نان (*nān*) bread.

نانوا (*nānvā*) baker.

ناو (*nāv*) boat; warship.

ناوبان (*nāvbān*) (naval) lieutenant.

ناورد (*nāvard*) battle.

ناو شکن (*nāv shekan*) destroyer.

ناوک (*nāvak*) small arrow.

ناوگان (*nāvegān*) fleet.

ناوی (*nāvi*) naval rating.

ناهار (*nāhār*) luncheon.

نا هنجار (*nā hanjār*) rough, coarse; abnormal.

ناهید (*nāhid*) Venus.

نای (*nāy*) reed, cane; flute.

نایاب (*nāyāb*) rare, scarce.

نایب (*nāyeb*) A. deputy, lieutenant.

نایب السلطنه (*nāyebo's-salṭaneh*) A. regent, viceroy.

نایل (*nāyel*) A. attaining.

نبات (*nabāt*) A. plant, vegetable.

نبرد (*nabard*) battle.

نبرد ناو (*nabard nāv*) battle cruiser.

نبشتن (*nebeshtan*) *i.q.* نوشتن.

نبض (*nabẓ*) A. pulse.

نبوت (*nobovvat*) A. prophecy; prophet's mission.

نبوغ (*nobugh*) A. genius.

نبی (*nabi*) A. prophet.

نبیذ (*nabiẕ*) A. date wine; wine.

نبیر (*nabir*), نبیره (*nabireh*) great grandchild.

نتایج (*natāyej* A. results, consequences. (*Pl. of* نتیجه.)

نتیجه (*natijeh*) A. result, consequence; descendant. در نتیجهٔ as the result of.

نثار (*neṣār*) A. money scattered at a feast.

نثر (*naṣr*) A. prose.

نجابت (*najābat*) A. nobility; gentleness; chastity.

نجات (*najāt*) A. deliverance, salvation. نجات دادن to save.

نجار (*najjār*) A. carpenter.

نجاست (*najāsat*) A. impurity, uncleanness.

نجاشی (*najāshi*) A. Negus.

نجبا (*nojabā*) A. nobles. (*Pl. of* نجیب).

نجس (*najes*) A. dirty, impure, unclean.

نجم (*najm*) A. star.

نجوم (*nojum*) A. stars; astrology, astronomy. (*Pl. of* نجم)

نجومی (*nojumi*) *a.* astrological, astronomical.

نجوی (*najvā*) A. whisper(ing). نجوی کردن to whisper.

نجیب (*najib*) A. noble; gentle; chaste.

نحریر (*neḥrir*) A. skilful; learned.

نحس (*naḥs*) A. sinister, unlucky.

نحو (*naḥv*) A. manner, way; syntax, grammar.

نحوست (*noḥusat*) A. inauspiciousness, unluckiness.

نخ (*nakh*) cotton (yarn); thread.

نخاع (*nokhā'*) A. spinal cord; marrow.

نخبه (*nokhbeh*) A. choice (part).

نخچیر (*nakhchir*) game, prey.

نخست (*nakhost*) first. نخست وزیر Prime Minister.

نخستین (*nakhostin*) first.

نخل (*nakhl*) A. date-palm.

نخلستان (*nakhlestān*) *a.* plantation of date-palms.

نخوت (*nakhvat*) A. pride.

نخود (*nokhod*) pea.

نخیل (*nakhil*) A. date-palm.

ندا (*nedā*) A. proclamation, voice.

ندبه (*nodbeh*) A. lamentation.

ندرت (*nodrat*) A. rareness. بندرت rarely, seldom.

ندرةً (*nodratan*) A. rarely, seldom.

ندیم (*nadim*) A. boon companion.

نذر (*nazr*) A. vow.

نر (*nar*) male.

نرخ (*nerkh*) rate, current price.

نرد (*nard*) backgammon.

نردبان (*nardebān*) ladder.

نرگس (*narges*) narcissus.

نرم (*narm*) soft.

نرم تن (*narm tan*) mollusc.

نرمی (*narmi*) softness.

نروژ (*norvezh*) F. Norway.

نره (*narreh*) male.

نرینه (*narineh*) male; male members of the family.

نزاع (*nezā'*) A. quarrel.

نزاکت (*nazākat*) *a.* courtesy, delicacy.

نزدِ (*nazde*) near; in the opinion of.

نزدیک (*nazdik*) near.

نزدیکی (*nazdiki*) proximity, neighbourhood. نزدیکیِ (در) near (to).

نزع (*naz'*) A. death agony.

نزول (*nozul*) A. (act of) descending alighting; lodging; borrowing on interest.

نزهت (*noz-hat*) A. pleasure.

نژاد (*nezhād*) race, breed.

نژاد شناسی (*nezhād shenāsi*) ethnology.

نژادی (*nezhādi*) racial.

نژند (*nezhand*) sad; dreadful; angry.

نسا (*nesā*) A. women.

نساج (*nassāj*) A. weaver.

نسب (*nasab*) A. lineage.

نسبت (*nesbat*) A. relation(ship). نسبت به with regard to.

نسبةً (*nesbatan*) A. comparatively.

نسبی (*nesbi*) A. relative.

نستعلیق (*nasta'liq*) *a. name of the Persian style of writing.*

نستوه (*nastuh*) brave, warlike.

نسج (*nasj*) A. tissue.

نسخ (*naskh*) A. abrogation, cancellation; copying; *name of the Arabic style of writing.*

نسخ (*nosakh*) A. copies. (*Pl. of* نسخه.)

نسخه (*noskheh*) A. copy; recipe. نسخهٔ خطی manuscript.

نسر (*nasr*) A. vulture.

نسق (*nasaq*) A. mode, style; torture by mutilation.

نسل (*nasl*) A. offspring; race.

نسوج (*nosuj*) A. tissues. (*Pl. of* نسج.)

نسیم (*nasim*) A. zephyr.

نسیه (*nesyeh*) A. (on) credit.

نشاسته (*neshāsteh*) starch.

نشاط (*nashāṭ*) A. joy, mirth.

نشان (*neshān*) mark, sign; emblem, order. نشان دادن to show.

نشاندن (*neshāndan*) to sit; to fix, implant; to extinguish.

نشانه (*neshāneh*) butt, target; mark, sign.

نشتر (*neshtar*) lancet.

نشخوار (*noshkhvār*) (chewing the) cud, rumination.

نشر (*nashr*) A. propagation, publication.

نشریات (*nashriyyāt*) A. publications.

نشست (*neshast*) sitting; sinking, subsidence. نشست و برخواست friendly intercourse.

نشستن (*neshastan*) to sit.

نشگون (*neshgun*) pinch. نشگون گرفتن to pinch.

نشو (*nashv*) A. growth.

نشیب (*neshib*) declivity.

نشیمن (*neshiman*) dwelling; nest.

نص (*naṣṣ*) A. text.

نصاری (*naṣārā*) A. Christians. (*Pl. of* نصرانی.)

نصب (*naṣb*) A. (act of) erecting, setting up.

نصر (*naṣr*) A. victory; *masc. proper name.*

نصرانی (*naṣrāni*) A. Christian.

نصرت (*noṣrat*) A. victory.

نصف (*neṣf*) A. half. نصف کردن to divide in half.

نصیب (*naṣib*) A. portion, share.

نصیحت (*naṣihat*) A. advice.

نصیر (*naṣir*) A. helper, defender; *masc. proper name.*

نطفه (*noṭfeh*) A. sperm.

نطق (*noṭq*) A. speech.

نظار (*nozzār*) A. spectators. (*Pl. of* ناظر.)

نظارت (*nazārat*) A. supervision, inspection, control.

نظافت (*nazāfat*) A. cleanness.

نظام (*nezām*) A. order, system; discipline; military service.

نظامنامه (*nezāmnāmeh*) *a.* regulations, constitution.

نظامی (*nezāmi*) A. military.

نظائر (*nazā'er*) A. similar things.

نظر (*nazar*) A. view, sight, look. بنظر رسیدن to seem. نظر به in view of. از نظرِ with a view to. در نظر گرفتن to take into account.

نظری (*nazari*) A. speculative; theoretical.

نظریه (*nazariyyeh*) A. view, opinion.

نظم (*nazm*) A. order, regularity; poetry, verse.

نظیر (*nazir*) A. equal, like.

نظیف (*nazif*) A. clean.

نعره (*na'reh*) A. cry, roar.

نعش (*na'sh*) A. bier, coffin.

نعل (*na'l*) A. horseshoe.

نعلبکی (*na'lbaki*) *a.* saucer.

نعم (*na'am*) A. yes.

نعمت (*ne'mat*) A. affluence, riches; boon, blessing.

نعوظ (*no'uẓ*) A. *erectio penis.*

نغز (*naghz*) excellent; elegant.

نغمه (*naghmeh*) A. melody.

نفاس (*nefās*) A. childbirth; lochia.

نفاق (*nefāq*) A. discord; hypocrisy.

نفت (*naft*) petroleum, oil.

نفتی (*nafti*) pertaining to petroleum.

نفخ (*nafkh*) A. (act of) blowing; swelling.

نفر (*nafar*) A. individual, person. دو نفر متخصص two specialists.

نفرت (*nefrat*) A. abhorrence.

نفرین (*nafrin*) curse, imprecation.

نفس (*nafas*) A. breath, respiration; moment.

نفس (*nafs*) A. self; soul; concupiscence.

نفسانی (*nafsāni*) A. sensual.

نفس تنگی (*nafas tangi*) *a.* asthma.

نفع (*naf'*) A. profit, gain; interest.

نفوذ (*nofuẕ*) A. influence, penetration.

نفور (*nofur*) A. abhorring.

نفوس (*nofus*) A. souls; population. (*Pl. of* نَفْس.)

نفی (*nafy*) A. negation, denial; negative.

نفیس (*nafis*) A. precious; exquisite.

نقاب (*neqāb*) A. veil.

نقاد (*naqqād*) A. critic.

نقار (*neqār*) A. enmity; quarrel.

نقاره (*naqqāreh*) A. kettledrum.

نقاش (*naqqāsh*) A. painter.

نقاشی (*naqqāshi*) *a.* painting.

نقاط (*noqāṭ*) A. points. (*Pl. of* نقطه.)

نقاهت (*naqāhat*) A. convalescence; indisposition.

نقب (*naqb*) A. burrow, tunnel.

نقد (*naqd*) A. cash.

نقداً (*naqdan*) A. in cash, for cash.

نقدی (*naqdi*) A. pertaining to cash.

نقره (*noqreh*) A. silver.

نقش (*naqsh*) A. picture, painting, design, embroidery.

نقشه (*naqsheh*) A. plan; map.

نقشه بردار (*naqsheh bardār*) *a.* surveyor.

نقشه برداری (*naqsheh bardāri*) *a.* topography; survey.

نقص (*naqṣ*) A. deficiency, defect.

نقصان (*noqṣān*) A. deficiency, shortage.

نقض (*naqẓ*) A. violation, breach.

نقطه (*noqṭeh*) A. point.

نقل (*naql*) A. transportation; quotation; narration. نقل کردن to transport; to quote; to narrate.

نقل (*noql*) A. sugar-plum; dessert.

نقلی (*naqli*) A. pertaining to transport.

نقیب (*naqib*) A. chief, leader.

نقیض (*naqiẓ*) A. contradictory, contrary.

نکات (*nekāt*) A. points, subtleties. (*Pl. of* نکته.)

نکاح (*nekāḥ*) A. marriage.

نکبت (*nakbat*) A. adversity, misfortune.

نکته (*nokteh*) A. point, subtlety.

نکو (*neku*) good.

نکوهش (*nekuhesh*) blame.

نکوهیدن (*nekuhidan*) to blame; to disregard.

نگار (*negār*) picture, painting; beautiful woman.

نگارنده (*negārandeh*) writer.

نگاشتن (*negāshtan*) to write; to paint.

نگاه (*negāh*) look. نگاه کردن to look.

نگاهداری (*negāhdāri*) keeping, preservation, protection, maintenance. نگاهداری کردن to keep, preserve, protect, maintain.

نگاهداشتن (*negāhdāshtan*) to keep, preserve, protect.

نگران (*negarān*) looking; anxious, uneasy.

نگرانی (*negarāni*) anxiety, uneasiness.

نگریستن (*negaristan*) to look.

نگون (*negun*) inverted, upside down.

نگهبان (*negahbān*) watchman, sentinel.

نگهبانی (*negahbāni*) watch, sentry.

نگهدار (*negahdār*) protector, guardian.

نگهداری (*negahdāri*) *i.q.* نگاهداری.

نگهداشتن (*negahdāshtan*) *i.q.* نگاهداشتن.

نگین (*negin*) stone in a ring; seal-ring.

نم (*nam*) moisture, dampness; moist, damp.

نماز (*namāz*) prayer.

نمام (*nammām*) A. talebearer, informer.

نمایان (*nomāyān*) apparent, visible.

نمایش (*nomāyesh*) representation, exhibition, demonstration.

نمایشگاه (*nomāyeshgāh*) exhibition.

نمایشنامه (*nomāyeshnāmeh*) play.

نمایندگی (*nomāyandegi*) representation, agency.

نماینده (*nomāyandeh*) representative.

نمد (*namad*) felt.

نمدار (*namdār*) moist, wet.

نمره (*nomreh*) F. number.

نمط (*namaṭ*) A. manner.

نمک (*namak*) salt.

نمکدان (*namakdān*) salt-cellar.

نمناک (*namnāk*) damp.

نمو (*nomovv*) A. growth. نمو کردن to grow.

نمودار (*nomudār*) apparent, visible; model, exemplar; chart, graph.

نمودن (*nomudan*) to show; to appear. (*Used as a synonym of* کردن *in compound verbs.*)

نمونه (*nomuneh*) sample, model, pattern.

نمی (*nami*) moisture, dampness.

ننگ (*nang*) shame, disgrace.

نو (*nou*) new. از نو anew.

نوا (*navā*) tune, melody; food, sustenance.

نواب (*novvāb*) A. deputies; nabob. *Pl. of* نایب.)

نواحی (*navāhi*) A. regions (*Pl. of* ناحیه.)

نواختن (*navākhtan*) to caress,

fondle ; to play (*a string instrument*).

نوار (*navār*) ribbon.

نوازش (*navāzesh*) caress, fondling.
نوازش کردن to caress, fondle.

نوازنده (*navāzandeh*) musician.

نواقص (*navāqeṣ*) A. defects, faults.

نوامبر (*novāmbr*) F. November.

نو آموز (*nou āmuz*) novice.

نو آورد (*nou āvard*) innovated ; innovation, invention.

نواهی (*navāhi*) A. prohibitions.

نوبت (*noubat*) A. turn, time ; change of guard.

نوبر (*noubar*) first fruits, early (fruits).

نوبه (*noubeh*) A. turn ; change of guard ; intermittent fever.

نوبهار (*noubahār*) early spring.

نوح (*nuḥ*) A. Noah.

نوحه (*nouḥeh*) A. mourning, lamentation.

نود (*navad*) ninety.

نور (*nur*) A. light.

نورانی (*nurāni*) *a.* luminous ; brilliant.

نورد (1) (*navard*) ply, fold ; cylinder, roller, rolling pin ; weaver's beam ; scroll.

نورد (2) (*navard*) battle.

نوردن (*navardan*), نوردیدن (*navardidan*) to travel over ; to fold, crease.

نوروز (*nouruz*) New Year's Day.

نوری (*nuri*) A. *masc. proper name.*

نوزاد (*nouzād*) new-born (baby).

نوزده (*nuzdah*) nineteen.

نوزدهم (*nuzdahom*) nineteenth.

نوش (*nush*) (pleasant) drink ; treacle ; antidote ; sweet, agreeable.

نوشتن (*neveshtan*) to write.

نوشته (*neveshteh*) written ; writing, document.

نوشروان (*noushervān*) *i.q.* انوشروان

نوشیدن (*nushidan*) to drink.

نوشیروان (*noushirvān*) *i.q.* انوشیروان

نوشین (*nushin*) sweet.

نوع (*nou'*) A. kind, sort, species.

نوع پرست (*nou' parast*) *a.*, نوع پرور (*nou' parvar*) *a.* philanthropist, philanthropic.

نوغان (*noughān*) silkworm seeds.

نوک (*nuk*) point, tip ; bill, beak.
نوک زدن to peck.

نوکر (*noukar*) M. servant.

نومید (*noumid*) hopeless, desperate.

نومیدی (*noumidi*) despair.

نوه (*naveh*) grandson.

نوی (*navi*) newness.

نوید (*navid*) glad tidings.

نویسنده (*nevisandeh*) writer.

نوئل (*no'el*) F. Christmas.

نوین (*novin*) new, recent, modern.

نه (*nah*) not ; no. (*The* h *is not pronounced.*)

نه (*noh*) nine.

نهاد (*nehād*) nature, character.

نهادن (*nehādan*) to put, place, lay.

نهار (1) (*nahār*) dinner.

نهار (2) (*nahār*) A. daytime.

نهال (*nehāl*) A. sapling.

نهان (*nehān*) hidden, secret; secrecy.

نهانی (*nehāni*) secret(ly).

نهایت (*nehāyat*) A. extremity, maximum, utmost.

نهائی (*nahā'i*) A. final.

نهج (*nahj*) A. manner.

نهر (*nahr*) A. river; canal.

نهضت (*nahẓat*) A. movement.

نهفتن (*nehoftan*) to hide.

نهم (*nohom*) ninth.

نهمار (*nahmār*) innumerable.

نهنگ (*nahang*) crocodile.

نهی (*nahy*) A. prohibition.

نهیب (*nehib*) dread.

نی (*nei*) reed, cane.

نیا (*niā*) grandfather.

نیابت (*niābat*) A. vicegerency, regency.

نیاز (*niāz*) need, necessity.

نیازمند (*niāzmand*) needy.

نیازمندی (*niāzmandi*) need, requirement, necessity.

نیام (*niām*) sheath, scabbard.

نیایس (*niāyesh*) blessing, praise.

نیت (*niyyat*) A. intention, desire.

نیر (*navyer*) A. luminary.

نیرنگ (*nirang*) magic; deceit.

نیرو (*niru*) strength, force(s).

نیرومند (*nirumand*) powerful.

نیز (*niz*) also.

نیزه (*neizeh*) lance.

نیسان (*nisān*) A. April.

نیست (*nist*) non-existence, non-existent.

نیستن (*neyestan*) reed-bed.

نیستی (*nisti*) non-existence; annihilation.

نیش (*nish*) sting; fang; sarcasm.

نیشتر (*nishtar*) lancet.

نیشکر (*neishakar*) cane sugar.

نیک (*nik*) good.

نیکبخت (*nikbakht*) fortunate.

نیکل (*nikel*) F. nickel.

نیکو (*niku*) good.

نیکی (*niki*) goodness.

نیل (*neil*) A. (act of) attaining.

نیل (1) (*nil*) Nile.

نیل (2) (*nil*) indigo; blue.

نیلوفر (*nilufar*) water-lily.

نیم (*nim*) half. دو نیم کردن to cut in half.

نیم تنه (*nim taneh*) coat, jacket.

نیمدار (*nimdār*) worn; second-hand.

نیم رخ (*nim rokh*) profile.

نیم رسمی (*nim rasmi*) *a.* semi-official.

نیمرو (*nimru*) fried egg(s).

نیم (*nim koreh*) *a.* hemisphere.

نیمه (*nimeh*) half.

نیوشیدن (*niushidan*) to listen.

نیو یورک (*niu york*) E. New York.

و

و (*va, o*) and.

وا (*vā*) back, again; open. وا کردن to open.

وا بسته (*vā basteh*) connected, dependent; attaché.

وات (*vāt*) F. watt.

وات سنج (*vāt sanj*) wattmeter.

واجب (*vājeb*) A. necessary, obligatory.

واجد (*vājed*) A. possessing.

واحد (*vāḥed*) A. unit.

واحه (*vāḥeh*) A. oasis.

وادار (*vādār*) persuaded, forced. وادار کردن to persuade, to force.

وا داشتن (*vā dāshtan*) to appoint; to set up; to prevent; to induce, persuade, force.

وادی (*vādi*) A. valley.

وار (*vār*) *a suffix equivalent to the English* -like. طوطی وار parrot-like.

وارث (*vāreṣ*) A. heir.

وارد (*vāred*) A. arriving, entering. وارد شدن to arrive. وارد آوردن to inflict.

واردات (*vāredāt*) A. imports.

وارسی (*vārasi*) investigation, inspection.

وارونه (*vāruneh*) upside down.

واژگون (*vāzhgun*) overturned, upset.

واژه (*vāzheh*) word, term.

واسط (*vāseṭ*) A. middle; mediator.

واسطه (*vāseṭeh*) A. means, medium; cause. بواسطهٔ because of.

واسع (*vāse'*) A. wide, spacious.

واصل (*vāṣel*) A. arriving. واصل شدن to arrive.

واضح (*vāẓeḥ*) A. clear, plain.

واضع (*vāẓe'*) A. founder.

واعظ (*vā'eẓ*) A. preacher.

وافر (*vāfer*) A. abundant.

وافی (*vāfi*) A. sufficient, ample.

واقع (*vāqe'*) A. lying, situated; happening, occurring. واقع شدن to happen.

واقعا (*vāqe'an*) A. really, indeed.

واقعه (*vāqe'eh*) A. event, incident.

واقعی (*vāqe'i*) *a.* real.

واقف (*vāqef*) A. aware, informed.

واکس (*vāks*) R. blacking, polish.

واکسن (*vāksan*) F. vaccine.

وا کنش (*vā konesh*) reaction.

وا گذار (*vā gozār*) made over. وا گذار کردن to make over.

واگذاری (*vā gozāri*) cession, making over.

وا گذاشتن (*vā gozāshtan*) to cede, turn over.

وا گرفتن (*vā gereftan*) to put by; to catch by contagion.

واگون (*vāgun*) F. railway carriage; tram.

واگیره (*vāgireh*) contagion.

واگیره دار (*vāgireh dār*) contagious.

والا (*va-ellā*) A. otherwise. والا فلا otherwise not.

والا حضرت (*vālā haẓrat*) *a.* His Royal Highness.

والد (*vāled*) A. father.

والده (vāledeh) A. mother.

والدین (vāledein) A. parents. (Dual of والد.)

والی (vāli) A. governor.

وام (vām) loan, debt.

واماندگی (vāmāndegi) fatigue.

واماندن (vāmāndan) to be fatigued.

وانمود (vānomud) (act of) feigning وانمود کردن to feign.

واهب (vāheb) A. giver.

واهی (vāhi) A. weak ; vain, futile, chimerical.

وای (vāy) woe ! alas !

وبا (vabā) A. pestilence ; cholera.

وبال (vabāl) A. sin ; trouble, mischief.

وتد (vatad) A. stake, peg.

وتر (vatar) A. string, chord.

وتو (veto) F. veto.

وتیره (vatireh) A. way, manner.

وثوق (voşuq) A. confidence.

وثیقه (vaşiqeh) A. security, pledge ; bond, document.

وجاهت (vajāhat) A. beauty.

وجب (vajab) A. span.

وجد (vajd) A. ecstasy.

وجدان (vejdān) A. conscience.

وجع (vaja') A. ache, pain.

وجنه (vajaneh) A. cheek ; outward appearance.

وجوب (vojub) A. necessity.

وجود (vojud) A. existence. با وجود داشتن to exist. با وجودِ in spite of.

وجوه (vojuh) A. manners, ways ; funds. (Pl. of وجه.)

وجه (vajh) A. manner, way ;

amount, sum. هیچوجه به by no means (with neg.).

وجیه (vajih) A. handsome.

وحدانی (vaḥdāni) A. single ; divine.

وحدانیت (vaḥdāniyyat) A. unity (of God).

وحدت (vaḥdat) A. unity.

وحش (vaḥsh) A. wild animal. باغ وحش zoological garden.

وحشت (vaḥshat) A. fear ; loneliness.

وحشی (vaḥshi) A. savage, wild.

وحشیت (vaḥshiyyat) A. savagery.

وحی (vaḥy) A. inspiration.

وحید (vaḥid) A. single, unique, only.

وخامت (vakhāmat) A. badness, dangerousness.

وخیم (vakhim) A. bad, dangerous.

وداع (vedā') A. farewell.

ودایع (vadāye') A. deposits. (Pl. of ودیعه.)

ودیعه (vadi'eh) A. deposit, trust.

ور (var) side. آن ورِ on the other side of, beyond.

وراثت (varāşat) A. heritage, inheritance.

ور انداز (var andāz) occurs only in the compound verb ور انداز کردن to eye up and down.

ورثه (varaşeh) A. heirs. (Pl. of وارث.)

ورد (vard) A. rose.

ورد (verd) A. (act of) telling one's beads, reciting mechanically. ورِد زبان habitual phrase.

ورزش (varzesh) exercise, gymnastics, sport.

ورزشکار (*varzeshkār*) athlete, sportsman.

ورزشکاری (*varzeshkāri*) athletics, sportsmanship.

ورزیدن (*varzidan*) to cultivate; to exercise, train; to do.

ورشکست (*varshekast*) bankrupt.

ورشکستگی (*varshekastegi*) bankruptcy.

ورشو (*varshou*) G. Warsaw.

ورطه (*varṭeh*) A. abyss, precipice.

ورق (*varaq*) A. leaf, sheet (of paper); playing-card.

ورقه (*varaqeh*) A. leaf, sheet (of paper); paper, document; card.

ورم (*varam*) A. swelling, inflammation.

ورنه (*varnah*) otherwise. (*The* h *is not pronounced.*)

ورود (*vorud*) A. arrival.

ورور (*verver*) (act of) jabbering, chattering.

ورید (*varid*) A. vein.

وزارت (*vezārat*) A. ministry.

وزارتی (*vezārati*) *a.* ministerial.

وزرا (*vozarā*) A. ministers. (*Pl. of* وزیر.)

وزغ (*vazagh*) A. frog.

وزن (*vazn*) A. weight; measure, metre.

وزنه (*vazneh*) A. weight.

وزیدن (*vazidan*) to blow.

وزیر (*vazir*) A. minister. وزیرِ مختار minister plenipotentiary.

وسائط (*vasā'eṭ*) A. means. (*Pl. of* واسطه.)

وسایل (*vasāyel*) A. means. (*Pl. of* وسیله.)

وسط (*vasaṭ*) A. middle, centre.

وسطی (*vasaṭi*) *a.* central.

وسطی (*vosṭā*) A. middle, central.

وسع (*vos'*) A. capacity, ability.

وسعت (*vos'at*) A. extent, space, amplitude.

وسمه (*vasmeh*) A. woad leaves (*for dyeing the eyebrows*).

وسواس (*vasvās*) A. scruple; temptation; tempter.

وسوسه (*vasvaseh*) A. temptation; scruple.

وسیع (*vasi'*) A. vast, broad.

وسیله (*vasileh*) A. means; pretext.

وصال (*veṣāl*) A. union.

وصایا (*vaṣāyā*) A. precepts. (*Pl. of* وصیت.)

وصایت (*vaṣāyat*) A. guardianship, tutorship.

وصف (*vaṣf*) A. description.

وصل (*vaṣl*) A. union.

وصلت (*vaṣlat*) A. marriage. وصلت کردن to marry.

وصله (*vaṣleh*) A. patch.

وصول (*voṣul*) A. arrival; collection.

وصی (*vaṣi*) A. guardian, tutor, executor.

وصیت (*vaṣiyyat*) A. will, testament, legacy; precept.

وصیتنامه (*vaṣiyyatnāmeh*) *a.* will, testament.

وضع (*vaẓ'*) A. (act of) laying; establishment, foundation; enactment; state, condition, position.

وضع کردن to lay; to establish, found; to enact. وضعِ حمل child-birth.

وضعیت (vaẓ'iyyat) A. position, situation.

وضو (voẓu) A. ritual ablution.

وضوح (voẓuḥ) A. clearness.

وضیع (vaẓi') A. mean, base.

وطن (vaṭan) A. native land.

وطن پرست (vaṭan parast) a., وطن دوست (vaṭan dust) a. patriot(ic).

وطن پرستی (vaṭan parasti) a., وطن دوستی (vaṭan dusti) a. patriotism.

وظائف (vaẓā'ef) A. duties. (*Pl. of* وظیفه.)

وظیفه (vaẓifeh) A. duty.

وعده (va'deh) A. promise. وعده دادن to promise.

وعظ (va'ẓ) A. (act of) preaching; sermon.

وغیره (vagheireh) A. etcetera.

وفا (vafā) A. loyalty, fidelity.

وفات (vafāt) A. death. وفات کردن to die.

وفا دار (vafā dār) a. loyal, faithful.

وفا داری (vafā dāri) a. loyalty, fidelity.

وفق (vafq) A. accordance, conformity. بر وفقِ in accordance with. وفق دادن to adapt.

وفور (vofur) A. abundance.

وقاحت (vaqāḥat) A. impudence.

وقار (vaqār) A. gravity, dignity.

وقایع (vaqāye') A. events, incidents. (*Pl. of* واقعه.)

وقایه (vaqāyeh) A. defence, protection, guard.

وقت (vaqt) A. time. آنوقت then.

وقت شناس (vaqt shenās) a. opportunist.

وقع (vaq') A. respect, esteem.

وقف (vaqf) A. pious legacy, pious foundation.

وقفه (vaqfeh) A. pause, standstill.

وقوع (voqu') A. occurrence. بوقوع پیوستن to happen.

وقوف (voquf) A. information, knowledge.

وکالت (vekālat) A. agency, deputyship.

وکالت نامه (vekālat nāmeh) a. letter of attorney.

وکلا (vokalā) A. deputies, delegates. (*Pl. of* وکیل.)

وکیل (vakil) A. deputy, وکیل مرافعه barrister.

ول (vel) (hanging) loose, free. ول کردن to let go.

ولادت (velādat) A. birth.

ولایت (velāyat) A. province.

ولایتی (velāyati) a. provincial.

ولت (volt) F. volt.

ولت سنج (volt sanj) voltmeter.

ولد (valad) A. son, child.

ولد الزنا (valado 'z-zenā) A. bastard.

ولع (vala') A. eager desire.

ولگرد (velgard) vagrant, vagabond.

ولوله (velveleh) A. howling, wailing; clamour.

ولی (1) (*vali*) A. guardian, tutor; saint.

ولی (2) (*vali*) *a.* but.

ولی عهد (*vali 'ahd*) A. crown prince.

ولیکن (*valikan*) *a.* but.

ونیز (*veniz*) F. Venice.

وهاب (*vahhāb*) A. bestower; God.

وهام (*vahhām*) A. sceptic(al).

وهله (*vahleh*) A. moment, instance.

وهم (*vahm*) A. imagination.

وهن (*vahan*) A. weakness.

وی (*vei*) he, she.

ویتامین (*vitāmin*) F. vitamine.

ویران (*virān*) desolate. ویران کردن to lay waste.

ویرانه (*virāneh*) ruin; ruined.

ویژه (*vizheh*) special; pure. بویژه specially.

ویس قنسول (*vis qonsol*) F. vice-consul.

ویسکی (*viski*) E. whisky.

ویلا (*vilā*) F. villa.

ویلان (*vilān*) wandering, vagrant.

وین (*vien*) F. Vienna.

ه

هاتف (*hātef*) A. voice out of the unknown.

هادی (*hādi*) A. leader, guide; *masc. proper name.*

هار (*hār*) mad, rabid.

هارون (*hārun*) A. Aaron.

هاضم (*hāzem*) A. digestive.

هال (*hāl*) goal (*in football*).

هاله (*hāleh*) A. halo.

هامون (*hāmun*) plain.

هاون (*hāvan*) mortar. دستهٔ هاون pestle.

هاویه (*hāvieh*) A. abyss; hell.

هائل (*hā'el*) A. terrible.

هبوط (*hobuṭ*) A. descent.

هبه (*hebeh*) A. donation.

هتاک (*hattāk*) A. defamer.

هتک (*hatk*) A. (act of) rending, tearing; violation, aspersion.

هتل (*hotel*) F. hotel.

هجا (*hejā*) A. syllable; spelling; satire.

هجده (*hejdah*) eighteen.

هجدهم (*hejdahom*) eighteenth.

هجر (*hajr*) A., هجران (*hejrān*) A. separation.

هجرت (*hejrat*) A. emigration, flight; hegira.

هجری (*hejri*) A. reckoned from the hegira.

هجو (*hajv*) A. satire, lampoon, libel.

هجوم (*hojum*) A. attack.

هجی (*heji*) A. spelling.

هخامنشی (*hakhāmeneshi*) Achaemenian.

هدایت (*hedāyat*) A. guidance, salvation; *masc. proper name.*

هدر (*hadar*) A. useless effort.

هدف (*hadaf*) A. target.

هدهد (*hodhod*) A. hoopoe.

هديه (*hadiyyeh*) A. present, gift.

هذه السنه (*hāzehe 's-saneh*) A. this year.

هذيان (*hazayān*) A. delirium; nonsense.

هر (*har*) every, each, any. هر كس everybody. هر كدام each.

هراس (*herās*) fear.

هراسان (*herāsān*) frightened.

هر آينه (*har āyeneh*) indeed, certainly.

هر جا (*har jā*) everywhere.

هرج و مرج (*harj o marj*) chaos, confusion.

هرچند (*harchand*) although.

هرچه (*harcheh*) whatever.

هرز (*harz*) vain, futile.

هرزه (*harzeh*) dissolute; vain; absurd.

هرگاه (*hargāh*) whenever; if.

هرگز (*hargez*) never (*with neg.*)

هرم (*haram*) A. pyramid.

هرمز (*hormoz*) *masc. proper name.*

هزار (*hazār*) thousand.

هزار پا (*hazār pā*) millipede.

هزبر (*hezabr*) A. lion.

هزل (*hazl*) A. joke, jest.

هزليات (*hazliyyāt*) A. facetiae.

هزيمت (*hazimat*) A. rout.

هزينه (*hazineh*) expenses.

هست (*hast*) existence.

هسته (*hasteh*) fruit-stone.

هستى (*hasti*) existence.

هسر (*hasar*) glazed frost (*verglas*).

هشت (*hasht*) eight.

هشتاد (*hashtād*) eighty.

هشتم (*hashtom*) eighth.

هشتن (*heshtan*) to leave; to put, place; to let, allow.

هشيار (*hoshyār*) intelligent.

هشيارى (*hoshyāri*) intelligence.

هضم (*hazm*) A. digestion. هضم كردن to digest.

هضمى (*hazmi*) A. digestive.

هفت (*haft*) seven.

هفتاد (*haftād*) seventy.

هفتم (*haftom*) seventh.

هفته (*hafteh*) week.

هفده (*hefdah*) seventeen.

هفدهم (*hefdahom*) seventeenth.

هكتار (*hektār*) F. hectare.

هكتو ليتر (*hekto litr*) F. hectolitre.

هلاك (*halāk*) A. perdition, ruin. هلاك شدن to perish.

هلاكت (*halākat*) A. ruin, destruction.

هلال (*helāl*) A. crescent.

هلاهل (*halāhel*) deadly, fatal.

هلند (*holand*) F. Holland.

هلندى (*holandi*) Dutch.

هلو (*holu*) peach.

هليدن (*helidan*) *i. q.* هشتن.

هم (*ham*) also; even; each other. باهم together.

هم (*hamm*) A. care, grief.

هما (*homā*) *name of a fabulous bird of good omen;* osprey.

همال (*hamāl*) equal; companion.

همان (*hamān*) same.

همانا (*hamānā*) indeed, certainly.

هم آورد (*ham āvard*) opponent, adversary, rival.

هم آهنگ (*ham āhang*) harmonious, concordant.

همايون (*homāyun*) auspicious ; royal.

همايونى (*homāyuni*) royal.

همت (*hemmat*) A. ambition ; endeavour.

همتا (*hamtā*) fellow, mate.

همجنس (*hamjens*) *a.* of the same kind, homogeneous.

همجوار (*hamjevār*) *a.* neighbouring.

هم چشم (*ham chashm*) rival.

همچنان (*hamchonān*) thus ; such.

همچنانکه (*hamchonānkeh*) such that, as.

همچنين (*hamchonin*) thus, in this manner.

همچو (*hamcho*) such, as.

همخوابه (*hamkhvābeh*) bedfellow, spouse.

همداستان (*hamdāstān*) companion ; accomplice.

همدرس (*hamdars*) *a.* classmate.

همدست (*hamdast*) accomplice.

همدم (*hamdam*) intimate friend, confidant.

همديگر (*hamdigar*) one another, each other.

همراه (*hamrāh*) fellow-traveller. همراهِ together with, along with.

همسايه (*hamsāyeh*) neighbour(ing).

همسر (*hamsar*) consort ; coeval.

همشيره (*hamshireh*) sister.

همكارى (*hamkāri*) cooperation.

همگى (*hamegi*) totality, all.

هموار (*hamvār*) level, smooth.

همواره (*hamvāreh*) always.

هموم (*homum*) A. cares. (*Pl. of* هَمّ.)

همه (*hameh*) all, every.

هميشه (*hamisheh*) always.

همين (*hamin*) same.

همينكه (*haminkeh*) as soon as.

هنجار (*hanjār*) way, manner ; plumb-line ; norm.

هند (*hend*) India.

هندسه (*hendeseh*) A. geometry.

هندو (*hendu*) Indian, Hindoo.

هندوانه (*hendovāneh*) water-melon.

هندو چين (*hendu chin*) Indo-China.

هندوستان (*hendustān*) India.

هندى (*hendi*) Indian.

هنر (*honar*) art ; virtue.

هنر پيشه (*honar pisheh*) artisan ; artist.

هنرستان (*honarestān*) industrial school.

هنرمند (*honarmand*) skilful.

هنگ (1) (*hang*) regiment.

هنگ (2) (*hang*) intelligence.

هنگام (*hangām*) time.

هنگامه (*hangāmeh*) crowd ; tumult.

هنگرى (*hongri*) F. Hungary.

هنگفت (*hangoft*) enormous.

هنود (*honud*) A. Indians.

هنوز (*hanuz*) still, yet.

هوا (*havā*) A. air ; weather ; desire, passion.

هوا پيما (*havā peimā*) *a.* aeroplane.

هوا پيما بر (*havā peimā bar*) *a.* aircraft carrier.

هوا پیمائی (*havā peimā'i*) *a.* pertaining to aircraft.

هوا خواه (*havā khāh*) *a.* partisan.

هوا سنج (*havā sanj*) *a.* barometer.

هوا نوردی (*havā navardi*) *a.* air navigation, aviation.

هوائی (*havā'i*) A. airy, aerial.

هودج (*houdaj*) A. camel litter.

هور (*hur*) sun.

هوس (*havas*) A. eagerness, yearning, craving.

هوش (*hush*) intelligence.

هوشمند (*hushmand*) intelligent.

هوشنگ (*hushang*) *name of a legendary king of Persia; masc. proper name.*

هوشیار (*hushyār*) vigilant; intelligent.

هوشیاری (*hushyāri*) caution; intelligence.

هول (*houl*) A. (sudden) fear.

هولناک (*houlnāk*) *a.* dreadful, terrible.

هویت (*hoviyyat*) A. identity, identification.

هویدا (*hoveidā*) manifest, evident.

هیاهو (*hayāhu*) tumult, uproar.

هیبت (*heibat*) A. majesty, awe, awe-inspiring presence.

هیجا (*heijā*) A. war.

هیجان (*hayajān*) A. excitement.

هیچ (*hich*) nothing; no; at all (*with neg.*)

هیچکس (*hichkas*) (*with neg.*) nobody.

هیچوقت (*hichvaqt*) *a.* (*with neg.*) never.

هیرمند (*hirmand*) (the River) Helmand.

هیزم (*hizom*) wood.

هیزم شکن (*hizom shekan*) woodcutter.

هیکل (*heikal*) A. figure; temple.

هیون (*hayun*) dromedary.

هیهات (*heihāt*) A. alas!

هیئت (*hei'at*) A. figure; body (of men), council, mission; astronomy. هیئتِ دولت , هیئتِ وزرا cabinet.

ی

یا (*yā*) or. ویا *id.*

یابنده (*yābandeh*) finding, finder.

یابو (*yābu*) pack-horse.

یاخته (*yākhteh*) cell.

یاد (*yād*) memory. یاد داشتن to remember. یاد آوردن to remind. یاد گرفتن to learn.

یاد آور (*yād āvar*) reminding.

یاد آوری (*yād āvari*) remembrance. یاد آوری کردن to remind.

یاد بود (*yād bud*) commemoration.

یاد داشت (*yād dāsht*) memorandum.

یادگار (*yādgār*) souvenir, memorial.

یار (*yār*) friend; sweetheart; helper.

یارا (*yārā*) power; courage.

یارستن (*yārastan*) to be able; to dare.

یاره (*yāreh*) collar, bracelet.

یاری (*yāri*) friendship; assistance.

یاز (*yāz*) cubit.

یازده (*yāzdah*) eleven.

یازدهم (*yāzdahom*) eleventh.

یازیدن (*yāzidan*) to stretch out.

یاس (*yās*) jasmine.

یأس (*ya's*) A. despair.

یاسا (*yāsā*) M. law, custom.

یاساق (*yāsāq*) M. prohibition, punishment.

یأس آمیز (*ya's āmiz*) *a.* desperate.

یاسمن (*yāsaman*) jasmine.

یاغی (*yāghi*) T. rebel(lious).

یافا (*yāfā*) A. Jaffa.

یافت (*yāft*) found. (*In the expression* یافت شدن to be found.)

یافتن (*yāftan*) to find; to obtain.

یاقوت (*yāqut*) ruby.

یال (*yāl*) neck; mane.

یاور (*yāvar*) major.

یاوه (*yāveh*) absurd, idle, vain; idle talk.

یبس (*yobs*) A. dryness; constipation.

یبوست (*yobusat*) A. constipation.

یتیم (*yatim*) A. orphan.

یحتمل (*yaḥtamel*) A. perhaps, probably.

یحیی (*yaḥyā*) A. John.

یخ (*yakh*) ice. یخ بستن to freeze.

یخچال (*yakhchāl*) icehouse.

ید (*yad*) A. hand; authority, possession.

یدک (*yadak*) led horse.

یدکی (*yadaki*) spare (part).

یراق (*yarāq*) T. lace, braid; trappings, harness.

یزدان (*yazdān*) God.

یزک (*yazak*) advance guard; patrolman.

یسر (*yosr*) A. ease, prosperity.

یشم (*yashm*) jasper.

یعقوب (*ya'qub*) A. Jacob.

یعنی (*ya'ni*) A. *i. e.*

یغما (*yaghmā*) plunder, booty.

یقه (*yaqeh*) T. collar.

یقین (*yaqin*) A. sure, certain; certainty; certainly. یقین داشتن to be certain.

یقیناً (*yaqinan*) A. certainly.

یک (*yak*) one.

یکباره (*yakbāreh*) all at once.

یکدیگر (*yakdigar*) each other, one another.

یکجا (*yakjā*) at once; in a lump.

یکدفعه (*yakdaf'eh*) *a.* once; all at once; simultaneously.

یکران (*yakrān*) chestnut, bay (horse).

یکسان (*yaksān*) equal, uniform.

یکسر (*yaksar*) entirely, totally; straight, direct(ly).

یکسره (*yaksareh*) one-sided; single (*ticket*).

یکشنبه (*yakshanbeh*) Sunday.

یکم (*yakom*) first.

یکنواخت (*yaknavākht*) monotonous.

یکه (*yakkeh*) single, singular ; shock.

یگانه (*yagāneh*) one, only, unique.

یگانگی (*yagānegi*) oneness, unity ; uniqueness.

یل (*yal*) hero.

یلدا (*yaldā*) longest night of winter.

یلوه (*yalveh*) T. woodcock.

یله (*yaleh*) released, abandoned ; bent, tilted.

یم (*yamm*) A. sea.

یمکن (*yomken*) A. perhaps, probably.

یمن (*yaman*) A. Yemen.

یمن (*yomn*) A. auspiciousness.

یمین (*yamin*) A. right (side) ; oath.

ینبوع (*yanbu'*) A. spring, fountain.

یواش (*yavāsh*) T. slow(ly), soft(ly).

یود (*yod*) F. iodine.

یورتمه (*yortmeh*) T. canter.

یورش (*yoresh*) T. attack.

یوز (*yuz*) greyhound. یوز پلنگ panther.

یوسف (*yusof*) A. Joseph.

یوغ (*yugh*) yoke.

یوگو اسلاوی (*yugo eslāvi*) F. Yugoslavia.

یوم (*youm*) A. day.

یومیه (*youmiyyeh*) A. daily ; daily pay.

یونان (*yunān*) Greece.

یونانی (*yunāni*) Greek.

یهود (*yahud*) A. Jew(s).

یهودی (*yahudi*) A. Jew(ish).

ییلاق (*yeilāq*) T. summer quarters.